John Quincy Adams
and the
Public Virtues of Diplomacy

John Quincy Adams

and the

PUBLIC VIRTUES OF

DIPLOMACY

Greg Russell

University of Missouri Press

Columbia and London

Copyright © 1995 by
The Curators of the University of Missouri
University of Missouri Press, Columbia, Missouri 65201
Printed and bound in the United States of America
All rights reserved
5 4 3 2 1   99 98 97 96 95

Library of Congress Cataloging-in-Publication Data

Russell, Greg, 1955–
    John Quincy Adams and the public virtues of diplomacy / Greg
  Russell.
      p.   cm.
    Includes bibliographical references and index.
    ISBN 0-8262-0984-X (alk. paper)
    1. Adams, John Quincy, 1767–1848—Contributions in diplomacy.
    2. United States—Foreign relations—1783–1865.   I. Title.
  E377.R87   1995
  973.5'5'092—dc20   94-38105
                                                                       CIP

♾™ This paper meets the requirements of the
American National Standard for Permanence of Paper
for Printed Library Materials, Z39.48, 1984.

Designer: Stephanie Foley
Typesetter: Connell-Zeko Type & Graphics
Printer and Binder: Thomson-Shore, Inc.
Typeface: Minion

Frontispiece: Portrait of John Quincy Adams, by Gilbert Stuart and Thomas Sully,
courtesy of the Harvard University Portrait Collection, Harvard University Art
Museums, bequest of Ward Nicholas Boylston, 1828.

Dedicated to the memory of Louisa Catherine Adams
Piscemur, venemur, ut olim

Contents

Acknowledgments / ix

Introduction / 1

1. Revolutionary Politics and Training for Statesmanship / 9
2. Ethics, Philosophy, and Religion in Adams's Worldview / 66
3. Adams's Realism and the Role of Domestic Ideals
   in Foreign Affairs / 114
4. American Nationhood and the Duty to Posterity / 142
5. Philosophy, Politics, and Statecraft at the Founding / 179
6. The Ethics of Power in American Diplomacy:
   The Statecraft of John Quincy Adams / 231

Conclusion / 265

Bibliography / 275

Index / 289

Acknowledgments

ANY NUMBER OF COLLEAGUES AND FRIENDS have been helpful in various ways during the preparation of this manuscript. Much of the research, as well as access to key source material, was made possible by a grant from the H. B. Earhart Foundation. I am also indebted to the Eric Voegelin Institute for American Renaissance Studies at Louisiana State University, the White Burkett Miller Center of Public Affairs at the University of Virginia, the Massachusetts Historical Society, and the Department of Political Science at the University of Oklahoma. I especially wish to single out a number of willing souls who offered their support and attention from the very beginning of this assignment: Kenneth W. Thompson, Ellis Sandoz, George Carey, Beverly Jarrett, and Cecil V. Crabb. I have also learned much from the comments, and related work, of Forrest Mc-Donald, Russell Kirk, Norman Graebner, David Clinton, Daniel G. Lang, Henry A. Kissinger, Arthur Schlesinger, Jr., and George F. Kennan. Jane Lago and Sara Fefer provided valuable editorial assistance in the final preparation of the manuscript.

Portions of this manuscript appeared in slightly different form in *Interpretation, Review of International Studies,* and *Review of Politics* and are reprinted by permission. Also, I am grateful to the Adams Manuscript Trust for permission to quote from John Quincy Adams's 1787 commencement address at Harvard University.

x

Acknowledgments

Shirley Russell, more mistress than wife, has been routinely kind enough to accommodate the worries and labors of this investment. Our two young children, Annelise and Caitlann, are another matter altogether, filled with the turbulence and bustle that easily overwhelm the simplest virtues of parenthood.

John Quincy Adams
and the
Public Virtues of Diplomacy

Introduction

THIS BOOK EXAMINES the philosophical and moral resources of nineteenth-century America's most accomplished diplomat and statesman—John Quincy Adams (1767–1848). The son of John and Abigail Adams enjoyed a career unsurpassed by that of any other American of his generation. A graduate of Harvard College (1787), he served as minister to the Netherlands (1794), minister to Prussia (1797), member of the Massachusetts senate (1802), United States Senator (1803), minister to Russia (1809), minister to Great Britain (1815), secretary of state (1817), president of the United States (1824), and member of the House of Representatives (1831–1848). His distinctive worldview—the product of an extraordinary life at the center of national affairs—substantiates a fundamental link between the internal goals of the American union and external principles of foreign policy conduct. Principles of statecraft could not help but embody the norms of democratic and republican rule. Throughout his life, Adams was drawn inexorably to the intersection of ethics and statesmanship. Moral reasoning enabled Adams to reflect upon the character of democratic foreign policy, in addition to the relationship between methods and purposes of diplomacy in a troubled world. More than any other public official of his day, he elaborated on that "equal station" which Jefferson suggested the "Laws of Nature and of Nature's God" entitled

America to assume in a world of great powers. He defined the nation's obligations to others as a function of the obligations of the nation to its citizens. Adams strengthened this connection through his deliberations on the conflicting vitalities of human nature, the meaning of history, the nature of virtue and happiness in politics and government, and the values of America's national interest in international affairs.

Adams joined with Jefferson in affirming natural rights as the moral compass of the union; he quoted Madison's "pride and boast of America, that the rights for which she contended, were the rights of human nature." As both politician and diplomat, Adams affirmed America's commitment to mankind as well as the existence of clear limits to the nation's moral authority in world affairs. As a realist, in the tradition of Alexander Hamilton, he understood the restraints imposed by an anarchic world arena in which America would only be a minor (but not always unimportant) player in the European balance. As an idealist, in the tradition of Thomas Jefferson, he exhorted his countrymen to uphold the public virtues of republican rule as a model for other nations to emulate. In other words, America's success in the world— for which a prudent and modestly conceived national interest was necessary—was a result of the nation's own moral and spiritual stamina in self-governance. America, Adams wrote in 1816, was "the strongest nation upon the globe for every purpose of justice." Yet he could not "ask of heaven success, even for my country, in a case where she would be in the wrong." He hoped America might "be armed in thunder for the defense of right, and self-shackled in eternal impotence for the support of wrong."[1] From the horizon of ethics, Adams was reluctant to condone any *essential* difference between public and private moral acts. Perhaps the most that can be said concerning the moral character of a private, as opposed to a political, action is that an individual acting in one capacity may be more or less moral than when acting in the other.

Adams forcefully accentuated the importance of national self-restraint

---

1. John Quincy Adams, *The Lives of James Madison and James Monroe*, 22; JQA to John Adams, August 1, 1816, *The Writings of John Quincy Adams*, 6:60–62; hereafter, correspondence cited is from this source unless otherwise indicated.

in his celebrated July 4, 1821, oration before the citizens of Washington. His address was in answer to the question, "What has America done for the benefit of mankind?" In the assembly of nations, the United States "held forth to them the hand of honest friendship, of equal freedom, of generous reciprocity." For over a half century, the nation "abstained from interference in the concerns of others, even when conflict has been for principles to which she clings." In remarks that have lost no relevance with the passage of time, Adams laid down an iron law of American statecraft: "Wherever the standard of freedom and Independence, has or shall be unfurled, there will her heart, her benedictions, and her prayers be. But she goes not abroad, in search of monsters to destroy. She is the well-wisher to the freedom and independence of all. She is the champion and vindicator only of her own."[2] Adams voiced a concern for the consequences of intervention in wars "of interest and intrigue, of individual avarice, envy, and ambition, which assume the colors and usurp the standard of freedom." America's glory "is not *dominion,* but *liberty.* Her march is the march of the mind." Adams's political philosophy and international ethics illustrate how principles of right and obligation in foreign policy take a direct bearing from the moral and political order of civil society.

The intellectual universe of John Quincy Adams, a compound of Christian faith and classical virtue, discloses the unique resources that molded the diplomatic achievements of America's greatest secretary of state in the nineteenth century. What has been described as the golden age of American statecraft, the 1814–1828 era, forms the backdrop for Adams's diplomacy during the Madison and Monroe administrations. During these years, the United States signed the treaty ending the War of 1812, issued the Monroe Doctrine, and strengthened its maritime power through an agreement with Britain to clear the Great Lakes of warships and by obtaining rights to fish off the coast of Labrador and Newfoundland. Americans extended their continental reach through the annexation of Florida, by removing Russian influence from the

2. John Quincy Adams, *An Address Delivered at the Request of a Committee of the Citizens of Washington; on the Occasion of Reading the Declaration of Independence, on the Fourth of July, 1821,* 30–31.

southwestern coast of North America, through the establishment of the American-Canadian boundary from the Great Lakes to the Rockies, and by staking their first claims to the Pacific coast.[3] Adams was a central figure in all these transactions and, in each instance, saw a larger moral message for the exercise of power in defense of the national interest. His inability to countenance an irremediable gap between the principles of ethics and diplomacy provides a useful point of departure for rethinking the moral responsibilities of American statesmen. Adams's quality as a human being has a direct and obvious relation to his political and social thinking.

That Adams as thinker has been largely ignored by most standard works on America's intellectual traditions may be explained by the manner in which his worldview cut across conventional theoretical guideposts. Henry Adams considered that his grandfather had been a political man, actuated by ordinary feelings; whereas Brooks Adams judged him an "idealistic philosopher who sought with absolute disinterestedness to put the Union upon a plane of civilization which would have averted the . . . recent [civil] war; who had failed, as all men must fail who harbor such a purpose, and who . . . resigned himself and his ambitions to fate."[4] Adams's social and political thought derived in great measure from his own reading of classical as well as seventeenth- and eighteenth-century thinkers. He was also obligated to the long tradition of medieval political thought, back to St. Thomas Aquinas, in which the reality of moral restraints on power, the responsibility of rulers to the communities they ruled, and the subordination of government to law were axiomatic. His combination of the Lockean position with an emphasis on the vigorous role to be played by government in a program of internal improvements; his combination of a strong nationalism based upon a sense of moral rectitude with an insistence on self-restraint, equality, and a recognition of moral laws in the relations of nations; his combination of a religious faith in natural law

---

3. Walter LaFeber, ed. *John Quincy Adams and the American Continental Empire*, 13.
4. Henry Adams, *The Degradation of the Democratic Dogma*, vii; Allan Nevins, ed., *The Diary of John Quincy Adams, 1794–1845*, ix.

with an empirical and skeptical view in the realm of science made Adams unique among public figures of his day in the United States.

Adams was aptly described by Hans J. Morgenthau as the classic example of the political moralist in thought and word, who cannot help being a political realist in action. His international thought was anchored in the realist tradition of Washington and Hamilton; yet he did the better part of his work in statecraft in an atmosphere saturated with Jeffersonian principles. Between Adams's moral principles and his conception of the national interest there was hardly ever a conflict. The moral principles, as Morgenthau noted, were nothing but political interests formulated in moral terms, and vice versa. Adams's seminal contributions to the American diplomatic tradition—freedom of the seas, the Monroe Doctrine, and Manifest Destiny—are evidence of this achievement. For example, the legal principle of freedom of the seas was a weapon through which an inferior naval power tried to safeguard its independence from Great Britain. Similarly, the Monroe Doctrine's moral postulates of nonintervention (and anti-imperialism) were negative conditions for the security and prestige of the United States. Their fulfillment insulated the young republic from the power struggles in Europe and, through it, ensured the predominance of the United States in the Western Hemisphere. Manifest Destiny was the moral and ideological incentive for American continental expansion and subjugation of native inhabitants.[5]

Morgenthau's analysis, however, speaks more to effect and less to cause. The implication of his commentary, and the argument of this book, is that realism and idealism need not be treated as mutually exclusive categories from which to judge the words and deeds of the statesman. Equally important in this connection is whether moral desiderata above the nation state function only as an ideological apology for the powerful (the homage that vice pays to virtue) or as an exercise in costly self-deception for the weak. Is the statesman ill-advised to derive norms of national conduct from some source other than mundane political reality? While Adams was by no means a

5. Hans J. Morgenthau, *In Defense of the National Interest*, 19, 22.

systematic thinker, he evolved a conception of life, God, and the universe into which his attitude on all the political problems of his time may be fitted.

Samuel Flagg Bemis's classic two-volume political biography of John Quincy Adams is unsurpassed to this day in its analysis and detail. Secondary historical works typically have focused on a particular facet of Adams's wide-ranging public service.[6] This book fills a void by bringing together Adams's political and literary careers, by looking to his statesmanship as an expression of distinct intellectual and diplomatic traditions. Foremost among these was Adams's reliance upon the classical and Christian backgrounds of American constitutionalism. His attempt to reconcile natural law with a vision of activist government committed to the public interest is highlighted through extensive reliance upon source materials in the Adams Papers Collection, in addition to his *Memoirs* (twelve volumes) and *Writings* (seven volumes).

The first chapter provides a broad overview of Adams's life and political career. An attempt is made in these pages to illuminate the many familial, institutional, and educational influences on his understanding of American government and the duties of citizenship.

The second chapter investigates Adams's political realism as an expression of classical and modern political thought, as well as an inquiry into the ethics of Christianity. Adams drew extensively upon Christian revelation as well as Greek (Socrates, Plato, Aristotle) and Roman (Virgil, Quintilian, Cicero) thought to explain the concept of virtue at the center of man's political nature. Human nature was the starting point for Adams's political theory. Alexander Pope's *Essay on Man*, and the symbol of the Great Chain of Being, was a powerful influence on Adams's diagnosis of the balance between reason and passion in man's political behavior. Other topics taken up here include

---

6. Samuel Flagg Bemis, *John Quincy Adams and the Foundations of American Foreign Policy* and *John Quincy Adams and the Union;* Mary W. M. Hargreaves, *The Presidency of John Quincy Adams;* Leonard Richards, *The Life and Times of Congressman John Quincy Adams;* Robert East, *John Quincy Adams, the Critical Years: 1785–1794.*

Adams's commentary on the social contract, the nature of representation, democracy, equality, and reconciling individual liberty with a clear concept of the public interest.

The third chapter evaluates Adams's contribution to the larger historical debate regarding the relationship between domestic and foreign obligations for republican governments. For early American statesmen, the heritage of classical and modern thought posed two essential questions: 1) whether internal or external affairs should have primacy in calculating the national interest; and 2) whether expansion and foreign involvement are compatible with republican principles of government. Thucydides' *History of the Peloponnesian War*, no less than the philosophy of Plato and Aristotle, enabled American thinkers to reflect on the priorities attributed to internal and external policies. At the same time, the Founders drew upon the insights of modern thinkers: Machiavelli, Francis Bacon, James Harrington, Algernon Sidney, Montesquieu, and David Hume. Adams embraced both traditions and added a greater diversity of thought to the facile distinction between "power politics" and "moral choice" in defending the normative foundations of the national interest.

The fourth chapter brings together Adams's writings and orations on the founding period and the values of the American nation. Adams wrote at length on the New England Confederacy, Declaration of Independence, Articles of Confederation, and federal Constitution. The documents of the American Revolution shaped his political views on the scope of federalism, separation of powers doctrine, and debate over state sovereignty. He also resorted to the language of classical politics and Anglo-Saxon Whiggery to defend the formal institutions of republican government.

The fifth chapter connects politics and statecraft by analyzing a number of Adams's youthful essays from the 1790s. The letters of "Publicola" (1791), inspired by the controversy between Thomas Paine and Edmund Burke concerning the French Revolution, point to Adams's reliance on natural law to defend minority rights in representative government. The letters of "Marcellus" and "Columbus" (1793) laid out a course of action that brought Adams into line with the foreign policy of Washington's Farewell Address, later reiterated in the Monroe Doctrine, and associated with the general concept of the two separate spheres, or systems, of policy.

The sixth chapter draws on Adams's unique diplomatic legacy as an important case study documenting the significance of moral reasoning in the statesman's obligation to uphold the national interest in a universal system of power politics. Recourse to political ethics afforded Adams a vantage point from which to evaluate the volatile problem of intervention—viewed in terms of the moral responsibilities and limits of American power—at a crucial turning point in the diplomatic history of the young republic. Attention is devoted to Adams's reaction to European intervention in the Western Hemisphere, American incursions into Spanish Florida, and American support for Latin American independence and the war with Mexico.

A conclusion outlines the enduring lessons and foreign policy principles of Adams's statesmanship. His realism was grounded in a tragic sense of politics; yet he realized that the very recognition of tragedy and human failing depends upon an appreciation of transcendent standards through which to gaze upon the misery *and* grandeur of the human condition. Part of Adams's contribution to the nation's intellectual life arises from his defense of religion and virtue as indispensable components of the American liberal mind. On the one hand, moral standards served as the relevant, objective, and constant goal of Adams's political universe. He argued that both individuals and states must judge political action by universal moral principles, such as that of liberty. On the other hand, political ethics enabled Adams to expose and moderate the temptation to hypocritical pretense in foreign policy. The prudent statesman, capable of distinguishing between the expedience of power and the realm of universal ethical norm, is less apt to commit the sin of equating political or military success with moral superiority.

ONE

Revolutionary Politics and Training for Statesmanship

John Quincy Adams was born in the North Parish of Braintree, Massachusetts, on July 11, 1767. Family lineage alone brought him into a world of great events with an excellent prospect for public service—*non sine dis animosus infans*. He was named after his great-grandfather on the maternal side, John Quincy, a long-serving Speaker of the House of Representatives in Massachusetts and a vigorous champion of colonial rights and liberties. Adams, in one of his letters, reflected on the meaning of his baptism, and how the passing of his ancestor carried an undying moral lesson for his existence.

> The incidence that gave rise to this circumstance is not without its moral to my heart. He was dying when I was baptized; and his daughter, my grandmother, present at my birth, requested that I . . . receive his name. The fact, recorded by my father at the time, has connected with that portion of my name, a charm of mingled sensibility and devotion. It was filial tenderness that gave the name. It was the name of one passing from earth to immortality. These have been among the strongest links of my attachment to the name of Quincy, and have been to me through life a perpetual admonition to do nothing unworthy of it.[1]

1. Adams quoted in William Henry Seward, *Life and Public Services of John Quincy Adams*, 23.

This honorable patronymic was renewed in 1833 at the birth of John Quincy Adams II, the son of Charles Francis and Abigail Brooks Adams. The joy of the newborn's grandfather was evident by the entry in his diary on September 30: "There is no Passion more deeply seated in my bosom than the longing for posterity worthily to support my own and my father's name. . . . For this I have done my part. My Sons must do theirs. There is now one Son of the next Generation, and my hopes revive."[2]

I.

Fate, which had made such good preparation for John Quincy Adams before his birth, was no less generous in shaping the circumstances of his early training and maturation. The career of this boy was to be filled with stirring and portentous events, "all of which he saw and much of which he was." The Hutchison riot over the Stamp Act had occurred just two years prior to his birth; the Boston Massacre was not quite three years into the future; the Boston Tea Party would transpire in six years; in seven years the boy's father would be one of the leaders of the First Continental Congress and in nine years one of the signers of the Declaration of Independence. On June 17, 1775, the seven-year-old lad stood at his mother's side on Penn's Hill and "heard Britannia's thunder in the battle of Bunker Hill, and witnessed the tears of my mother . . . at the fall of [Joseph] Warren, a dear friend of my father, and a beloved physician to me." In the days of Rome's imperialism, Cicero speaks of war being detested by Roman mothers,—*Bella matronis detesta*. Adams recalled how his own mother, "bred in the *faith* of deliberate detestation of war," supervised his daily recitation of "the Ode of [William] Collins on the patriotic *warriors* who fell in the war to subdue the Jacobite rebellion of 1745."

> How sleep the *brave*, who sink to rest,
> By all their Country's wishes blest!
> When Spring, with dewy fingers cold,

2. Jack Shepherd, *The Adams' Chronicles, Four Generations of Greatness*, 320.

Returns to deck their hallow'd mould,
She there shall dress a sweeter sod
Than Fancy's feet have ever trod
By Fairy hands their knell is rung,
By forms unseen their dirge is sung,
There *Honour* comes, a pilgrim grey,
To bless the turf that wraps their clay,
And Freedom shall awhile repair,
To dwell, a weeping Hermit, there.[3]

Recalling these lines seventy years later, Adams affirmed his revulsion of war waged "by tyrants and oppressors, against the rights of human nature and . . . the rightful interests of my country." Never a pacifist, however, he judged that war in defense of these principles, "far from deserving my execration, is . . . a religious and sacred duty." *Dulce et decorum est, pro patria mori.*[4]

With John Adams away at the Continental Congress, the boy had no regular schooling apart from family connections and young law clerks under the tuition of his father. Yet the extensive guidance and tutelage both parents provided for their son would later serve John Quincy well in his own paternal counsel that his two children "have some single great end or object to accomplish." Edward Everett, in his eulogy on John Quincy Adams, commented that there seemed to be no such stage as that of boyhood. When a mere nine years old, he wrote his father the following letter:

Dear Sir,
I love to receive letters very well; much better than I love to write them. . . . Mamma has a troublesome task to keep me steady, and I own I am ashamed of myself. I have but just entered the 3d volume of Smollet, tho' I had designed to have got it half through by this time. I have determined this week to be more diligent. . . . I have Set myself a Stent & determine to read the 3d volume Half out. If I can but keep my resolution, I will write again at the end of the week and give a

3. Bennett Champ Clark, *John Quincy Adams, "Old Man Eloquent,"* 16–17; *Memoirs of John Quincy Adams, Comprising Portions of His Diary from 1795 to 1848,* 1:5–6; W. Moy Thomas, ed., *The Poetical Works of William Collins,* 51.
4. *Memoirs,* 1:6.

better account of myself. I wish, Sir, you would give me some instructions, with regard to my time, & advise me how to proportion my Studies & my Play, in writing, & I will keep them by me, & endeavour to follow them. . . .

P. S.—Sir, if you will be so good as to favour me with a Blank book, I will transcribe the most remarkable occurrences I mett with in my reading, which will serve to fix them on my mind.[5]

Making due allowance for precocity of genius, the early maturity of the younger Adams proves the signal advantage of pure and intellectual associations in childhood.

The education of John Quincy Adams was an introduction to the principles of heroic action and to the moral ties that bind men together in an associated state of happiness. His father insisted that human nature, in all its infirmities, is still capable of great things. Education made greater differences between man and man than nature made between man and brute. The virtue and moral examples "to which men may be trained, by early education and constant discipline, are truly sublime and astonishing." Both "Newton and Locke" could be profitably read as "examples of the deep sagacity which may be acquired by long habits of thinking and study." It should be Abigail's care and his, therefore, to "elevate the minds of our children, and exalt their courage, to accelerate and animate their industry and activity, to excite in them an habitual contempt of meanness, an abhorrence of injustice and inhumanity, and an ambition to excel in every capacity, faculty, and virtue. If we suffer their minds to grovel and creep in infancy, they will grovel and creep all their lives."[6] Timing was also a factor in the education of the young; early youth was the period to inculcate taste and judgment, before any unchaste sounds had fastened on children's ears, and before any affectation or superfluous vanity was settled on their minds.

For Abigail, the "school mistress," a curriculum of study should enable children to rivet "their Attention upon great and glorious Ob-

5. Ibid., 1:8–9; Edward Everett, *A Eulogy on the Life and Character of John Quincy Adams*, 13–17.

6. John Adams to Abigail Adams, October 29, 1775, *Adams Family Correspondence*, 1:317–18; Phyllis Lee Levin, *Abigail Adams, A Biography*, 41–43.

jects, to root out every little Thing, . . . [and] make them great and manly." With an admixture of puritan and patriotic resolve, she acted upon the recommendation of her husband: "Let them revere nothing, but Religion, Morality and Liberty." What Abigail described as "first principles" encompassed norms and mores which would provide the young with the strength of character "to [resist] such examples as would tend to corrupt the purity of their words and action." She would rather "they . . . chill with horror at the sound of an oath and blush with indignation at an obscene expression." Writing to her son in 1778, Abigail suggested that the "most useful disposition in a young mind is diffidence of itself." Diffidence, understood not as the absence of self-confidence but as openness to "advice and instruction from . . . your natural guardian," is the precondition for present and future happiness. Great learning or superior abilities are of little service "unless virtue, truth, and integrity are added to them." She exhorted her son to "adhere to those religious sentiments and principles which were early instilled" in his mind and to recognize that his words and actions are accountable to a superintending deity. There was no truth more certain than "that the welfare and prosperity of all countries, communities, and . . . individuals, depend upon their morals." America's revolutionary struggle with Britain was one such epoch whereby civic virtue and personal sacrifice might combine to crown political success and ennoble the human character.

> These are the times in which a genius would wish to live. It is not in the still calm of life, or the repose of a pacific station, that great characters are formed. Would Cicero have shone so distinguished an orator if he had not been roused, kindled, and inflamed by the tyranny of Catiline, Verres, and Mark Anthony? Great necessities call out great virtues. When a mind is . . . animated by scenes that engage the heart, then those qualities, which would otherwise lie dormant, wake into life and form the character of the hero and statesman.[7]

Abigail Adams advised her son that his earthly duties were given "in the first place, to your great Preserver; in the next to society in general;

7. John Adams to Abigail Adams, April 15, 1776, *Adams Family Correspondence,* 1:384; *Letters of Mrs. Adams, the Wife of John Adams,* 18, 95–96, 110–11.

in particular, to your country, to your parents, and to yourself." The only sure and permanent foundation of individual virtue is religion. Moreover, the only certain foundation of religion "is the belief in the one . . . God, and a just sense of his attributes, as a being infinitely wise, just, and good." Reverence of the Almighty who governs nature "more particularly regards man, whom he created after his own image, and breathed into him an immortal spirit capable of a happiness beyond the grave." The experience receives elegant portrayal by Alexander Pope in his *Essay on Man.*

> Remember man, the universal cause
> Acts not by partial, but by general laws,
> And makes what happiness we justly call,
> Subsist not in the good of one, but all.
> There's not a blessing individuals find,
> But some way leans and hearkens to the kind.[8]

Thus the Supreme Being makes the goodwill of man toward his fellow creatures an example of his regard to Him, "and for this purpose has constituted him a dependent being and made his happiness to consist in society."[9]

Justice, humanity, and benevolence are the duties owed to society and country. The latter carries "the additional obligation of sacrificing ease, pleasure, wealth, and life itself for its defence and security." One of the most useful lessons of all life, said Abigail Adams in a letter to her son, is the knowledge and study of yourself. "Passions are the elements of life," but elements which are subject to the control of reason. Hence an inspired writer observes, "He that is slow to anger, is better than the mighty; and he that ruleth his spirit, than he that taketh a city." Throughout his life, John Quincy Adams fought to govern and control himself while observing the effects of lawless power and malignant passions in his own homeland. Self-government was to be the key to both individual happiness and his usefulness to mankind. "Virtue

---

8. *Letters of Mrs. Adams,* 18, 95–96, 110–11; Alexander Pope, *Collected Poems,* 206.
9. *Letters of Mrs. Adams,* 114.

alone is happiness below"; and it "consists in cultivating and improving every good inclination, and in . . . subduing every propensity to evil."[10]

II.

Over a seven-year period, from 1778 to 1785, the parochial attachments of an American youth would undergo cosmopolitan refinements in travel to the leading capitals and artistic centers of Europe. In February 1778, on board the frigate *Boston*, John Quincy accompanied his father on a brief diplomatic mission to Paris, the latter receiving a commission to join Benjamin Franklin and Arthur Lee in negotiating treaties of commerce and alliance with France. Late in 1779, once again, John Adams—now Minister Plenipotentiary instructed to negotiate a treaty of peace with Great Britain—set out for France on the leaky *La Sensible*. John Quincy, hesitant about a second voyage, was persuaded by his mother's insistence: "In all human probability," she said, "it will do more for your education to go back to France with your father than to prepare for college at Andover." After six months of schooling at Passy, he transferred to the Latin School in Amsterdam and pursued classical studies at the University of Leyden. By the age of ten, he had read two volumes of Smollett's *Complete History of England*, some Shakespeare and Pope, and James Thomson's *The Seasons* and had attempted Milton's *Paradise Lost*. Two years earlier, John Adams recommended that his son study Thucydides' *History of the Peloponnesian War*, for future times might require new wars, councils, and negotiations. His lifelong obsession with books was evident in the earliest of entries in his stupendous diary. In addition to describing routine matters of travel, he copied extensively from Samuel Garth ("Epilogue to the Tragedy of Cato"); Joseph Addison's translation of Horace; Edmund Waller ("Of the Fear of God"); and William Guthrie's *Geographical Grammar*.[11]

10. Ibid., 115–16.

11. Abigail Adams quoted in Bemis, *John Quincy Adams and the Foundations of American Foreign Policy*, 11; *Diary of John Quincy Adams*, ed. David Grayson Allen, Robert J. Taylor, Marc Friedlaender, and Celeste Walker, 1:xxxv–xxxvi, xxxix.

Adams's apprenticeship to the diplomatic craft began on July 7, 1781, when the fourteen-year-old became the private secretary to Francis Dana, newly appointed American representative in Russia. Dana, later chief justice of the Massachusetts Supreme Court, attempted unsuccessfully to persuade Catherine the Great to receive his country into the League of Armed Neutrality by a treaty that would include formal recognition of the fledgling republic. The American minister, who could not speak French, was assisted by the French ambassador, Marquis de Verac, who could not speak English. Adams's command of the diplomatic language made him a useful interpreter and copyist in performing the duties of the legation in St. Petersburg. With a keen eye for social evil, he wrote to his father about the difficulty of advancing his education in a country without schools; he complained, "There is nobody here but princes and slaves, the slaves can not have their children instructed, and the nobility that choose to have theirs, send them into foreign countries." According to his letters and diary, Adams seems to have spent a large portion of his year in Russia reading English and European history by such authors as Hume, Macaulay, and Robertson. In the third volume of Hume's *History of England*, Adams found "an exact description of the present state of" Russian society.

> If we consider the antient state of Europe, we . . . find that the far greater part of society were every where bereaved of their *personal* liberty and lived entirely at the will of their masters. Everyone that was not noble was a slave. The peasants were sold along with the land. . . . Even the gentry . . . were subjected to a long train of subordination, under the greater barons or chief vassals of the crown, who tho' . . . placed in a high state of splendor, yet, having but a slender protection, of the law, were exposed to every tempest of the state, and by the precarious condition in which they lived, paid dearly for the power of . . . tyrannizing over their inferiors.[12]

Because he had not brought a Latin dictionary, and could not find one in St. Petersburg for several months, he was unable to continue his classical studies until after 1782.

12. Adams quoted in Clark, *John Quincy Adams*, 22; *Adams Family Correspondence*, 4:286–87.

From October 1782 until April 1783, when he returned to his father's residence at The Hague, John Quincy embarked on a seven-month journey through Sweden, Denmark, and Germany. He wrote of Frederick the Great's unfavorable reaction to German *belles-lettres*, made inquiries on the prospect of commercial relations between the United States and Scandinavian countries, and advised merchants on the most desirable exports to America. The bright years in Paris, when he served as his father's private secretary, introduced him to the extravagances of Versailles and the protocol of the diplomatic corps. He contributed, in a small and confidential capacity, to the preparation of papers used in the diplomatic exchanges for the Treaty of Paris. In addition, he pondered politics and science with Franklin and Jefferson, delighted in the Paris theater and opera, and attended the dinners that Lafayette gave every Monday for his American friends. His education was not neglected. He renewed his interest in French literature: he read the works of Voltaire, Molière, Beaumarchais, Rousseau, Rabelais, La Fontaine, Laplace and Le Sage's *Gil Blas*. Evenings at home afforded John Adams the opportunity of exposing the youth to algebra, plane and solid geometry, and trigonometry. Later sent to England to meet his mother, he spent hours listening to debates in the House of Commons. That great age of English eloquence—Fox, Pitt, Burke, Sheridan, and North—allowed John Quincy to act upon his father's recommendation to scrutinize the principal orators. He preferred the younger Pitt to Fox, though adding with customary censoriousness: "But they are both very great men, and it is a real misfortune . . . that those talents which were made to promote the honor and power of the nation should be prostituted to views of interest and ambition."[13]

In 1785, John Adams received an appointment as the first American minister to the Court of St. James (a position which later would be filled both by his son and grandson); the prospect of extending his European visit prompted the younger Adams to see his own career in relationship to the people and ideas of his own country.

---

13. JQA to John Adams, June 18, 1784, 1:15–16; Bemis, *John Quincy Adams and the Foundations of American Foreign Policy*, 15–16.

I am determined that so long as I shall be able to get my own living in an honorable manner, I will depend on no one. . . .
>*But still . . . Oh! how wretched*
>*Is that poor man, that hangs on Princes' favors.*

My father has . . . taken up all his lifetime with the interests of the public, that his own fortune has suffered by it: so that his children will have to provide for themselves, which I shall never be able to do if I loiter my . . . time in Europe. . . . With an ordinary share of common sense, which I hope I enjoy, at least in America, I can live *independent* and *free*; and rather than live otherwise, I would wish to die before the time when I shall be left at my own discretion.[14]

After a brief stopover in New York, where he was entertained by Richard Henry Lee and John Jay, he returned to Cambridge and was admitted to the junior class at Harvard, in March 1786. Harvard and John Quincy Adams were a perfect match. "A person who wishes to make any figure as a scholar at this University, must not spend much time either in visiting or being visited." Education taught him "that inseparable connection between knowledge, and virtue and liberty, which characterized . . . the Puritan settlers of New England." Even as the child is to "be educated for manhood upon earth, so the man must be educated upon earth, for heaven; and . . . where the foundation is not laid in Time, the superstructure cannot rise for Eternity." Adams recorded the verses from Pope with which his philosophy professor concluded a memorable lecture.

>All are but parts of one stupendous whole
>Whose Body, Nature is, and God, the Soul;
>That, chang'd through all, and yet in all the same;
>Great in the Earth, as in the ethereal frame;
>Warms in the Sun, refreshes in the breeze,
>Glows in the stars, and blossoms in the trees,
>Lives through all Life, extends through all extent,
>Spreads undivided, operates unspent;

14. *Diary of John Quincy Adams,* 1:256–57; *King Henry VIII,* act 3, scene 2, lines 366–67.

To him no high, no low, no great, no small;
He fills, he bounds, connects and equals all.[15]

Adams's participation in a series of "forensic disputations" at the university provides clues to the formative beliefs that would mold his judgment on perennial questions of politics, religion, and human existence. In September 1786, he took the affirmative stance on the question, "Whether inequalities among Citizens, be necessary to the Preservation of the Liberty of the Whole?" He identified two views on how inequality relates to the citizens of a state—inequality "of Fortune, or of Rights, Privileges and Dignities." Of the former, he had no doubt that inequality follows from "the natural Course of Things." The proper question, Adams said, is "whether a pure democracy [can] be the most favorable Government to the Liberties of a People."[16] His distrust of the multitude led him to embrace the ancient maxim that men can never possess a great degree of power without abusing it. His estimate of human nature was supplemented with commentary upon the classical schema of government by one (monarchy), few (aristocracy), or many (democracy).

Of all the variations of tyranny, the most dreadful is that form that rises in the name of an entire population; "and in a Government, where all men are equal, the People will infallibly become tyrants." Laws cannot afford citizens protection where every person "has a right of altering and annulling them . . . and where nothing is wanting, but the capricious whim of a vile Rabble." It may be supposed that a single despot has learned "in some measure, the Art of governing an Empire"; similarly, aristocratic leaders may be expected to uphold the dignity of the state and "take . . . measures for the safety of the majority . . . though they may be unjust to individuals." When the passions of the people are aroused, however, "they hurry into the greatest extremities . . . and their Ignorance serves only to increase their Obstinacy, and their Inconsistency." Inequalities in temperament and skill—and the

---

15. JQA to John Adams, May 21, 1786, 1:25; John Quincy Adams, *Discourse on Education*, delivered at Braintree, Thursday, October 24, 1839, 36; Pope, *Collected Poems*, 188–89.

16. *Diary of John Quincy Adams*, 2:99.

rewards individuals thereby achieve—do not create a presumption that "they ought all to share an equal degree of Power." In addition, the poor, who claim to have been injured by those who "have amassed too large a Proportion of Wealth," do not suffer their misfortune because of political oppression. On the contrary, the experience of his own commonwealth convinced Adams that the reason "is because other Persons have been more industrious, more prudent and more success-ful than they." His was a plea neither "for an excess of inequality" nor against "an equal right to Justice, and to the Protection of the Laws." Individual virtue could and should rise above hereditary distinctions.

> Wealth may with Propriety be transmitted from Father to Son. *But Honour and Dignities, should always be personal.* [italics added] The Man who to the greatest natural and acquired Abilities unites the greatest Virtues, should certainly not be view'd as on a Par with a vicious Fool, but the absurdity would I confess be equally great, if any one was obliged to enquire who were the Ancestors of a Citizen, to know whether he be respectable.[17]

Adams, recalling Thucydides' account of the war between Athens and Sparta, suggested that the "History of Lacedaemon certainly can produce no Argument in favour of equality." First, Sparta grew from the seeds of hereditary monarchy. The myths of antiquity record that two branches of a family "descended from Hercules, were in Possession of the Throne for nine-hundred years." Second, the twenty-eight–member senate formed an aristocratic body with power equal to that of kings. Third, the authority of the Ephori, "who were chosen annu-ally among the People was superior even to that of Monarchs." Fur-thermore, the lawgiver Lycurgus sought "to establish by Force, a Con-stitution which could form nothing but warriors." Adams found it impossible to read Thucydides' chronicle of the factions and confu-sions throughout all Greece—"introduced by a want of equilibrium among classes"—without horror.

> During the few days that Eurymedon, with his troops, continued at Corcyra, the people of that city extended the massacre to all whom

17. Ibid., 100, 102.

they judged their enemies. The crime alleged was their attempt to overturn the democracy. Some perished merely through private enmity; some by the hands of the borrower, on account of the money they had lent. Every kind of death, every dreadful act, was perpetrated. Fathers slew their children; some were dragged from altars, some were butchered at them. . . . The contagion spread through the whole extent of Greece; factions raged in every city; the licentious many contending for the Athenians, and the aspiring few for the Lacedaemonians.[18]

"Such things will ever be," says Thucydides, "so long as human nature continues the same." For Adams, those "fine feelings of the Heart which render human Nature amiable" can only be protected by a constitution "which might unite all the advantages, severally possessed by each of those Systems [monarchy, aristocracy, democracy], without having their Defects."[19]

In April 1787, Adams took the affirmative position in debating the question, "Whether the introduction of Christianity has been serviceable to the temporal interests of mankind." A liberal system of religion, "unlike the forcible arguments of an infallible inquisition," does not stifle every sentiment that can counterbalance the vices and follies of human nature. Adams conceded that his adversaries would "have a rich plunder of argument" in juxtaposing the Christian religion to "the bloodiest and most devastating wars that ever afflicted the human race." From the days of Nero to those of Constantine, "the bloody banner of Persecution was . . . continually display'd against the peaceful standard of Christ." The Crusades, calculated to consolidate the faith, "increased the importance of religion, by the murder of millions: and when the Christian world grew weary of contending with foreign enemies, they soon discovered, that they had sufficient to do, to defend the glory of Christ against one another."[20]

Christian ethics, then, must be sharply distinguished from every form of moralistic program and ideological credo that would claim for

18. Cited in John Adams, *A Defence of the Constitutions of Government of the United States of America*, 1:iv–v; Thucydides, *The Peloponnesian War*, 236–45.

19. *Diary of John Quincy Adams*, 2:102–3.

20. Ibid., 2:191–92; Adams, *A Discourse on Education*, 17.

their partial insights a more ultimate standing than they deserve. For Adams, religion was not just a matter of doing good, feeling holy, or experiencing the transcendent; it was also grasping the tincture of evil in one's efforts to do good, recognizing one's mortality, realizing that the transcendent was not attainable in society. Moral judgments can easily spill over into Pharisaism, exemplified by the priggish moralizers Christ condemned in the Gospels. One can turn to the parable of the Pharisee and the publican in the eighteenth chapter of the Gospel according to St. Luke.

> Two men went up to the temple to pray; the one a Pharisee, and the other a publican. The pharisee stood and prayed thus with himself, God, I thank thee, that I am not as other men are extortioners, unjust, adulterers, or even as this publican. . . . And the publican standing afar off, would not lift so much as his eyes unto heaven, but smote upon his breast, saying, God be merciful to me a sinner. I tell you, this man went down to his house justified rather than the other: for every one that exalteth himself shall be abased, and he that humbleth himself shall be exalted.[21]

Admitting all these facts to be incontestable, Adams did not believe that "every trifling deviation of sentiment" invalidated the advantages rendered by Christianity to mankind. From St. Augustine on, churchmen elaborated the precepts of natural law and the Ciceronian doctrine of just and unjust war. The source of discord among men should be attributed "to an infernal spirit which cannot be rooted from their hearts, and not to a religion whose main object is to oppose that spirit." Christianity, Adams admitted, may have been the immediate object of many contests; however, "when mankind have an inclination to quarrel with one another, a motive is early found." Eminent jurists—Pufendorf, Vattel, and Grotius—record how "the Christian institution" inspired the intellect and will of men to reduce the frequency of war and to mitigate its cruelties. Christianity holds both men and nations subject to a transcendent moral and political order, one that prompts them to treat individuals as more than means to an end. The

---

21. Kenneth W. Thompson, *Political Realism and the Crisis of World Politics*, 140–41.

moral criteria of the Judeo-Christian tradition, Adams argued, "has vindicated the rights of nature" insofar as

> it has enlarged our views and taught us, not to confine our goodwill and friendship, to the small circle from whom we have received, or to whom we have granted favours, but to embrace in the arms of our affection the whole human race: it has inculcated the sublime maxim of loving our enemies, and of praying for those who persecute, and in short, if it does not enable us to reach the summit of perfection, it is because we wilfully depart from its guidance and direction.[22]

Like the Founding Fathers, Adams opposed any system of dual morality in the uses of politics and diplomacy—i.e., by setting the political sphere apart from the private one for purposes of ethical evaluation. In his Harvard commencement address upon graduating (second in his class) in 1787, Adams took up the problem in a speech on the "Importance of Public Faith to the Well-Being of a Community." The inspiring essay induced a person then so esteemed as Dr. Jeremy Belknap to apply for a copy to be inserted in the *Columbian Magazine* of Philadelphia. A few days afterward a sharp rebuttal appeared in one of the Boston newspapers. The controversy that the speech precipitated was even more important than its successful publication. It portended, as Charles Francis Adams noted, the rise of a power to be developed throughout life "much more by the opposition it aroused than by the favor it conciliated." Political history is ripe with examples whereby antagonism helps to bring to view the high qualities of a statesman much more than the most zealous friendship.[23]

Adams was troubled by the intimation "that nations are not subjected to those laws which regulate the conduct of individuals; that national policy commands them to consult their interest, though at the expense of foreigners, or of individual citizens." Expedience was the rule for political cynics who insist "that it is the duty of every government to alleviate the distresses of the people, over whom it is placed; and that a violation of the public faith cannot subject any individual to

---

22. *Diary of John Quincy Adams*, 2:193.
23. *Memoirs*, 1:22.

censure." This conclusion, Adams retorted, is based upon "no other principle than the probability of escaping the punishment due to the most flagrant enormities." Could there, he asked, be more than one kind of justice and equity? Could "honor and probity be qualities of such an accommodating nature that they will, like the venal sycophant of a Court, suit themselves at all times to the interests of the prevailing party?" The very existence of political rights, whether possessed by an individual or by a society, implies a corresponding obligation. A nation, then, can have no right to "form treaties, or to enter into contracts of any kind without being held by every bond of justice to the performance." Any man who could "be regardless of his country's faith, must always be regardless of his own."[24]

Deciding halfheartedly upon law as a profession, Adams spent the next three years (before being admitted to the bar in 1790) in study with Theophilus Parsons, of Newburyport, later chief justice of the Massachusetts Supreme Court. Judge Parsons advised his disciple "to read a number of ethic writers." Studying such orators as "Quintilian, and the best writers upon Christianity," was indispensable for wise legal counsel. It was necessary for a person going into the legal profession to have principles firmly established; otherwise, "however amiable and however honest his disposition might be, the necessity he is under of defending indiscriminately the good and the bad, the right and the wrong, would imperceptibly lead him into universal skepticism." Ethics was a natural calling for one who had "an opportunity to observe the effects of the passions, how despotically they rule! how they bend and master the greatest and wisest geniuses! 'Tis a pity . . . that prudence should desert people when they have most need of it." Adams's lament notwithstanding—"Human Nature, how inexplicable art thou!"—he realized that human beings cannot help *but* bring a political dimension to the study of ethics.[25]

24. John Quincy Adams, "An Oration upon the Importance and Necessity of Public Faith, to the Well-Being of a Community," delivered at Harvard University on July 17, 1787, Adams MSS; Adams to Jeremy Belknap, August 6, 1787, 1:34–35.

25. *Diary of John Quincy Adams*, 2:319–20; Josiah Quincy, *Memoir of the Life of John Quincy Adams*, 64–65.

During these critical years, in the shadows of the federal convention and Washington's first administration, Adams endured the sometimes agonizing rite of passage from his private station to an imposing public stage. This was a period of conscious formulation of his basic political concepts. Regarding the work accomplished at Philadelphia in 1787, he wrote, "If the Constitution be adopted, it will be a grand point gained in favour of the aristocratic party. There are to be no titles of nobility; but there will be great distinctions and these distinctions will soon be hereditary." Although Adams was "willing to take [his] chance under any government whatever," he had always held free government to be inconsistent with human nature. Yet time worked great changes in his political outlook. The influence of his father led to a change in attitude after John Quincy read an extract from the third volume of *A Defence of the Constitutions of Government of the United States of America*. The argument therein "speaks very favourably of the System proposed by the Federal Convention. . . . I did not expect it, and am glad to find I was mistaken since, it appears probable, the plan will be adopted."[26]

This was also a period in Adams's life, as revealed by personal sketches published as *Life in a New England Town, 1787–1788*, of purgatorial self-doubt about himself and his world. Whatever twisting of the ego and hypochondria accompanied the inward labors of his mind, he had no illusions about the existence of genuine public standards of service. Fretting about his "state of useless and disgraceful insignificancy," he looked upon his twenty-fifth year as a time when others "who were born for the benefit of their fellow creatures . . . rendered themselves conspicuous among their contemporaries." Adams confronted his own ambition, constant and unceasing, but without "a desire to establish either fame, honor, or fortune upon any other foundation than that of desert."

> Labor and toil stand stern before the throne,
> And guard—so Jove commands—the sacred place.[27]

26. *Diary of John Quincy Adams*, 2:302–3, 371–72; John Adams, *A Defence of the Constitutions of Government of the United States of America*, 3:502–6.
27. Quoted in Seward, *Life of John Quincy Adams*, 55–56.

The legal profession was by no means well suited to satisfy the object of his ambition. Moreover, Adams objected to the separation of man's political and intellectual virtues in the calculation of praiseworthy deeds. The typical conviction that "extraordinary genius cannot brook the slavery of plodding over the rubbish of antiquity (a cant so common among the heedless votaries of indolence) . . . is one of the most powerful ingredients in the Circean potion which transforms . . . promising young men into the beastly forms which . . . feed upon the labor of others." Soon the country would have higher claims on Adams's duties than "making writs," and "haranguing juries," and "being happy."[28]

It is not surprising that John Quincy Adams's first public notice derived from a series of published essays defending America's domestic and foreign obligations with the onset of the French Revolution and war in Europe. The revolution in France appeared to him as the work of a blind giant, urged to fury by the remembrance of wrongs endured for generations. The "Altar of Liberty" was raised amid seas of blood, and stained with the gore of innocent victims. A people who would enjoy freedom, Adams believed, must learn to merit the privilege by the study of its principles and by exercising power "under those salutary restraints which man can never throw off and be happy." He thought the revolution would prove a costly failure; and that it was engendering an influence which, if not countered, would be injurious to American liberties. Jeffersonian Republicans justified the revolution as the lawful attempt of an oppressed people to secure their inalienable rights—that Americans were bound by both honor and duty to render all assistance to the French egalitarians. Challenging this strain of idealism, Adams published in the *Boston Centinel*, in 1791, a series of articles, signed "Publicola," in which he explored the meaning of natural rights and their bearing upon America's national interest. These articles were republished in England, as an answer to several points in Thomas Paine's *Rights of Man*. The style of reasoning led more than a few to suspect the hand of the elder Adams at work. John Adams wrote

28. Ibid.

to his wife, from Philadelphia, on December 5, 1793: "The Viscount Noailles . . . seemed very critical in his inquiries concerning the letters printed as mine in England. I told him . . . that I did not write them, and . . . in confidence, who did. He says they made a great impression upon the people of England; that he heard Mr. Windham and Mr. Fox speak of them as the best thing that had been written, and as one of the best pieces of reasoning and style they had ever read."[29]

Having found his temporary milieu, Adams followed the "Publicola" papers with the "Marcellus" articles. Here Adams emphasized the complementary relation between balance of power politics and international legal norms in defending American neutrality between France and Great Britain. During the winter of 1793 and 1794, Adams next lashed out at the inflammatory appeals of Citizen Genêt, who had publicly flouted Washington's neutrality. Under the pseudonym "Columbus," he outlined principles of the law of nations and their applicability to the privileges and immunities of diplomats. In reference to the controversy, John Adams wrote to his wife on December 19, 1793: "The President has considered the conduct of Genêt very nearly in the same light with 'Columbus,' and has given him a bolt of thunder. We shall see how this is supported by the two Houses. There are those who gnash their teeth with rage which they dare not own as yet. We shall soon see whether we have any government or not in this country."[30] The younger Adams insisted that strict neutrality was "alike the dictate of duty and policy" for the United States. However strongly American sympathies were elicited in behalf of the French Revolution—however the United States was bound in gratitude for French support during its own revolution—still, self-preservation is the first law of nature. Intervention in European conflicts would only prostrate the interests of the country and imperil the very existence of its government. In these essays, Adams developed the political creed—and two great principles—that governed his life's work: union at home, and independence of all foreign entanglements and alliances.

29. Ibid., 52.
30. Ibid.

III.

Jefferson, before his retirement from the State Department, commended the young statesman to the favorable regard of President Washington. The president himself soon became fixed on John Quincy Adams; he saw in him not only views of policy in harmony with his own, but also a familiarity with the languages and customs of foreign courts. In a letter to John Adams, Washington wrote of a promising future for the vice president's son: "[he] must not think about retiring from the path he is now in . . . and I shall be . . . mistaken if, in as short a time as can well be expected, he is not found at the head of the Diplomatic Corps, be the government administered by whomsoever the people may choose." Accordingly, in his twenty-seventh year, Adams was appointed minister of the United States at The Hague. While residing in Holland, he traveled to London on two separate occasions, once between October 1795, and June 1796, to exchange ratifications of the Jay treaty, and again the following June 1797. The young minister sat with Chief Justice John Jay and Thomas Pinckney, minister of the United States to Great Britain, prepared a detailed study of the treaty and, at Jay's request, passed judgment on one of the most important diplomatic instruments of American history. During the second visit, on July 26, he married Louisa Catherine Johnson, daughter of Joshua Johnson, a Marylander serving as the United States consul in London. Knowledge of the Anglo-American treaty of 1794—an articulation of American neutrality owing to such international law as was universally accepted—proved invaluable to Adams when he arrived back in the Netherlands, melancholy battleground of French and British power in the midst of European turmoil and strife.[31]

Adams arrived in Holland when General Pichegru, no unworthy forerunner to Napoleon in soldierly skills, crossed the Maas and the Waal to occupy Utrecht and Amsterdam. By the end of 1795—less than three months after Adams presented his credentials to Their High

---

31. Ibid.; Bemis, *John Quincy Adams and the Foundations of American Foreign Policy*, 46–48.

Mightinesses—the old Dutch Republic was pulled down and a Batavian Republic, proxy of France, was empowered. For the United States, Adams served as an important diplomat-observer as the tide of ideas and physical change emanating from Paris swept over the Low Countries. The prophecy of Rousseau, that the ancient monarchies of Europe could not survive much longer, became a settled proposition in Adams's mind. Yet the discordant vigor of mob republicanism in France was not without its lesson for the moral foundations of the American union: "Our laws, our liberties, everything that has ever been dear to our hearts, will be brought into question." The moral code of one nation flings the challenge of its universal claim with messianic fervor into the face of another. Compromise, the virtue of the old diplomacy, becomes the treason of the new; for the mutual accommodation of conflicting claims within a common framework of moral standards, amounts to capitulation when the moral standards themselves are the stakes of the conflict.[32] Adams was among the first to witness and describe the modern phenomenon of "nationalistic universalism"— i.e., the tendency of nations to act on the lighthearted equation between a particular nationalism and the counsels of Providence.

In the unlimited sovereignty of the people, the "sublime inventions of the noyades and of the Republican nuptials shed a new gleam of light upon the brilliant illumination of the eighteenth century." Every advantage in the war with England seemed to be on the side of France. Adams reported that the French armies were inexhaustible, "and the loss of ten thousand men had no other effect than that of calling out myriads more." Everything that could be the subject of human possession—both property and conscience—was absorbed by the nation, and "this maxim is most thoroughly reduced to practice." The struggle between the Jacobins and Royalists, in a world where political hypocrisy "has been to some an asylum, to others a weapon," left an indelible impression on Adams; "it . . . annihilated all confidence between man and man, and introduced . . . universal distrust in its stead." The French Revolution epitomized how the arts and sciences themselves are

32. JQA to John Adams, September 21, 1797, 2:214–16; Morgenthau, *Politics among Nations*, 241–56.

"liable to become objects of proscription to political fanaticism." The myrmidons of Robespierre "were as apt to pillage libraries as the followers of Omar"; and "if the principle is . . . to prevail, which puts the scepter of sovereignty into the hands of the European Sans Culottes, [then] they will reduce everything to the level of their own ignorance." If even in ideal situations "the perfection of . . . legislation is scarcely adequate to the construction of a government which may be at the same time strong to enforce the law and weak for any abuse of its power," then the task "may . . . be pronounced *impossible* in France."[33]

President Washington, toward the close of his second term in 1796, appointed Adams minister plenipotentiary to Portugal. Before departing for Lisbon, and after his father's election as president, his diplomatic assignment was changed to Berlin. The main objective of his mission, in 1798 and 1799, was to safeguard the rights of neutral commerce through treaties negotiated with the Prussian and Swedish governments. While attending to these public duties, he did not forego the more congenial pursuits of literature. His letters during this time disclose a restless mind seldom, if ever, satisfied, and always moved by aspirations after something higher and better than he could accomplish. His translations included the satires of Juvenal and Wieland's *Oberon* from the original into English verse. The publication of this work, designed for press, was superseded by the version of Sotheby. He also translated a treatise by Friedrich von Gentz, on the origins and principles of the American Revolution. This work provided "one of the clearest accounts . . . of the rise and progress of the American Revolution, in so small a compass; rescuing it from the . . . imputation of its having proceeded from the same principles, and of its being conducted in the same spirit, as that of France." Before leaving Europe, he made a lengthy tour through Silesia, during which he described his impressions in letters to his brother, Thomas Boylston Adams. These letters, published in the United States and Great Britain, offer more than extensive details about manufacturing establishments in Silesia; they reveal his basic political philosophy and values in the context of the

---

33. JQA to John Adams, July 27, 1795, 1:384–85, 387–90.

changing political landscape of Europe and the relation of the United States to these events. He depicted an unmistakable lesson for America's national interest:

> The experience of the last six years has . . . shown how impossible it is to keep disconnected with the affairs of Europe, while we have . . . essential mercantile connections with the great maritime states; and the numerous injuries we have suffered . . . from both parties amply prove how essential it is to our interests to have other friends than either. In every naval war it must be the interest of Britain and France to draw or force us into it as parties, while it must be our unequivocal interest to remain neutral. . . . I am confident we have suffered more for want of a free intercourse, communication and concert with the neutral states in Europe than would discharge five times the expense of maintaining ministers with them, and if we should finally be . . . compelled to engage in hostilities for our own defence, it may be . . . attributed to the neglect of a good understanding with the nations which have . . . an interest similar to ours, that is a neutral interest.[34]

In early 1801, following his bitter electoral defeat, President Adams recalled his son from Berlin to the United States, thereby dramatizing the gulf of animosity separating the politics of the elder Adams and Jefferson. Adams's voyage homeward was punctuated by additional reflections upon his commitment to public service. No man of civic virtue could ever shrink from the performance of public duties simply because the required service might be disagreeable or even dangerous. Steadfast conviction and the belief in objective standards of right political conduct are obligatory even though "the severest of all trials of virtue is . . . finding benefits returned with injuries, and her devotion with ingratitude." Universal reproach was, indeed, "far worse to bear than violence." Furthermore, the statesman's primordial struggle against popular clamor was not without its charms to Adams's mind. Nothing great or valuable among men was ever achieved, he thought, without the counterpoise of strong opposition, "and the persecution that proceeds from [public] opinion becomes itself a title to esteem

34. Friedrich von Gentz, *The Origin and Principles of the American Revolution, Compared with the Origin and Principles of the French Revolution*, 3–4; JQA to John Adams, January 31, 1798, 2:250–51.

when the opinion is found to have been erroneous." In an early auto-biographical sketch, Adams used a Shakespearean idiom to depict his career as a "mingled yarn." The narrative of his life had "something to commend, and enough to censure." He reproached himself for having "too much indulged the suggestions of [his] own judgment, and paid too little deference to that of other men." The agency of party was so entrenched in the land "that [any] undertaking to pursue a course . . . independent of it as a public man is perhaps impracticable." Yet he adamantly refused to separate either his public or his private life from the "unalterable determination to abide by the [moral] principles which have always been my guides."[35]

In the Massachusetts of his day, John Quincy Adams, the son of a president, himself an ex-foreign minister and one of the ablest men in the state, could not be ignored politically. His return to legal prac-tice coincided with being appointed a commissioner of bankruptcy by the judge of the district court, only to be removed by Jefferson. In an exchange of letters with Abigail Adams in 1801, Jefferson acknowl-edged that his decision was unintentional—the appointments of bank-ruptcy commissioners having recently been placed in the hands of the president. In making the new appointments he had not inquired of the former incumbents. John Quincy Adams was by conviction and birth a Federalist on the issues that had originally divided the nation's two parties; on the other hand, he had little sympathy for the British tilt in foreign affairs taken by the followers of Alexander Hamilton, toward whom he harbored an enduring resentment for their intrigue against his father in the election disaster of 1800. While Massachusetts was the stronghold of Federalism, it was also headquarters for the Essex Junto, a group of loyal Hamiltonians, led by George Cabot, Fisher Ames, and Theophilus Parsons. As early as 1799, Adams was prepared to part company with the Federalist party should it become divided over the issue of war and servile to the restrictive commercial policies of Britain.[36]

35. JQA to Thomas Boylston Adams, December 20, 1800, 2:488–90; Seward, *Life of John Quincy Adams*, 86; JQA to Skelton Jones, April 17, 1809, 3:298–305.
36. JQA to William Vans Murray, December 10, 1799, 2:244.

In April 1802, he was elected by the Federalists in Boston to represent them in the Massachusetts State Senate. Adams soon demonstrated his fierce independence from the shackles of party discipline. At a Federalist caucus, only three weeks after his election, he angered party leaders by proposing that Republicans be allowed minority representation on state councils. His willingness to vote with the Republicans by opposing a bill to create a bank, favored by all the moneyed men, confirmed Fisher Ames's summary of Adams as "too unmanageable." Writing about this period many years later, Adams alluded to "the novitiate of my legislative labors, during which I was not able to effect much good, or to prevent much evil. I wanted the authority of experience, and I discovered the danger of . . . exposing corruption." Although his opposition proved unavailing, it illustrated that the integrity of the man was superior to the policy of the mere politician. On one occasion, Adams was asked, "What are the recognized principles of politics?" He replied, that there were no *principles* in politics—there were recognized *precepts*, but they were bad ones. But, continued the inquirer, is not this a good one—"To seek the great good of the greatest number?" No, said Adams, that is the worst of all, for it looks specious, while it is ruinous. What, then, shall become of the minority? This is the only principle to seek—"the greatest good of all."[37]

On February 3, 1803, at the age of thirty-six, Adams was elected by the Massachusetts House of Representatives to be a United States Senator, besting Timothy Pickering in the contest. Fisher Ames conceded that the former was chosen "in consequence of a caucus pact, that if Col. Pickering should not be elected on two trials, then the Feds. would combine and vote for J. Q. A. This happened accordingly." Adams arrived in the capital city when the streets were little more than clearings of mud in which ambassadorial carriages would get mired to the hubs and have to be abandoned by exasperated diplomats. The city, as Gouverneur Morris once observed, "was wholly in the future." Adams was unpopular because he was his father's son; because he was unbending and seldom casual even at the most uneventful moment; and because he

37. The exchange, cited in the *Massachusetts Quarterly* (1848), is contained in Seward, *Life of John Quincy Adams*, 86; James Truslow Adams, *The Adams Family*, 132–33.

proved unamenable to familiar partisan distinctions. Soon the unmanageable son of the even-more-unmanageable father experienced the treatment summarized in these words: "The Republicans trampled upon the Federalists, and the Federalists trampled upon John Quincy Adams." The country, he wrote in his diary at the end of his first senatorial year, "is so totally given up to the spirit of party, that not to follow blindfold the one or the other is an inexpiable offence." Adams could not steer his way clear to pursue the dictates of his own conscience "without sacrificing every prospect, not merely of advancement, but even of retaining that character and reputation I have enjoyed." If independent judgment and public service could not "give satisfaction to my country, I am . . . determined to have the approbation of my own reflections."[38]

It was said of Adams that he considered every measure to be voted on as he would a proposition in Euclid, utterly divorced in solving it from any thought of party. His stance on the Louisiana Purchase (1803) is an important example of Adams's political analysis, particularly the manner in which he juxtaposed ethical and legal claims to political exigencies. A few months after his entrance to the Senate, a law was passed by Congress authorizing the acquisition of Louisiana and its admission as a state. The Federalists were bitterly opposed to the measure, seeing it as a strengthening of slavery and the South. Adams questioned the constitutionality of the second provision of the statute enabling the president to take possession of Louisiana.

> And be it . . . enacted, that until the expiration of the present session of Congress, unless provision for the temporary government of the said territories be sooner made by Congress, *all the military, civil and judicial powers* exercised by the officers of the *existing government* of the same shall be vested in *such person* and *persons*, and shall be *exercised in such manner, as the President of the United States shall direct*, for maintaining and protecting the inhabitants of Louisiana in the free enjoyment of their liberty, property, and religion.[39]

He was joined by a minority of six in opposing the measure.

On the one hand, Adams opposed neither the acquisition of Louisi-

---

38. *Memoirs*, 1:282–83; Adams, *The Adams Family*, 134.
39. JQA to the editors of the *National Intelligencer*, 7:339.

ana nor ratification of the treaty by which it was required. The constitutional authorization to make treaties, provided in Article 2, sec. 2, is "given to the President with concurrence of two-thirds of the Senate . . . *without limitation.*" Of the power to make the treaty, then, he "had no doubt [of it], as having been granted by the constitution." On the other hand, Adams was compelled to distinguish between the power to make a treaty and the power to carry that treaty into effect. To have limited the former would amount to "an abdication by the nation itself of . . . the powers appertaining to sovereignty, and [to] have placed it on a footing of inequality with other nations." Executing the treaty, however, "imports the exercise of internal powers of government and was subject to all the limitations prescribed by the constitution to the exercise of these powers." In communicating the treaty to the Senate after ratifications had been exchanged, President Jefferson declared, "You will observe that some important conditions cannot be carried into execution but with the aid of the legislature." Adams observed that much of the nation's brief diplomatic history had been a record of debates by elected officials as to "how far they are bound to sanction in their legislative capacity stipulations with foreign nations . . . ratified by the treaty-making power."[40]

The implementation of the Louisiana convention required, from Adams's point of view, something much more fundamental. Congressional authority to confer upon the president such extraordinary power could only be accomplished by an act of construction. The Constitution of the United States was a charter of limited powers; that "some of these powers must be *constructive* I never doubted; but that this construction must itself have limits I was equally convinced." Carrying the treaty into execution entailed the exercise of powers not granted to Congress itself, of powers reserved by the people of the United States, and of powers inherent by natural right in the people of Louisiana. The union of the two groups required the express and formal consent of both, a step that Adams thought required amending the Constitution. Enlarging the social compact "between the people of the United States

40. Ibid., 340–42.

and the people of Louisiana was, according to the theory of human rights I had learned . . . , an act, the satisfaction of which could only be consummated by themselves." Adams's hesitancy was not whether—or by what instruments—the sense of the people could be obtained; the consent of the people, he later wrote to his father in 1811, "may be subsequent by their acquiescence as well as antecedent by express grant." Rather the fundamental challenge to democracy, and to the nation's foreign policy, was "that powers in themselves of a transcendental nature, cannot be assumed by *construction* as incidental to expressed powers of apparent import so much more limited than themselves." A time would come when the people's representatives would have to face "the consequences of the principles then settled" in 1803 in order to: "determine whether the territories of Ceylon or Madagascar, of Corcisca or of Cuba, shall be governed by rules and regulations emanating from your Congress; whether the inhabitants of those *territories* shall be governed for a discretionary time . . . in such manner as the President . . . shall direct, and whether their *people* shall ultimately be constituted into states, represented upon the floor of your national legislative assemblies."[41]

A crisis in Adams's senatorial career soon arrived in the midst of repeated violations of American neutrality in the war between Britain and France. Napoleon proclaimed his Continental System, a self-blockade of French-controlled Europe against British commerce declared by the Berlin and Milan decrees (November 21, 1806, and December 17, 1807); and England cut off all commerce with countries from which France caused the British flag to be excluded, unless the trade proceeded by way of British ports under British license and toll (Orders-in-Council of January 7 and November 11, 1807). Despite concerns raised by the impressment of American seamen, and the confiscation of their ships' cargoes, the New England Federalists were opposed to any decisive break with Britain. John Quincy Adams, as early as 1798, rejected the Federalist contention, expressed by Timothy Pickering, then secretary of state, that "Britain appears to be the only bulwark

---

41. Ibid., 345; JQA to John Adams, August 31, 1811, 4:204–9.

against the universal domination of France by sea, as well as by land." Adams found no plausible defense of the balance of power by the "unprovoked aggression upon the property of citizens of these United States, a violation of their natural rights, and an encroachment upon their natural independence." His introduction of resolutions condemning Britain's claim to the right of seizure of neutral vessels, no less than his support of the Non-Importation Act of 1806 and the embargo of 1807, made his breach with the Federalists unavoidable. "On most of the great national questions under discussion," he admitted, "my sense of duty leads me to support the Administration, and I find myself . . . in opposition to the federalists in general."[42]

From this moment onward, Adams argued that the Federalists were barely able to conceal "the glaring absurdity and hypocrisy of their professed veneration for the policy of Washington" and their "actions which were aiming at a fatal blow to the Union." This allusion harked back to an alleged conspiracy of Federalist leaders, in 1804, to effect a withdrawal of the northern states from the republic. The plan of a New England combination was the work of "small statesmen who, feeling like Caesar, and finding that Rome is too large an object for their grasp . . . strike off a village where they might aspire to the first station, without exposing themselves to derision." Unlike the biblical lesson of David, adding all the tribes of Israel to Judah and Benjamin, the New England divisionists walked in the "ways of Jeroboam—the son of Nabat—who made Israel to sin by breaking off Samaria from Jerusalem." Preferring to view the matter "in reference to moral considerations," Adams noted that this secessionist scheme obliged the conspirators "to practice continual deception, and to work upon the basest materials, the selfish and dissocial passions of their instruments." He acknowledged his own excommunication from Federalist ranks with "that congenial spirit which . . . considers temperance as one of the first political duties, and which can perceive a very distinct shade between political candor and political hypocrisy." On June 3,

---

42. Secretary of State (Pickering) to John Quincy Adams, March 17, 1798, 2:240–41; Bemis, *John Quincy Adams and the Foundations of American Foreign Policy*, 138–39; *Memoirs*, 1:497–98.

1808, the Massachusetts legislature, anticipating the end of his term by nine months, elected a successor and adopted resolutions against Jefferson's embargo. Adams's resignation a few days later left even his sympathetic father convinced that, politically, he was "among the dead." John Adams advised his son to return to his Harvard professorship (in 1805 John Quincy had been elected Boylston Professor of Literature and Rhetoric), "but above all to your office as a lawyer . . . and the education of your children."[43]

Adams regarded his university discourses, published in two volumes, as the greatest literary effort of his life. He turned to three volumes of Leland's *Demosthenes* and two volumes of Guthrie's *Quintilian* and organized a scholarly curriculum of seven years' duration. Students in well-attended classes were met with a stern exhortation at their professor's inaugural lecture: "Call up the shades of Demosthenes and Cicero to vouch your words; point to their immortal words [for] . . . these are not only the sublimest strains of oratory . . . ; they are at the same time the expiring accents of liberty in the nations which have shed the brightest lustre on the name of man." The rhetorical works of Cicero, especially, "have a recommendation to students beyond all others; because they are the lessons of a consummate master on his own art." The rhetoric of Greek and Roman statesmen "was the instrument and spur to ambition. The talent of public speaking was the key to the highest dignities; the passport to the supreme dominion of the state."

> A faculty thus elevated, given us for so sublime a purpose, and destined to an end so excellent, was not intended by the Supreme Creator to be buried in the grave of neglect. As the source of all human improvements, it was itself susceptible of improvement by industry and application, by observation and experience. Hence, wherever man has been found in a social state, and wherever he has been sensible of his dependence upon a supreme disposer of events, the

43. JQA to William Plumer, August 16, 1809, 3:339–42; JQA to William Plumer, October 6, 1810, 3:508; JQA to Abigail Adams, June 30, 1811, 4:127. For John Adams's remarks, see *Writings*, 3:189 n.1.

value and the power of public speaking . . . has at least been universally felt.[44]

On this same subject, Cicero proclaims, "Or what is so striking, so astonishing, as that the religious feelings of judges, the gravity of the senate, should be swayed by the speech of one man."[45]

Adams's devotion to literary pursuits was destined for early termination. In December of 1808, he related his thoughts on public service in a letter to Orchard Cook, who had intimated the possibility of an appointment in the new Madison Administration. His duty to country was analogous to "that which philosophers teach us should guide our views of death—never to be desired, never to be feared."[46] Few other American statesmen have been as quietly compulsive about high office as John Quincy Adams; however, until the last day of his life, he would never lift a finger to obtain it. While in Washington on legal business before the Supreme Court, Adams received a note on March 6, requesting his presence at the White House. Madison offered him the post of minister to Russia, asking for a timely response, inasmuch as the nomination was to be placed before the Senate within thirty minutes. Although the Senate withheld confirmation at first—deeming it inappropriate to establish a mission at this time—a second prompting by President Madison, on June 26, 1809, led to Adams's approval. Timothy Pickering, who had voted against the appointment, concluded that probably the best thing to do with his former colleague was to send him out of the country. Ezekiel Bacon had written to him that the post was "somewhat like an honorable exile," and Adams himself had conceded that foreign duty was a hindrance to an American career. America's first minister to Russia departed Boston in August, aboard the *Horace*, and arrived in St. Petersburg on October 23, 1809.

Adams entered Russia during the colorful and dramatic time of Tsar Alexander I—the exact period of Tolstoy's *War and Peace*. Frequent and congenial meetings with the tsar, and diplomatic dinners hosted

---

44. John Quincy Adams, *Lectures on Rhetoric and Oratory*, 1:13–14, 19, 98; Lousene G. Rousseau, "The Rhetorical Principles of Cicero and Adams," 397–99.

45. Cicero quoted by Rousseau, "The Rhetorical Principles of Cicero," 398.

46. Quoted by Adams, *The Adams Family*, 138.

by the imperial chancellor, Count Rumiantzov, provided the American ambassador with a unique position from which to survey the turbulent scenes of Napoleonic Europe.

> There is not a republic left in Europe. The very name of the people is everywhere buried in oblivion. In England the great concerns . . . are intrigues and cabals of princes and foreign ministers to supplant one another, and the prices of seats at the playhouses. In France and the rest of Europe, king-making and king-breaking, orders of chivalry and dissolutions of marriage, blanchisseuses, princesses, and Jacobin grubs bursting into butterfly princes, dukes, and counts, conscriptions and contributions, famine grinding the people into soldiers . . . and an iron harrow tearing up the bowels of the nations. This is the present history of the times.[47]

The débacle of the Grand Armée, in the early winter of 1812, was a spectacular testimony to the brutal ravages of war. From Moscow to Prussia, "eight hundred miles . . . have been strewed with [Napoleon's] artillery, baggage wagons, ammunition chests, dead and dying men, whom he has been forced to abandon to their fate—pursued . . . by three regular armies . . . and by an almost numberless militia of peasants . . . spurred to revenge . . . themselves, their country, and their religion." Adams, convinced that Napoleon's reign had "kindled into tenfold fierceness . . . the flames of individual ambition throughout Europe," was not surprised "to see the Corsican Alexander shrinking into his natural dimensions . . . and meeting . . . a reverse of destiny as great and almost as wonderful as his elevation." Bonaparte, no less than "General [William] Hull and his [British] conqueror [Sir Isaac] Brock" in the American War of 1812, all exemplify: "*On what foundation stands the warrior's pride!*"[48]

An amazing interlude of Adams's stay in Russia was President Madison's offer to him of a place on the Supreme Court of the United States and his declination of it. Political considerations within the administration favored the elevation of Adams over rival Republican candidate Gideon Granger. In a letter to Jefferson, Madison noted that

---

47. JQA to Thomas Boylston Adams, February 14, 1810, *Writings*, 3:397–98.
48. JQA to Abigail Adams, December 31, 1812, 4:421–25.

"the soundest Republicans are working hard against him [Granger], as infected with Yazooism and intrigue. They wish for J. Q. Adams, as honest, able, independent and untainted with such objections." Studies in the law, Adams admitted in responding to the president, "were never among those most congenial to my temper." The great proportion of his time had been absorbed by "occupations so different from those of judicial tribunals" that Adams could not avoid "a deep and serious distrust" of his qualifications for a seat on the bench. As Adams confided to his brother, neither he nor the country could escape the consequences of his reputation as a "political partisan." He could perhaps aspire to the impartiality of an "umpire in their controversies"; less certain, however, was whether the people's representatives could be sufficiently impartial toward him "to make them fit to be judged by [him]."[49]

In addition to the predicament of having to support a lavish household on the beggarly salary allotted to his mission, the ostentatious diplomatic amenities of the Russian capital failed to satisfy Adams's intellectual cravings. "I had always," he wrote at this time, "an eager relish for the pursuits of literature, and acquired at any early period of life a taste for the fine arts." Painting, music, the decorations of drama—and the elegant arts that are combined in its representations—are beneficial and molding influences to which the human spirit may turn for nourishment. It was his invariable custom to read the Bible through once every year, and while in St. Petersburg he did so twice in English and once each in French and German. The relation of political ethics to Christian faith was the lengthy subject of eleven letters sent by John Quincy Adams, beginning on September 1, 1811, to his son George Washington Adams. Published as *Letters of John Quincy Adams to His Son, on the Bible and Its Teachings*, their purpose was to "inculcate a love and reverence for the Holy Scriptures, and a delight in their perusal and study." While Adams was in Russia, he encountered the notorious Madame de Staël, a bitter opponent of Napoleon and literary provocateur of Europe's best salons. Adams's anti-British animus made it difficult for him to accept her comment that Britain was a "moral nation." His

---

49. JQA to the President of the United States (James Madison), June 3, 1811, 4:95; JQA to Thomas Boylston Adams, April 10, 1811, 4:47–48; JQA to John Adams, 4:145.

reservations about the capricious Frenchwoman had been kindled earlier, however, when he found her in league with Paine, Madame Roland,
and Benjamin Constant, laboring "to wind up the drunkenness of a club
or tavern into a frenzy."[50]

At this time, Adams's diplomacy in Russia—and trusting friendship
with Alexander—paid important dividends. The political balance in
Europe was delicate: Russia, fighting the French, remained close to
England, which was at war with America. The United States was prepared to negotiate, through the proffered mediation of the tsar, a treaty
of peace with Great Britain. Yet the mercurial temperament of the
Russian monarch taught Adams the cunning of power in defense of
national and international ideals. Metternich described Alexander as "a
strange combination of masculine virtues and feminine weaknesses. Too
weak for true ambition, but too strong for pure vanity." Alternatively
idealistic and calculating, he constituted an ambivalent mixture of universal principles justifying specifically Russian gains, of high motives
supporting aspirations considered selfish in lesser men. "He was not
for nothing the son of [the mad] Tsar Paul," Talleyrand said of him.[51]
Accordingly, James A. Bayard and Albert Gallatin, secretary of the treasury, joined Adams in St. Petersburg on July 21, 1813, as members of
a mission to negotiate with the British. The British rejected the mediation but informally proposed a meeting the following year. A new American peace commission—with Adams, Gallatin, and Bayard assisted by
Henry Clay and Jonathan Russell—opened negotiations with British
commissioners at Ghent on August 7, 1814.

Throughout protracted negotiations lasting six months, Adams's fierce
nationalism was often nuanced by a concern for both accepted norms
of international law and the nation's vital interests. He referred his
colleagues "to Martens, book vii, chap. iv. section 3, of his Summary"
(in the massive *Receuil des traités*) to find the prescription for opening

50. JQA to Skelton Jones, April 17, 1809, 3:298–305; John Quincy Adams, *Letters of John Quincy Adams, to His Son, on the Bible and Its Teachings*, 6–7; JQA to John Adams, March 22, 1813, 4:451; JQA to John Adams, September 11, 1797, 2:201.

51. Metternich and Talleyrand quoted by Henry A. Kissinger, *A World Restored: Europe after Napoleon*, 90.

negotiations with the British. In addition to defending American rights to the fisheries on the Newfoundland coast, Adams resisted the British charge that the United States was guilty of "perpetual encroachment upon the Indians under the pretense of purchases." Adams took "the ground of the moral and religious duty of a nation to settle, cultivate, and improve their territory—a principle . . . recognized by the law of nations." Bayard, "since he has been reading Vattel, agreed in the argument," while such metaphysics "Clay thought were canting." In Adams's mind, it was incompatible with both the moral and physical nature of things to "condemn vast regions of territory to perpetual barrenness and solitude" when a nation of eight million were pressing against them for means of subsistence. The successful conclusion of negotiations produced a political stalemate. Nothing for which the United States had gone to war (e.g., a favorable maritime code and an end to impressment) was gained, but no right previously acknowledged was infringed upon. "We have abandoned no essential right," he wrote to his mother, "and if we left everything open for future controversy, we have at least secured our Country the power at her option to extinguish the war." Yet the future would be perilous unless the United States took bold steps to become a great naval and military power. This prospect, Adams thought, "must be forced upon us. And as we have . . . made some progress in it already, I doubt whether we shall ever have again so favorable an opportunity for accommodating our . . . political system to it as the present."[52]

No extraordinary accomplishments marked Adams's tenure as American minister to the Court of St. James, from 1815 until 1817, although he initiated proceedings resulting in the Rush-Bagot Agreement of 1817. The treaty, the first reciprocal naval disarmament in modern history, limited naval arsenals on the Great Lakes and demilitarized the frontier between the United States and Canada. English society threw open its doors to Adams. He made the acquaintance of Fox's political heir, the pro-American Lord Holland, and enjoyed lively exchanges with intellectual leaders, including Jeremy Bentham and Sir James

52. *Memoirs*, 3:41–42; "Answer to the British Commissioners," *Writings*, 5:98–99; JQA to William Harris Crawford, September 14, 1814, 5:140–41; JQA to Abigail Adams, December 24, 1814, 5:247–48.

Mackintosh. His relationship with English statesmen—Castlereagh, Bathurst, Liverpool, and most of all, George Canning—familiarized him with their characters and methods; this familiarity later was to prove invaluable when he was called to direct American foreign policy. Informing his father that his "principal inquiries are not after the inside but the outside of heaven," Adams took time for regular lessons in physical astronomy, in addition to pouring over Bode's *Uranographia* and the astrology of Manilius. Yet his mind was never far from American affairs, and this stay abroad seemed to clear all traces of provincialism. Writing to his father in 1816, when it was rumored that the District of Maine was to be split off from Massachusetts, he said, "If I were merely a Massachusetts man I should deeply lament this dismemberment. . . . But the longer I live the stronger I find my national feeling growing upon me, and the less my affections are compassed by partial localities."[53] Adams's political motivation looked to strengthen the union and its government. Rumors reached him that he might be appointed secretary of state by the incoming president, James Monroe, and on April 16, 1817, Adams received a letter notifying him of his appointment and requesting his earliest return to Washington.

IV.

Adams's selection as secretary of state had a certain bipartisan logic in the "Era of Good Feeling," an interval of stagnant politics in which it became increasingly hard for Republicans to maintain party discipline and party zeal. Of this appointment, President Monroe wrote to General Jackson: "Mr. Adams, by long service in our diplomatic concerns appearing to be entitled to the preference, supported by his acknowledged abilities and integrity, his nomination will go to the Senate." In response, Jackson felt little hesitation in affirming that Adams "will be an able helpmate," the president having "made the best selection to fill the Department of State that could be made." Adams acted on the principle that public office should be accepted but not striven for;

53. JQA to John Adams, August 1, 1816, 6:58–62, 111–14.

however, this appointment brought the more difficult task of having "to conciliate the duties of self and the spirit of personal independence, with the deference of personal obligation and the fidelity of official subordination." Recalling the political misfortunes of his father's presidency, John Quincy Adams suffered few illusions about his new station. Service in the cabinet carried "the difficulty of moving swiftly along with associates . . . disdainful of influence, yet eager to exercise it, impatient of control, and opposing . . . stubborn resistance to surmises and phantoms of encroachment."[54]

Adams possessed, without doubt, more experience in diplomacy and world affairs than any other man who has ever filled the post of secretary. His stature as a diplomat, examined at length in a subsequent chapter, encompassed major initiatives in both the formulation and administration of foreign policy in the executive branch. For example, alluding to "a maxim of Mr. Jefferson's," young diplomats were advised against serving long "in a public capacity at the courts of Europe," in the "air of those regions so unfriendly to American constitutions" without returning "to be renovated by the wholesome republican atmosphere of their own country." American representatives were to report on the affairs and interests of each country, not only on their direct relation with the United States but also with other parts of Europe and with the rest of the world. Each ambassador was instructed to assess any particular characteristics of the administrations and those in power, the relations of the latter with their subordinates, the qualities of those next in the line of succession to office, the names of those closest to the seats of power. For his part, Adams promised that all public dispatches or private letters would be answered. His instructions to American diplomats concerning their duties were masterpieces, many analyzing in minute detail the workings of the Holy Alliance and European balance of power following the Congress of Vienna.[55]

In his deportment as a diplomat, Adams often exhibited a disposi-

54. Both letters are cited in Seward, *Life of John Quincy Adams*, 115; JQA to Abigail Adams, May 16, 1817, 6:181–82.

55. JQA to Christopher Hughes, June 22, 1818, 6:357–58; JQA to Alexander Hill Everett, August 10, 1818, 6:427–28; JQA to Henry Middleton, July 5, 1820, 7:46–50.

tion to abrupt and irritable judgment. His description of Spain's foreign minister, Luis de Onís, was not uncharacteristic: "I have seen slippery diplomatists . . . but Onís is the first man I have met who made it a point of honor to pass for more of a swindler than he was." He could barely contain his impatience with Spain's delay in ratifying the Transcontinental Treaty of 1819. "The Government of the United States [acting through Adams], by a forbearance perhaps unexampled in human history, has patiently waited for your [Onís's] arrival [with news of the ratification of the treaty by the Spanish monarch], always ready to give in candor . . . every explanation that could with any propriety be demanded." Yet Adams summoned the tact and reserve to calm his adversary when the Spanish minister arrived one morning to complain of a dead chicken tied to his bell rope the night before—"a gross insult to Spain and the Spanish monarchy, imputing that they were of no more import than a dead old hen." His colleagues in the cabinet, and the president himself, took pains to modify the occasional severity of the secretary's language. Secretary of the Treasury William Crawford complained of having to tone down the "asperities" of the State Department's official notes. President Monroe, studying Adams's official response in 1823 to Tsar Alexander and the autocratic principles of the Holy Alliance, gave his opinion: "The direct attack which [Adams] makes on the recent movements, of the Emperor, and of course, censure, on him, and its tendency to irritate, suggest the apprehension that it may produce an unfavorable effect. The illustration of our principles, is one thing; the doing it, in such a form, bearing directly, on what has passed, and which is avoided in the [historic] message [before Congress], is another."[56]

Every secretary of state inherits problems not of his own choosing, even though he may create or have new ones thrust upon him. The Florida question—interwoven with that of the western boundary of

56. JQA to Charles Jared Ingersoll, August 7, 1821, 7:167; JQA to Don Francisco Dionisio Vives, May 8, 1820, 7:23. See the words in brackets struck out by the president or the members of the cabinet in the notes To Hyde de Neuville, July 28, 1821, 7:137–60; JQA to Don Joaquin De Anduaga, April 15, 1822, 7:222–24; Worthington C. Ford, "John Quincy Adams and the Monroe Doctrine," 45.

Louisiana, with Spain's inability to suppress privateers on Amelia and Galveston islands, with spoilation claims, and with the problem of neutrality in the contest between Spain and her revolting colonies—was so complex and pressing that even the European powers threatened to intervene. Adams's most impressive achievement as secretary of state was orchestrating policies that culminated in securing the outright possession of the Florida territories, which Jefferson and others before him had failed to achieve. He advocated open defiance of Spain by justifying Andrew Jackson's lawless invasion of Spanish territory and by supporting the outright seizure of the disputed lands. With the entire cabinet lined up against him, the secretary "achieved victory by a series of papers unique in the annals of American diplomacy for their sophistical reasoning and special pleading."[57] On February 22, 1819, a treaty was concluded between the United States and Spain, by which east and west Florida, along with the adjacent islands, were ceded to the United States. An unquestioned American victory, the Adams-Onis Treaty set the stage for the nation's longest-lived foreign policy—the Monroe Doctrine.

During this period in London, Albert Gallatin and Richard Rush—acting on orders from Adams—reached an agreement with the British that resulted in the Convention of 1818. Although the accord said nothing about impressment of American seamen or indemnity for American slaves carried off during the War of 1812, it renewed United States fishing privileges off the coasts of Newfoundland and Labrador. The convention also defined the American-Canadian border along the forty-ninth parallel from the Lake of the Woods to the Rocky Mountains. As John Jacob Astor's settlement at the mouth of the Columbia River did not survive the recent war, both nations agreed that the Oregon territory would be jointly occupied for up to ten years. In December 1820, a committee of the House of Representatives issued a report setting forth American claims to the whole Pacific Northwest as far north as 60°. British Minister Stratford Canning called upon Adams for an explanation of the congressional debates about further American settlements in the region. Adams, in no mood for conciliation, asked what the British

---

57. *The Selected Writings of John and John Quincy Adams,* ed. Adrienne Koch and William Peden, xxix.

prime minister would think if an American diplomat—after hearing before Parliament a speech calling for troops to be sent to the Shetland Islands or a new colony to New South Wales—were to request an explanation. Canning, then, asked if the secretary of state considered the cases as parallel with that of the Columbia River. Adams's account of the stormy interview that followed is too characteristic to be omitted.

> "So far as any question of right is concerned," said Adams, "perfectly parallel." "Have you," said Canning, "any *claim* to the Shetland Islands or New South Wales?" "Have you any *claim*," said Adams, "to the mouth of the Columbia River?" "Why, do you not *know*," replied Canning, "that we have a claim?" "I do not *know*," said Adams, "what you claim or what you do not claim. You claim India; you claim Africa; you claim—" "Perhaps," said Canning, "a piece of the moon." "No," said Adams, "I have not heard that you claim exclusively any part of the moon; but there is not a spot on *this* habitable globe that I could affirm you do not claim; and there is none which you may not claim with as much color of right as you can have to [the] Columbia River or its mouth." "And how far would you consider," said Canning, "this exclusion of right to extend?" "To all the shores of the South Sea," said Adams. "We know of no right that you have there." "Suppose," said Canning, "Great Britain should undertake to make a settlement there, would you object to it?" "I have no doubt we should," said Adams. . . . "And in this," said Canning, "you include our northern provinces on this continent?" "No," said Adams; "there the boundary is marked, and we have no disposition to encroach upon it. Keep what is yours, but leave the rest of this continent to us."[58]

This vigorous statement of the American attitude contains the germ of the famous principle that Adams later was to evolve, that the American continents are not subject to European colonization.

Of primary importance during this period was Adams's wise reluctance, in the face of Henry Clay's robust insistence, to acknowledge the independence of South American republics before the "chances of [Spain] . . . to recover [them] had become utterly desperate." The House of Representatives, in 1820, passed a resolution expressing "the deep

---

58. Dexter Perkins, "John Quincy Adams," in *The American Secretaries of State and Their Diplomacy*, ed. Samuel Flagg Bemis, 4:90–91; *Memoirs*, 5:250–53.

interest which [Americans] feel for the success of the Spanish Provinces . . . which are struggling to establish liberty and independence." There was certainly no more ardent lover of liberty than John Quincy Adams; however, he questioned America's obligation to export democratic principles as well as the capacity of South American colonists to sustain enlightened self-government. After strenuously opposing before the cabinet a proposal to sell arms to Colombia, he concluded "that moral considerations seldom appear to have much weight in the minds of our statesmen, unless connected with popular feelings." Adams was distressed that "giving secret aid to the revolutionists, while openly professing neutrality, was barely not denied in the [in the cabinet]." This course of action would be seen as an act of war against Spain, "for which the Executive was not competent [to undertake], by the Constitution, without the authority of Congress." Adams saw no middle ground between adherence to neutrality and intervention in every European national war; the latter held out no other "prospect for this nation than a career of washing their blood-stained hands" in every principle "of right, of justice, or policy, and of humanity." Both in politics and diplomacy, "the more of pure moral principles is carried into the policy and conduct of a Government the wiser and more profound that policy will be."[59]

There were only two completely independent nations in the New World in 1815, the United States and Haiti. The eruption of new republics in South America produced an unstable situation, rich in possibilities of trouble. Anything might happen—armed intervention by the Holy Alliance, a new balance of power, an Anglo-American entente, or a Pan-American alliance. Adams wisely believed that the Holy Alliance would not intervene with arms to aid Spain subdue her revolting colonies. New questions were opened in 1823, however, when George Canning proposed that the United States join Britain in recognizing the new nations and in passing a self-denying ordinance on any further acquisitions. John Calhoun, secretary of war, wanted to follow Canning, even at the cost of renouncing Cuba and Texas. The president wavered between the extremes of doing nothing, for fear of the Holy

59. *Memoirs*, 5:46–47.

Alliance, and of carrying the war into Turkey to aid Greece, whose struggle for independence was followed in the United States with greater interest than was shown for South America. While contemplating Canning's overture, Adams knew that Russia was pushing her trading posts from Alaska southward to San Francisco Bay. In September 1821, Alexander issued a ukase extending Alaska to latitude 51° N, well within the Oregon territory and declaring *mare clausum* the waters thence to the Bering Strait. In October 1823, Adams received two notes from the tsar that included a characteristic homily on the Holy Alliance and disdainful references to "expiring republicanism."

Adams had no wish to follow in the wake of England; in addition, he had no desire to have the United States make any immediate acquisitions either in the West Indies or South America. He would not, however, tie the hands of the United States in future contingencies. American diplomacy was at a crossroads, confronted by the European balance of power with a clear challenge to the limits of the national interest. The secretary of state, for the better part of two days, led the way in persuading Monroe to simultaneously take a stand against the Holy Alliance and to decline the British offer. The passages on foreign relations from Monroe's historic message to Congress, delivered on December 2, 1823, expressed exactly the concepts championed by Adams before the cabinet. The president's own words may be cited to illumine the seminal principles of the Monroe Doctrine:

—The American continents . . . are henceforth not to be considered as subjects for future colonization.

—The political system of the allied powers is essentially different . . . from that of America. . . . We should consider any attempt on their part to expand their system to any portion of this hemisphere as dangerous to our peace and safety.

—With the existing colonies or dependencies of any European power we have not interfered and shall not interfere.

—In the wars of the European powers in matters relating to themselves we have never taken any part, nor does it comport with our policy so to do.[60]

60. Morison, Commager, and Leuchtenburg, *The Growth of the American Republic*, 1:410–11.

Monroe's second term led to a struggle among the contenders within the administration for political advantage in the next election. Adams's often-expressed disdain for office seeking could only partially conceal his ambition; the very reiteration of disinterestedness belied his presidential preoccupation. He often alluded to other candidates who had not the delicacy of restrained ambition he proposed to manifest. With almost self-righteous assurance he asked, "Do they call it aristocratic hauteur and learned arrogancy? Why, so be it, my worthy friends and approved good masters. It is not then cringing servility, nor insatiate importunity." Adams's temperament was exemplified when he called upon Robert Walsh, Jr., a close friend and powerful editor of the *National Gazette*, to avoid partisanship and to observe two principles: "a view of the question [the next presidential election] as connected with the public welfare only," and "the discharge of his own duty as a public journalist." Adams was not disingenuous in saying to his wife: "It is my situation that makes me a candidate, and you at least know that my present situation was neither of my own seeking, nor of my choice." Yet the secretary of state was not immune occasionally from seeing history as himself writ large.

> Of the public history of . . . Monroe's administration, all that will be worth telling to posterity . . . has been transacted through the Department of State. The treaties with Great Britain, with Spain, with France, and with Russia, and the whole course of policy with regard to South America, have all been under the immediate management of that Department. . . . The acquisition of Florida and the extension of the territories . . . to the Pacific Ocean have been accomplished through the Department, and the formal admission of our right to border upon the South Sea, both by Spain and Great Britain, has been first obtained, I might confidently say by me.[61]

From the beginning, the presidential election of 1824 was contested amid angry cries of conspiracy and bitter recriminations against the opportunism of John Quincy Adams. His three chief opponents were Andrew Jackson, whom Adams had stoutly defended on the issue of

61. JQA to Louisa Catherine Adams, September 29, 1822, 7:308–9; JQA to Louisa Catherine Adams, October 7, 1822, 7:315–16.

Florida, William Crawford, and Henry Clay. The tabulation of votes in the electoral college denied each candidate a majority. Jackson led with ninety-nine; Adams was second with eighty-four; and Crawford was third with forty-one. Prior to the election, Adams knew of rumors that alleged an understanding had been reached between the secretary of state and Clay concerning the presidency, rumors that Adams always denied. In fact, the charge hounded Adams until the closing years of his life, when he was forced to listen to speeches in the House of Representatives reviving the old legend. The issue of who would be president was not settled until Clay, Adams's longstanding rival, swung his influence to the New Englander. A confidential interview with Clay led Adams to record few details of this historic controversy: "In the question to come before the House . . . he [Clay] had no hesitation in saying that his preference would be for me."[62] The election in the House of Representatives did not take place until February 9, 1825. On the first ballot, Adams received thirteen votes, Jackson received seven, and Crawford received four. The day after his inauguration, the president, undaunted by charges of bargain and corruption behind this "unholy alliance," nominated Clay as his secretary of state.

Historians have not been generous in their assessment of the presidency of John Quincy Adams. Critics have described his administration as a failure, marked by exclusion of the United States from the British West Indian trade, the ineffectiveness of its export policy to promote strong Pan-American relationships, and the enactment of the "tariff of abominations." Others have argued that it generated the sectionalism that terminated the "good feelings" of that bygone era. Few would quarrel with the judgment of one historian that "his administration was as uneventful as any in American history."[63] For Adams's political and ethical vision of a rejuvenated America, however, a four-year martyrdom had commenced. What Adams confronted in the last two decades of his life, both as a president and as a congressman, was not just a nation that failed to embrace the national commitments he

62. *Memoirs*, 6:113–14, 12:16, and 12:21.
63. Mary W. M. Hargreaves, *The Presidency of John Quincy Adams*, xiii; *The Selected Writings of John and John Quincy Adams*, xxxiv.

considered vital for preserving the general welfare. He also confronted, in tragic and often dramatic detail, his own failure to find a religious or philosophical explanation for the meaning of his life's work.

A constellation of forces made it virtually impossible for President Adams to govern by balancing political necessity and moral principle. First, there was no sense of party allegiance to the man in the White House. The old Federalist party was dead and the Republicans, having moved away from Jeffersonian principles after 1815, were racked by internal divisions. For example, the Republican party established a National Bank five years after it had been declared unconstitutional; it adopted Hamilton's theory of a high protective tariff; and it had supported internal improvements on a grand scale. In his *Memoirs*, which took on the character of a "treasury of damnations," he noted the mortifying majority against him, particularly mortifying to the patriot in his own country.[64] Gadflies like the "reptile John Randolph" lost no time in castigating the reigning member of the American "House of Stuart" and his supposedly disgraceful confederation with Clay—the alliance of "Blifil and Black George." Second, his refusal to remove political enemies and appoint in their place his own cadre alienated most of his influential adherents. He refused point-blank to use any office as a reward for political support or to build political machines. "Efforts," he confided in his diary, "had been made by some Senators to obtain different nominations, and to introduce a principle of . . . rotation in office at the expiration of these commissions; which would make the government [an] unremitting scramble for office. A more pernicious expedient could scarcely have been devised." Third, the tide of democracy was rising, and it was not a critical audience to which elected officials had to address their arguments as the scope of the franchise was steadily widened.

Fourth, Adams's own political philosophy ran counter to the democratic impulses of his time. He could never bring himself to accept the popular theory of representation that the statesman was more the delegate, and less the leader, of the people. The closing sentence in his

64. *Memoirs*, 7:474.

first annual message to Congress invoked a standard to which few would rally: "While foreign nations, less blessed with that freedom which is power than ourselves, are advancing with gigantic strides in the career of public improvement, are we to slumber in indolence or fold up our arms and proclaim to the world that we are palsied by the will of our constituents?" Growing industrialism, the expansion of the West, and a constantly widening electorate had all powerfully deflected the social forces of John Quincy Adams's day. In the midterm election of 1827, and for the first time in the nation's history, a majority opposed to the administration was returned to both houses of Congress. Moreover, Adams's proposal for a vigorous plan of internal improvements was not limited to roads and canals. The object of government, Adams always believed, was to improve the condition of the people. Economic improvement was essential; however, "moral, political, and intellectual improvement are duties assigned by the Author of our Existence to social, no less than to individual man."[65] He suggested that the government should maintain a national university, finance scientific explorations, establish a uniform standard of weights and measures, create a department of the interior, reform the patent laws, explore the coasts and interior country, and erect astronomical observatories ("lighthouses of the skies"). The government's refusal to use all its power for the benefit of the people would amount to a "treachery to the most sacred of trusts." Adams's program offended just about every special-interest group in the country. The Crawford-Calhoun-Jackson forces, championing states' rights and strict construction, brought the South and West together in alliance against the president.

Branded as everything from a thief who plundered the public domain to a pander who once delivered an American temptress to the Russian tsar, Adams was soundly defeated by Andrew Jackson in the election of 1828. It seemed to him that the forces of evil had triumphed over the forces of virtue. An entry in his diary three days before vacating the White House dramatizes his political isolation:

65. John Quincy Adams, "First Annual Message," in *The State of the Union Messages of the Presidents, 1790–1966*, 1:246–47; *The Selected Writings of John and John Quincy Adams*, 361.

I shall be restored to private life . . . though certainly not of repose. I go into it with a combination of parties and public men against my character . . . such as I believe never before was exhibited against any man since the Union existed. . . . [And] so it is, that this combination . . . is now exulting in triumph over me, for the devotion of my life and of all the faculties of my soul to the Union, and to the improvement, physical, moral, and intellectual, of my country. The North assails me for my fidelity to the Union; the South, for my . . . aspirations of improvement. Yet "bate I not a jot of heart and hope." Passion, prejudice, envy, and jealousy will pass. The cause of Union and of improvement will remain, and I have duties to it and to my country to discharge.[66]

Adams thought of himself as a leader "made by circumstances, and not by . . . volition." Only this rationale seems to account for "the agony of mind" that he took care faithfully to suppress in the face of repeated political disappointments. Not surprisingly, Adams was haunted almost daily by the French opera of Richard Coeur-de-Lion, where the minstrel, Blondel, sings under the walls of his prison a song, beginning

> Oh Richard! O, mon Roi!
> L'univers t'abandonne.

Returning to Quincy, he turned to his books—Cicero, Plutarch, Shakespeare, even Bulwer-Lytton's novel of *Pelham*, then just off the press. He also began to gather source material and write his father's political biography, which would be completed in 1871 by his son, Charles Francis Adams.

V.

The high political stations Adams occupied in no way diminished his unceasing philosophical, literary, and religious researches. On March 3, 1817, the United States Senate assigned to Adams the task of preparing a study on the standards and regulations of "weights and measures in the several States, and relative to proceedings in foreign countries." His

---

66. *Memoirs*, 8:101.

treatise of two hundred and forty-five printed pages, pronounced a monument of research by a series of European scholars, was as notable for its history and moral principles as for its mathematical computations emphasizing the need for international uniformity. As president, he took time each day to "read two chapters of Scott's Bible and Commentary, and the corresponding commentary of Hewlett"; in addition, the translation of the Psalms of David into English was a frequent exercise. Adams's lifelong interest in astronomy was nurtured by his familiarity with the works of Schubert, Lalande, Biot, and Lacroix. From Langlet's and Dufresnoy's tables, he compared the Arabian and Turkish computations of time with those of Christian nations. Astronomy and chronology led him to the study of mathematics and the logarithms in the tables of Collet. Works of the ancient philosophers and orators—Plato, Aristotle, Demosthenes, Isocrates, and Cicero— were read and compared. Moreover, Adams's religious perspective on the human condition was enlivened by his tireless reading of works by Butler, Bossuet, Tillotson, Massillon, Atterbury, and Watts. With such an ardor for the universality of knowledge, it is not surprising that his enthusiasm was tempered by a keen sense of his own shortcomings: "I feel nothing like the tediousness of time. I suffer nothing like *ennui*. Time is too short for me, rather than too long. If the day was forty-eight hours, instead of twenty-four, I could employ them all, if I had but eyes and hands to read and write."[67] His humble pretensions as a poet provided another glimpse of the eternal truths that had direct relevance to the lives of men; the following verse was inscribed to the sundial under the window in the hall of the House of Representatives:

> Thou silent herald of Time's silent flight!
> Say, couldst thou speak what warning voice were thine?
> Shade, who canst only show how others shine!
> Dark, sullen witness of resplendent light
> In day's broad glare, and when the noontide bright
> Of laughing fortune sheds the ray divine,
> Thy ready favor cheers us—but decline

67. Quincy, *Memoir of the Life of John Quincy Adams*, 52–53, 174. Adams quoted by Seward, *Life of John Quincy Adams*, 237–38.

> The clouds of morning and the gloom of night.
> Yet are thy counsels faithful, just and wise;
>   They bid us seize the moments as they pass—
> Snatch the retrieveless sunbeam as it flies,
>   Nor lose one sand of life's revolving glass—
> Aspiring still, with energy sublime,
> By virtuous deeds to give eternity to Time.

Adams's retirement to Quincy was both temporary and shaken by old political recriminations. William B. Giles, of Virginia, published a story contending that Adams believed Massachusetts Federalists were guilty of fomenting secessionist designs during the Jefferson administration. The controversy prompted thirteen prominent leaders—including Harrison Gray Otis, Henry Cabot, John Lowell, William Prescott, and T. H. Perkins—to call on Adams publicly to name the men who he had claimed were plotting treason in 1808. Adams's rejoinder, part of which was withheld from publication until 1877, only tarnished further his reputation in the eyes of the financially and socially select of Boston. One ray of sunshine amid the dark clouds was his election to the Board of Overseers of Harvard College. Adams himself could not foresee the course of events that would soon liberate him from his political exile. In September 1830, he was asked to stand as a candidate for the House of Representatives from the farming district of Plymouth. He replied that, if the people wished him to, he would serve them, but "I shall not ask [for] their votes. I wish them to act at their pleasure." In view of the two-term precedent, he thought it inevitable that ex-presidents should generally survive beyond the termination of their terms of office. Their election to Congress would in no manner signal a "derogatory descent." "For myself," he wrote to Charles Adams, "taught in the school of Cicero, I shall say, '*Defendi respublicam adolescens; non deseram senex.*'—'I will not desert in my old age the Republic that I defended in my youth.'"[68] Of the 2,565 votes cast in twenty-two towns, 1,817 were cast for Adams, and the rest were scattered among several candidates.

68. *Memoirs*, 8:287, 8:401; Shepherd, *The Adams Chronicles*, 317.

In a record of public service unequaled to this day, ex-President Adams served as a member of Congress from 1831 until his death seventeen years later in the very hall of Congress itself. Despite his seeming wish not to be elected, he recorded that his election "as President . . . [had not] been half so satisfying to [his] inmost soul." Long years of "incessant intercourse with the world [had] made political movement to [him] as much a necessary of life as atmospheric air." The oldest member of the House, Adams was at the same time the most punctual—the first at his post; the last to retire from the labors of the day. He remarked upon the habitual absence from the chamber of some of his colleagues paid from the public treasury, "as if they had been present fulfilling their obligations twelve hours a day." Adams disavowed any basic change in his foreign policy orientation—from those early views laid out in the *Marcellus* papers to his strong support of President Jackson's demand that France comply with the treaty of indemnity signed on July 4, 1831. In a speech before Congress on January 22, 1836, he answered Daniel Webster on the French crisis in an assault that he claimed "demolished" his opponent, "drove him from the field, and whipped him and his party into the rank and file of the nation in the quarrel with the French king."[69]

In internal affairs, Adams said he "had lived and shall die a federalist of Washington's . . . school and of the Republican School of John Marshall and John Jay." He never had been "a federalist of the School of Hamilton, Ames, Pickering, or Webster, or a Republican of the School of . . . Paine, Jefferson, or Calhoun." Moreover, he was dubious about Adam Smith's laissez-faire as the linch-pin of national prosperity: only fools or traitors would let the nation's economy be governed by the invisible hand of the international marketplace. The government, he agreed, should not meddle with the sacred right of private property or

69. By the 1831 treaty, France had agreed to pay the United States five million dollars to settle spoilation claims. Following a four-year delay in French payment, Jackson recalled the American minister to Paris and recommended to Congress that the United States issue letters of marque against French commerce—that is, declare war. Adams was virtually alone in defending the use of force in order to insure treaty provisions and rescue the nation's honor. See Summary of the Year, *Memoirs*, 9:339; *Memoirs*, 11:538.

individual initiative. Yet if the United States were to follow Smith's doctrine and concentrate on what it could produce best and most efficiently, meeting the rest of its needs through trade, then it would remain a nation of cotton planters and farmers at the mercy of industrial England. Both economic well-being and political independence required the government to take positive steps to develop a balanced, self-sufficient economy.[70]

The major domestic and foreign policy problems to come before Congressman Adams were modified in their solution by the problem of slavery. For years, he had considered slavery a "great and foul stain upon the North American Union." As secretary of state, he described the Missouri Compromise as the "title page to a great tragic volume." In a conversation with the secretary of war, John C. Calhoun, in 1820, Adams warned that "the dissolution of the Union [if it should result from the slave question] . . . must shortly afterwards be followed by the universal emancipation of the slaves." One of his first acts before the first session of the twenty-second Congress was to present a petition to abolish slavery and the slave trade in the District of Columbia. While Adams was always antislavery, he often took exception with the indiscriminate moral fervor of the abolitionists. For example, he believed that the Constitution conferred upon Congress the power to abolish the slave trade and to proscribe slavery in a territory seeking statehood; yet he also acknowledged that there was no constitutional justification for abolishing slavery in states where it already existed. The abolition of slavery "where it is established must be left entirely to the people of the state itself." The healthy "had no right to reproach or to prescribe for the diseased." Until his last years, he cautioned that the "premature agitation of slavery in the national councils" would retard, rather than facilitate, the abolition of this great evil—"as the most salutary medicines, unduly administered, were the most deadly poisons." The nuances of his position seldom survived the political tidal wave engendered by the Sable Genius of the South, an example being his characterization

70. "Report of the Committee of Manufactures," *Register of Debates*, 22nd Congress, 1st Session, (1831–1832), Appendix, 85; Leonard L. Richards, *The Life and Times of Congressman John Quincy Adams*, 69.

of the allegations made by Henry Wise of Virginia: "Abolition, abolition, abolition, was the unvarying cry; and he represented me as a
friend, the inspirer and leader of all abolition."[71]

Closely related to the issue of slavery was the fight in Congress for
the unsolicited right to petition. Such action was limited at this time
by the infamous "gag rule," imposed in 1836 by the dominant southern
representatives in Congress. The rule, drawn up by Henry Pinckney of
South Carolina, stated that "all petitions, memorials, resolutions, propositions, and papers relating . . . to the subject of slavery, or the
abolition of slavery, shall . . . be laid upon the table, and no further
action . . . shall be had thereon." Pinckney's resolution passed, 117 to
68, over the bitter denunciation of John Quincy Adams, who attacked
the measure as "a direct violation of the constitution of the United
States, the rules of this House, and the right of my constituents." Over
the next eight years, Adams made the repeal of the gag rule a cause
célèbre, offering petitions at the opening of every session of Congress
and soon becoming a symbol of emancipation. When a representative
from Virginia said that the Negroes in one petition were of an inferior
stock, Adams replied, "I adhere to the right of petition. . . . Petition is
supplication—it is entreaty—it is prayer!" Where, Adams asked, "is
the degree of vice or immorality which shall deprive the citizen of the
right to supplicate for a boon, or to pray for mercy?" The right of
petition was vouchsafed by natural law; "and so far from refusing to
present a petition because it might come from those low in the estimation of the world, it would be an additional incentive if such an incentive were wanting." Adams also drew the momentous distinction
between the wartime and peacetime powers of Congress, with the
consequence that the elimination of slavery—through the use of wartime governmental powers—could be *lawfully* accomplished.[72] In a
sense, this idea provided the seed from which Lincoln's Emancipation

71. *Memoirs*, 4:502–3, 4:530–31; JQA to Jonathan Jennings, July 17, 1820, 7:53–54;
Register of Debates, 22nd Congress, 1st Session, December 12, 1831, 1424–26; *Memoirs*,
8:434, 10:479.

72. Seward, *Life of John Quincy Adams*, 289; Alfred Kelly and Winfred Harbison,
The American Constitution, 336; *Memoirs*, 11:103.

Proclamation developed. Adams was finally successful in obtaining the repeal of the gag rule in 1844, largely because the growth of the northern antislavery movement had convinced the northern congressmen that it would be politically unwise to support the rule any longer.

At the beginning of his term as a representative, Adams was willing to cut the tariff, less drastically than Jackson, but enough to make concessions to the South and to eliminate obvious inequities in the Tariff of Abominations, a document he signed as president but never regarded as above reproach. This did not prevent him from opposing Jackson's presidential message of December 1832, which, in effect, gave way to the pressure embodied in the Ordinance of Secession and Nullification of the convention in South Carolina. Adams insisted that no tariff action be taken until it became clear whether the Union was the master or the slave of states. A compromise would "directly lead to the final and irretrievable dissolution of the Union." Nullification "drew its first breath in the land where the meaning of the word democracy is that a majority of the people are the goods and chattels of the minority." Nothing was so absurd to Adams as the political amalgamation of nullification and democracy. In the first place, the true spirit of democracy has "its foundations in a generous theory of human rights," one based "on the natural equality of mankind." What communion, Adams wondered, can there be between "self-government . . . by the conjoint will of the majority" and nullification, the latter inspired by "the despotism of a corporation—unlimited, unrestrained, *sovereign* power." In the second place, nullification erected barriers against internal improvements of the country by the federal government, no less than obstructing the sale of public lands to fund commercial and scientific achievements on a national scale. "Slavery stands aghast at the . . . promotion of the general welfare, and flies to nullification for defense against the energies of freedom, and the inalienable rights of man."[73]

Both in and outside Congress, Adams spoke of those transcendent political principles founded in the American conscience and threat-

73. Quincy, *Memoir of the Life of John Quincy Adams*, 379–80; 382–83; 384–87.

ened by the hotbed of slavery. Nowhere was his intellectual temperament more apparent than during his appearance in 1841 before the
United States Supreme Court. In his first case before the court since
1809, Adams defended thirty-nine Africans who had been shipped as
slaves on the *Amistad* for Cuba. The Africans had rebelled on board,
killed the captain and cook, and taken their two Spanish masters
prisoner. Led by the slave Cinqué, they had hoped to sail back to West
Africa, only to be victimized in a clever ruse by the Spaniards that
landed them instead on Long Island Sound, where they were captured.
Adams fought against violation of the fundamental right to judicial
safeguards, which entailed a demand by the Spanish minister that the
slaves be delivered up to Spanish authority. The right of habeas corpus,
Adams pleaded, is the all-encompassing feature of British and American liberty, without which the power of arbitrary imprisonment could
make all other rights a mockery. Adams's legal brief made reference to
a philosophical principle, associated with southern interests, and recently argued in national print to sway the court's judgment: "The
truth is, that property in man has existed in all ages of the world, and
results from the *natural* state of man, *which is war*. . . . War, conquest,
and force, have produced slavery, and it is state necessity and the
internal law of self-preservation, that will ever . . . defend it." Adams's
rebuttal looked to a different interpretation of human nature and
natural rights.

> If these rights [in the Declaration] are inalienable, they are incompat-
> ible with the rights of the victor to take the life of his enemy in war,
> or to spare his life and make him a slave. If this principle is sound, it
> reduces to brute force all the rights of man. It places all the sacred
> relations of life at the power of the strongest. No man has a right to
> life or liberty, if he has an enemy able to take them from him . . . but I
> say that the doctrine of Hobbes, that *War* is the natural state of man,
> has for ages been exploded, as equally disclaimed . . . by the philoso-
> pher and the Christian.[74]

74. *Argument of John Quincy Adams before the Supreme Court of the United States, in
the Case of the United States, Appellants vs. Cinque, and Others, Africans, February 24, and
March 1, 1841*, 116–19.

Accordingly, Adams argued that the Hobbesian state of nature is incompatible with the notion of justice as defined in the Institutes of Justinian: *Constans et perpetua voluntas, jus suum cuique tribuendi* (The constant and perpetual will to secure to everyone his own right). The right of habeas corpus, which he thought in jeopardy in the case, he asserted to be the all-encompassing feature of British and American liberty, without which the power of arbitrary imprisonment could make all other rights a mockery. In March 1841, the court ruled that the Africans were free. Judge Joseph Story described Adams's argument as "extraordinary, for its power, for its bitter sarcasm, and its dealing with topics far beyond the record and points of discussion."[75]

His stand on the annexation of Texas, a serious qualification of his expansionist nationalism, was likewise a product of his antislavery, northeastern views. Less than ten years before General Sam Houston's rout of Santa Anna's Mexican forces at San Jacinto in 1836, the Adams administration tried a number of desperate ploys to persuade Mexico to sell as much of Texas as possible. The goal of Jackson, Calhoun, and other slavemasters, he claimed, was nothing short of outright intervention in the Mexican civil war. The "perfidious robbery and dismemberment of Mexico" would by 1845 triumph over all constitutional objection. "The Constitution," Adams wrote just prior to President John Tyler's signing of the joint resolution for annexation, "is a menstruous rag, and the Union is sinking into a military monarchy, to be rent asunder like the empire of Alexander or the kingdoms of Ephraim and Judah." Arguing that President James Polk had used his powers as commander in chief to create a situation that guaranteed war with Mexico in 1846, Adams favored the withdrawal of all American troops and the negotiation of a treaty without any demands for territorial concessions or reparations.[76]

During his last years of service in the House, John Quincy Adams never slackened in his advocacy of government as an instrument of

75. Shepherd, *The Adams Chronicles*, 333.

76. *Memoirs*, 12:171. Richards, *The Life and Times of Congressman John Quincy Adams*, 193; *Congressional Globe*, 30th Congress, 1st Session (1847–1848), January 3, 1848, 93–94.

social progress. As chairman of the committee on manufactures, he labored in vain for an appropriation to advance government-sponsored exploitation of natural resources. In 1835, an Englishman, James Smithson, bequeathed his estate, valued at over a half-million dollars, to the United States for the purpose of establishing an institution "for the increase and diffusion of knowledge among men." For the next eight years, Adams chaired a select committee that funded the creation of the Smithsonian Institution, although he was not successful in applying part of the money to an astronomical observatory for the extension of the "sublimest of the physical sciences." In fact, one of Adams's final public acts was dedicating the Cincinnati observatory in 1843. He was then seventy-six and far from well. Invoking the spirit of science as typified by the great figures of Tycho Brahe, Kepler, and Newton, Adams celebrated the occasion as the dawn of a new epoch of enlightenment in America. He contended that the laws of nature and of nature's God "are laws of duty, as well as laws of right." The divine workings of nature recommended "a point of view from which this new modeling of the institution of civil society" would lead directly to a national obligation to patronize scientific investigation. Adams's view was captured best in one of the immortal conceptions of Shakespeare.

> Nature never lends
> The smallest parcel of her excellence.
> But like a thrifty goddess she determines
> Herself the glory of a creditor—
> Both thanks and use.[77]

Man's reason, then, is his immortal part, and its best use must be devoted to analyzing the relationship between unseen causes and observable effects, with the heavens the proper object of initial inquiry.[78]

Even a paralytic stroke that befell Adams in 1846 could not keep him

77. Quoted in *The Selected Writings of John and John Quincy Adams,* 399.

78. John Quincy Adams, *An Oration, Delivered before the Cincinnati Astronomical Society on the Occasion of Laying the Corner Stone of an Astronomical Observatory,* 12–19, 61–63.

from constant attendance in the House of Representatives. On February 21, 1848, he was at his seat as usual, when he was seen to partially rise. The Speaker was putting a question before the chamber, only to be interrupted by shouts of "Stop! Stop! Mr. Adams!" The old man had fallen insensible and was removed to the Speaker's room. The shock of it saddened Henry Clay, who visited the family and held the dying man's hands, his eyes filled with tears. Adams lived only two more days, recovering speech long enough to declare, "This is the end of earth, but I am composed."[79] Until the twenty-fifth, his body lay in state in the committee room of the House in a coffin surrounded by evergreen boughs and spring flowers. His remains were carried back to the Stone Temple in Quincy, the family tomb, where he was laid to rest beside his parents.

79. For Henry Clay's reaction, see Remini, *Henry Clay*, 699–700.

TWO

Ethics, Philosophy, and Religion in Adams's Worldview

The normative foundations of American foreign policy inhere in philosophical conceptions of politics, human nature, and the meaning of history. Politics is an art, not a science, and what is required for its mastery is not the rationality of the engineer but the wisdom and moral strength of the statesman. From the deeds of the great diplomatists throughout the ages, politics achieve coherence by the wisdom born out of the experience of insecurity and heroic fulfillment of human possibilities. In the words of Hans Morgenthau: "The statesman must cross the rubicon not knowing how deep and turbulent the river is. . . . He must commit himself to a . . . course of action in ignorance of its consequences, and he must be capable of acting decisively in spite of that ignorance. . . . Rather than seeking unattainable knowledge, he must reconcile himself to ineluctable ignorance. His is the leading part in a tragedy, and he must act the part."[1] The statesmen who became masters of events and conscious creators of history—the Washingtons and Adamses, the Lincolns and Roosevelts— had one quality in common: they combined a general conception of foreign policy, of its direction and aim, with the ability to manipulate concrete circumstances in light of that conception. The actor on the

1. Hans J. Morgenthau, *The Restoration of American Politics*, 103.

political stage carries within his mind a political philosophy, however inchoate and fragmentary and unacknowledged. That philosophy makes him understand the political scene and act with regard to it. The enduring value of Adams's international thought can be explained by his command of the statesman's historic task of seeking victory while situated at an uneasy juncture between fate and freedom, necessity and chance.

Adams's political thought illustrates that there is no deliverance from the inescapable tension between reason and experience, between theoretical and practical knowledge. As Morgenthau explained the tragic conception of realism,

> The philosopher . . . knows more than the king . . . [but the philosopher] cannot act according to his knowledge. The king, even if he knew all the philosopher knows, would still not know for certain what action the concrete situation requires. No theoretical knowledge but only the experience of acting can teach him that. Yet even that experience will teach him only how to avoid the repetition of yesterday's blunder, not how to not commit a new one tomorrow.[2]

The sources of Adams's statesmanship must begin with his awareness of the existential human condition from which the religious impulse, made rational in dogma and visible in organization, springs: the finiteness of man in knowledge and action. Adams thought incessantly about the perennial challenge to man in his social and political existence—his heroic struggle to be and to be more than he is and to know that he can be more than he is. Political wisdom, he believed, begins with the experience of this insecurity—a recognition of the hapless social forces that man's own unstilled desires have created—as the test that pushes great men to the limits of their human possibilities. A concern for both the good and evil in human nature—the belief in miserably selfish and parochial man transcending himself by God's grace—was Adams's starting point in ethics, religion, science, and politics.

2. Hans J. Morgenthau, *Dilemmas of Politics,* 321.

I.

Adams believed that "moral principle should be the alpha and omega of all human composition, poetry or prose, scientific or literary . . . and emphatically of every discourse." One vital and seminal principle—"the discharge of some duty to God or man"—should animate the particular tasks of the poet and dramatist. Pope makes this duty a point of self-glorification:

> That not in fancy's maze he wander'd long,
> But stoop'd to truth, and moralized his song.[3]

Adams's love of Shakespeare prompted him to analyze the human tragedy that molded the moral and intellectual character of Hamlet. In fact, Shakespeare's creation was a "masterpiece of the human mind."

Adams understood tragedy as the imitative representation of human action and passion, designed to purify the heart of the spectator through the dramatization of terror and pity. This, he said, was "the definition of Aristotle; and Pope's most beautiful lines in the prologue to [Addison's tragedy of] Cato, are but an expansion of the same idea." Hamlet is the personification of a man crushed to extinction by the pressure of calamities inflicted, not by nature, but against nature; not by physical, but by moral evil. The symptoms of this mortal coil are evident in Hamlet's colloquy with Guildenstern:

> What a piece of work is a man! how noble in reason! how infinite in faculty! in form and moving how express and admirable! in action how like an angel! in apprehension how like a god! the beauty of the world! the paragon of animals! And yet, to me, what is this quintessence of dust? man delights not me.[4]

Hamlet represents both the heart and soul of man, "in agonizing conflict with human crime in its highest pre-eminence of guilt." His

---

3. *Memoirs*, 11:372.
4. John Quincy Adams and James H. Hackett, *The Character of Hamlet*, 3; Pope, *Collected Poems*, 57–58; *The Complete Works of William Shakespeare*, ed. William George Clark and William Aldis Wright, 1022.

passions—filial affection, youthful love, and manly ambition—are in conflict with his principles—filial duty, generous friendship, love subdued, ambition and life surrendered to avenge his father.

Hamlet's right to the throne had been violated, and his suspicions aroused, by the marriage of his mother to his uncle, so soon after his father's death. His love for Ophelia is first trammeled by the conflicting pride of his birth and station. Although he "made many tenders of his affection to Ophelia," and "hath importuned her with love in honourable fashion," he offered no proposal of marriage. Cautioned both by her brother and her father, she repulses the advances of Hamlet. Instead of attributing this to its true cause, he assumes that she mocks his affections; "and his first experiment of assumed madness is made upon her." He ends up treating her with a sickening "mixture of ardent passion, of gross indelicacy, and of rudeness, little short of brutality." At one moment, he is worshipping at her feet; at the next, he is taunting her with sneering advice to seek refuge in a nunnery. The language of splendid intellect, in alliance with acute feeling, accentuates the anguish of Hamlet—"a throne lost by usurpation—a father murdered by a mother and an uncle—an incestuous marriage between the criminals—and the apparition from the eternal world, of his father's spirit, commanding him to avenge the deed." A marked characteristic from the outset is Hamlet's own self-dissatisfaction:

> The time is out of joint—O cursed spite,
> That ever I was born to set it right.[5]

The revelation of the ghost is the climax of the tragedy; "it unsettles that ardent and meditative mind." Hamlet's disgrace is evident in the tone of levity that creeps into his words at the departure of the "perturbed spirit." His determination to "put on an antic disposition," Adams remarks, is the "expedient of a deadly but irresolute purpose." He will execute the command of his father by premeditating the time, place, and occasion. The execution of the deed leads him to feign occasional madness amid intervals of steady and rational conversation.

5. Adams and Hackett, *The Character of Hamlet*, 4, 7.

And thus it is that "the native hue of resolution is sicklied o'er with the pale cast of thought." The action and reaction between mind and heart—the feeling spurring him on and the reflection holding him back—constitute "that most admirable portrait of human nature in its highest state, little lower than the angels, little above the Hottentot of the African Cape, which pervades every part of the character and conduct of Hamlet." According to Adams,

> He reflects upon life, upon death, upon the nature of man, upon the physical composition of the universe; he indulges in minute criticism upon the performance of the players; he . . . comments upon a satire in Juvenal; he quibbles with a quibbling grave digger; he commemorates the convivial attractions of an old jovial table companion, whose bones the good man Delver turns up in digging the grave for Ophelia, and philosophizes upon the dust of imperial Caesar, metamorphosed into the bung of a beer barrel.[6]

Yet the man whom Hamlet has murdered is Ophelia's father, Polonius; Ophelia's madness and death are the consequences of the crime. Furthermore, Hamlet takes no notice at the burial scene—over which he "so pathetically and humourously disserts upon the bones of Yorick, the king's jester"—that the sepulcher is about to receive the corpse of Ophelia. The reasoning faculty of Hamlet "always takes the tinge of passion under which he is labouring, but his conduct is always governed by the impulse of the moment." His reflections are as sportive and playful as they are sorrowfully indignant and melancholy. Hamlet's real madness is towering passion, the furor *brevis*, which is the ancient definition of anger. His tragic character consisted of the ideal perfection in man's intellectual and moral nature "struggling with calamity beyond his power to bear, inflicted by the crime of his fellow man . . . sinking under it to extinction."[7]

Adams looked upon man's rational faculty as the peculiar and highest characteristic that distinguishes him from other animals. This attribute of the human species constitutes "the great link between the physical and intellectual world." Man's passions and appetites place

6. Ibid.
7. Ibid., 5.

him "on a level with the herds of the forest; by our REASON we participate of the divine nature itself." In the scale of creation, man ranks "higher than the clod of the valley" though "lower than the angels." The gift of reason alone enabled man to enjoy the "privilege of progressive improvement" that follows from "the advantages of individual discovery." The ubiquitous symbolism of the "Great Chain of Being" had a profound impact on the worldview of the American Founding Fathers, including John Quincy Adams. In the words of Pope:

> Vast chain of being! which from God began,
> Nature's aethereal, human, angel, man,
> Beast, bird, fish, insect, what no eye can see,
> No glass can reach; from Infinite to thee,
> From thee to nothing.[8]

The universe presented the spectacle of a continuous chain, or ladder, of creatures extending without a break from the worm to the seraph. Benjamin Franklin, upon selecting the motto for his dissertation, chose the following lines from Dryden:

> Whatever is, is in its Causes just,
> Since all Things are by, Fate; but Purblind Man
> Sees but a part o' th' Chain, the nearest link,
> His Eyes not carrying to the equal Beam
> That poses all above.[9]

The consequences of this worldview for the political thought of Adams may be noted briefly. Man formed the middle link between the lower and higher creatures. John Locke supposed he stood closer to the lower creatures than to God from whom he is infinitely remote. If the depravity of human nature (i.e., original sin) had been banished (though, as Pope points out, not without a new innocence that prompts man to praise the Creator and the Creation), so had man's striving for redemp-

---

8. John Quincy Adams, *Lectures on Rhetoric and Oratory*, 1:13–14. Pope, *Collected Poems*, 188.
9. James Parton, *Life and Times of Benjamin Franklin*, 1:605.

tion, man's aspiration for perfection. With the emancipation of man's anxiety from original sin came the lowering of the goals of human life. A. O. Lovejoy noted that the "imperfection of man is indispensable for the fullness of the hierarchy of being." With no room left for millenarian prophesy or fanaticism, Pope's ethical perspective amounted to a counsel of imperfection, an "ethics of prudent mediocrity." In the poet's words: "In pride, in reas'ning Pride, our error lies." Pope sought to elaborate the "science of human nature" and, thereby, "vindicate the ways of God to man." Politics becomes a sort of mediocre thing, neither the noblest nor the meanest realm but an in-between sphere; it is not the way to salvation, either in the beyond or in the world.

> Plac'd in this isthmus of a middle state,
> A being darkly wise and rudely great,
> With too much knowledge for the skeptic side,
> With too much weakness for the Stoic's pride,
> He hangs between; in doubt to act or rest;
> In doubt to deem himself a god or beast;
> In doubt his Mind or body to prefer;
> Born but to die, and reasoning but to err; . . .
> Chaos of thought and passion all confused,
> Still by himself, abused, or disabused;
> Created half to rise, and half to fall,
> Great lord of all things, yet a prey to all;
> Sole judge of truth, in endless error hurl'd;
> The glory, jest and riddle of the world![10]

Statecraft inhered in the recognition and application of the two premises underlying the political method of *counterpoise*: that men never act exclusively from disinterested and rational motives, and that it is possible to fashion a good "whole," a happy and harmonious state, by mixing and counterbalancing those antagonistic parts. Human reason enables one to judge the means by which the passions—all "Modes of Self Love"—can be gratified, but it has no driving power.

---

10. John Locke, *An Essay Concerning Human Understanding*, 2:50; A. O. Lovejoy, *The Great Chain of Being*, 199–200; Pope, *Collected Poems*, 185, 189–90; Sandoz, *A Government of Laws*, 223–24.

> On life's vast ocean diversely we sail,
> Reason's the card, but Passion is the gale.[11]

The chart, or compass, neither propels the ship nor determines the destination; it merely allows the mariner to know in which direction the ship is moving, or in what direction to steer in order to reach the port he desires. Conflicting passions, however, can be combined so as to ensure social peace and tranquility, the very purpose of the Creator in making man.

> Passions, like elements though born to fight,
> Yet, mix'd and softened, in his work unite:
> These, 'tis enough to temper and employ;
> But what composes man, can man destroy? . . .
> Each individual seeks a several goal,
> But Heavens great view is one, and that the whole.
> That counterworks each folly and caprice;
> That disappoints the effect of every vice.[12]

The statesman's assignment is to carry out this divine mission by so adjusting the parts of "the whole" that "jarring interests" will

> of themselves create
> Th' according music of the well-mix'd State.

This design will enable the legislator to

> build on wants, and on defects of mind,
> The joy, the peace, the glory of mankind.[13]

Readers of the *Federalist Papers* will recognize that the framers of the Constitution applied the same two presuppositions in planning a system of government not yet in existence. The delegates at the 1787 Convention sought a blend of political ethics and practical psychology—to preach to Americans about what they *ought* to do, as well as to

---

11. Lovejoy, *The Great Chain of Being*, 192.
12. Ibid., 192, 195.
13. Ibid., 195.

predict successfully what they *would* do, supposing certain governmental mechanisms were established. James Madison's writing, in particular, drew upon the method of counterpoise to attenuate "the spirit of faction" and promote the public welfare. "Faith in the people" is plainly repudiated by Madison; however, what he did have faith in was the efficacy of checks and balances as a corrective to the evils resulting from "government on the popular model," a "republican remedy for the diseases most incident to republican government." In *Federalist* #51, Madison defended the philosophical basis for republican government:

> The great security against a gradual concentration of the several powers in the same department, consists in giving to those who administer each department the necessary means, and personal motives, to resist the encroachments of others. . . . Ambition must be made to counteract ambition. The interests of the man must be connected with the constitutional rights of the place . . . But what is government itself but the greatest of all reflections on human nature? . . . The policy of supplying by opposite and rival interests, the defects of better motives, might be traced through the whole system of human affairs, private as well as public.[14]

John Quincy Adams saw a natural connection between Jefferson's self-evident truths in the Declaration and Madison's profile of political man in the *Federalist*. While all men are born with certain unalienable rights, these rights can be enjoyed only on the condition that they be respected in others. The law of nature and of nature's God "are laws of duty, as well as laws of right." The pursuit of happiness calls for the institutions of government to regulate and adjust the collisions of interests and passions incident to the existence of civil society—"to secure, as far as . . . human nature will admit, the rights of every one, by the organized and co-operating energy of all, and to harmonize the discordant elements of the social compact." Adams described a true republic as "the only actual or imaginable human government, in which self-love and social [concord] are the same." The use of self-love in this passage, as a bridge between individual and civic virtue, illus-

14. Jacob E. Cooke, ed. *The Federalist*, 349.

trates the confluence of classical and Christian components in Adams's political philosophy. While men are sinful and depraved, their self-love is not so radically evil and egotistic as in Hobbes, Hume, and Augustine. No less an authority than John Witherspoon, one of the more influential teachers in the entire history of American education,[15] argued that the key to human nature is realizing that the depravity of man is balanced by a part of God's creation that offers hope for the continuing improvement of human society.

For Adams, the ethics of political society begin with an anthropological distinction between nature and person. By his nature, man is the epitome of the whole range of material and spiritual being. In his person, however, man bears the seal of God as it is imprinted on his nature, by means of which he participates in Divine Being. Man's duty to himself, beyond the law of self-preservation and advancement, is to nurture that very dignity that puts him into a personal relationship with God. Nature and grace are not juxtaposed. The love of self, in the words of one political philosopher, "presumes a natural *desire* of the creature for communion with the Creator and with fellow beings who also bear the divine image as part of their very selfhood." Man's freedom is the freedom to choose among the actions, natural willings, and knowledge available in the potential of one's nature as a man. God or the good remain the natural end of fellow beings created for communion with the divine Creator. Moreover, Adams's position parallels Aristotle's argument—in Book 9 of the *Nicomachean Ethics*—that self-love constitutes the basis of friendship within the polity: "The friendly relations which we have with our neighbours and which serve to define the various kinds of friendship seem to be derived from our relations to ourselves." The good man, Aristotle observes, "wishes for and does what is good for himself and what appears good to him—for the mark of a good man is to work hard to achieve the good—and he does so for his own sake, for he does it for the sake of the intellectual part of himself, which . . . is thought to constitute what each person really is. Further . . . he wishes

15. Adams, *Cincinnati Oration*, 21–22; Garry Wills, *Explaining America: The Federalist*, 16; Sandoz, *A Government of Laws*, 179–86.

for his own life and preservation, and he wishes it especially for that part of him with which he thinks."[16]

Along similar lines, Adams observed that the natural equality and unalienable rights of mankind were preserved in "the true republic of Montesquieu—the government of which *virtue* is the seminal principle." Montesquieu did not abandon the older identification of liberty with civic virtue (as opposed to the private or nonpolitical life of the individual); in fact, he makes the argument at one point that liberty can in no sense be equated with the ability to do what one wills, but "can only consist in the ability to do what one ought to will, and in not being constrained to do what one ought not to will." Virtue in a republic expresses itself as a "love of the republic; it is a sensation, and not a consequence of acquired knowledge, a sensation that may be felt by the meanest as well as the highest person in the state." The less individuals are able to satisfy their private passions, "the more we abandon ourselves to those of a general nature." When virtue is banished, however, then

> ambition invades the minds of those who are disposed to receive it, and avarice possesses the whole community. The objects of their desires are changed; what they were fond of before has become indifferent; they were free while under the restraint of laws, but they would fain now be free to act against the law; and as each citizen is like a slave who has run away from his master, that which was a maxim of equity he calls rigor; that which was a rule of action he styles constraint; and to persecution he gives the name of fear. Frugality, and not the thirst of gain, now passes for avarice. . . . The members of the commonwealth riot on the public spoils, and its strength is only the power of a few, and the license of many.[17]

Democracy, Montesquieu argued, requires *love of country* and the allied passion of *love for equality*, the latter an inward sentiment, like that praised by classical thinkers, which involves a devotion to the good of the whole such that all "serve with alacrity" even though they cannot serve equally. What matters is not difference of talent but equal

16. Sandoz, *A Government of Laws*, 182; Ellis Sandoz, *Political Apocalypse, A Study of Dostoyevsky's Grand Inquisitor*, 194–95; Aristotle, *Nicomachean Ethics*, 252–53.

17. Montesquieu, *The Spirit of the Laws*, 2:21, 41, 150.

devotion to the common good. These sentiments were echoed by Adams's conviction that "intense patriotism must be the vital spark" for republican government. Like Montesquieu, Adams spoke of a transcendent principle that limits, as it directs, the vital impulses of republican rule. Christian benevolence "enjoins self-love as the standard of brotherly affection, and proclaims all mankind as a brotherhood of one kindred blood." Equality understood in these terms means that "every citizen of such a republic must be devoted to improve the condition of his country and of mankind." Liberty, far from jeopardizing equality, stimulates within each citizen "the constant exercise of all the faculties of body and of mind, with which he has been endowed by his Creator, to elevate . . . and beautify the land of his nativity, or of his choice."[18]

II.

The puritan's sharp distinctions between right and wrong, of election and damnation, of belief and unbelief, point to the dynamic opposition between the higher love of God and the rival loves that threaten the dominion of the human heart. "I see therefore," said John Winthrop, "I must keepe a better watch over my heart, & keepe my thoughts close to good things, & not suffer a vaine or worldly thought to enter, etc.: least it drawe the heart to delight in it." The puritan's life, as Ralph Barton Perry observed, entails the making of some harmonious purpose out of impulses each of which is endowed with an independent bias that must be countered if the purpose is to be maintained. The puritan's struggle against human enemies or the forces of nature was sustained by his belief that he was "battling for the Lord." It is not surprising, then, that the puritan, like other moralists, associated virtue with disinclination. It was said of John Quincy Adams, as evidence of his taint of puritanism, that "the fact that . . . action involved an enormous sacrifice would have been to his mind strong evidence that it was a duty; and the temptation to perform a duty, always strong with

18. Wilson Carey McWilliams, "On Equality as the Moral Foundation for Community," 300–301; Adams, *Cincinnati Oration*, 12–19, 61–63.

him, became ungovernable if the duty was exceptionally disagreeable." Puritan doctrine had lost much of its extreme edge by the end of the eighteenth century. John Adams, the father, was one of New England's first Unitarians. John Quincy Adams, growing up as an independent Congregationalist, came to believe in the existence of one God, Creator and Governor of the universe, particularly of mankind. The Bible taught obedience to the will of God, which was sometimes inscrutable, but always good.[19]

God was, for Adams, neither a rarefied philosophical abstraction nor a mere designation for the unknown, but a Being who ruled the universe. If His rule were not a beneficent one, then all meaning would pass from human existence and human morality. No amount of material comfort or well-being, either for the individual or for the nation, could compensate for the void created by a denial of a purposeful universe. Even as the United States was torn asunder by slavery, Adams never lost faith in God and in the fundamental morality of mankind. It was possible, even probable, that his dream of a free people wisely governing themselves, and advancing by gigantic strides in comfort and spiritual welfare, might have been shattered for the country to which he and his father had devoted the whole of their energies. This tragedy led not to his withdrawal but inspired him to fight harder against the forces and individual leaders who were arrayed against the genuine good of the nation. He was the servant of God, fighting God's enemies and his own, with his back against the wall. His fight was for human freedom—freedom from shackles in the South, freedom for the right to petition in Congress, freedom to pursue knowledge and advance science.[20]

From the vantage point of Christian ethics, Adams alluded to the fundamental existential contradiction of man in history—where there is, on the one hand, man's aspiration to the law of love as the true

19. Quoted by E. D. Hanscom, ed., *The Heart of the Puritan*, 252. J. T. Morse, *John Quincy Adams*, 175–76; J. H. Allen, *Christian History in Its Three Great Periods: Third Period, Modern Phases*, 89; Bemis, *John Quincy Adams and the Foundations of American Foreign Policy*, 7–8.

20. Adams, *The Adams Family*, 213.

essence of *humanitas* and, on the other hand, the tragedy of his consistent betrayal of that law. He traced the source of this contradiction to man's being situated at an uneasy juncture between necessity and freedom, spirit and nature, the human and divine. On the balance between reason and passions in human nature, Adams quoted from Ecclesiastes 6:11–12: "Seeing there be many things that increase vanity, what is man the better? For who knoweth what is good for man in this life, all the days of his vain life which he spendeth as a shadow?" There is, he thought, a natural disposition in man to brood over his afflictions, and to make himself more unhappy than he is. The scriptures add the sanction of religion to this sentiment because of man's imperfect nature. The life of Solomon provides a striking example of the tension between man as sinner and man as image of God. Few mortals have been more favored with higher and nobler intellectual achievements. He contributed perhaps as much as any statesman to an improvement in the human condition. Yet his old age was wasted in "impotent excitement, in idolatrous dotage, and in helpless repining at the nothingness of delights which he could no longer relish." His concubines found him as Madame Maintenon found Louis XIV—a "not amusable man." Human existence, Adams wrote, is "a condition of happiness in the main, interrupted by frequent sorrows."[21] He subscribed to the Christian experience of man as capable of virtue and faith but inclined to vice and sin. He aspires to divinity but knows that he is, indeed, lower than the angels.

Although ancient mythology speaks of the moral and physical depravation of man, "the vanity of human life is not inculcated among the moralists of Greece and Rome." A notable exception was the satirist Persius, who observed: "*O curas hominum! O quantum est in rebus inane!*" (O, the vanity of human cares! O what a huge vacuum man's nature admits). Adams saw the influence of Christian ideas upon this poet, and "still more upon Juvenal" and "the opinions of the age." In general, however, he thought that Greek and Roman perspectives on human nature overly accentuated the uniqueness of man's rational

21. *Memoirs*, 7:286.

faculties (*nous*). The Bible said nothing of a good mind and evil body; the dualism of the classical philosophers identifies the body with evil and assumes the essential goodness of mind or spirit. While the classical view of human virtue is optimistic when compared with the Christian perspective (as the former finds no defect in the center of human personality), it lacks the confidence of the modern view, which holds that *all* men can be either virtuous or happy. "There is nothing, methinks, more piteous than a man, of all things that creep and breathe upon the earth," declares Zeus in the *Iliad*. Aristotle confessed that "not to be born is the best thing and death is better than life," and gave as his opinion that melancholy was a concomitant of genius. The Stoic Chryssipus could conceive of happiness only for the wise and was certain that the common lot of men were fools. Seneca, despite his pious universalism, prays, "Forgive the world: they are all fools."[22]

The fragmentary character of human life is not regarded as evil in biblical faith. Man's existence is seen as having a center of life and meaning in which each fragment is related to the plan of the whole, to the will of God. The evil arises when a fragment seeks, by its own unaided wisdom, to comprehend the whole or attempts, by its own power, to substitute man's will for the mystery of God's creation. Adams took seriously the message in Psalm 37—"Fret not thyself because of evil doers, neither be thou envious against the workers of iniquity." The "excellent and profound morality" of the scripture was superior to Plutarch's *Treatise on the Delays of Divine Justice*, in addition to Juvenal's thirteenth *Satire*. In particular, this psalm lays out the duty of an individual's reliance upon the retributive justice of God, "without being staggered either by the transient properties of the wicked or by the afflictions of the good." There is no reference in these lines to the rewards and punishments of another life, the matter being left to the improvement of Christian doctrine. Adams noted that one of the promises of blessedness (to the meek, for they shall inherit the earth) is quoted and repeated by Christ in his Sermon on the Mount (Matt., 5:5). With "so much prosperity to the wicked in this world," a tran-

---

22. *The Satires of A. Persius Flaccus*, ed. H. Nettleship, 380–81; *Memoirs*, 7:285; Reinhold Niebuhr, *The Nature and Destiny of Man: A Christian Interpretation*, 1:9–11.

scendent reference point strengthens individual faith as it moderates the temptation to hypocrisy in all human achievements. Even "the good— as far as human nature can be called good—are followed by such . . . afflictions that some consolatory principle of truth upon divine justice is necessary to the comfort of existence."[23]

The pragmatic spirit of Adams's faith is evident by the questions he raised in response to a sermon from John 3:16: "For God so loved the world, that he gave his only begotten Son, that whosoever believeth in Him should not perish, but have everlasting life." What, Adams asked, is the meaning of the term *loved*, as an attribute of God toward the world? If God loved the world, was the gift of his Son the only way in which His commitment could be manifested? How could belief in the Son of God save the believer from perishing and confer upon him everlasting life? These questions remain "hidden mysteries buried under the text." The teachings of Christ all convey the idea that life is enjoyment; "animated existence is a gift of God demonstrating his goodness; intellectual life given to man is a . . . blessing granted . . . to man alone." Everlasting life, then, is a perpetuation of this blessing, even though the way that it is effected remains imperfectly disclosed to the imperfect understanding of man. In the language of I Corinthians 13:12: "We now see as through a glass darkly, but then face to face!" A sense of hope and humility guided Adams's understanding of the complex interplay between faith and reason:

> Warned of the imperfections of my own reason, I discount its conclusions, as I do those of others; and when I consider what man is, whence he comes, and where he goes, physically, I wonder only *at the degree* in which he does possess the power of linking cause and effect; that he should form the conception of God, of eternity, of a future state, of a state independent of matter; and I cannot account for the passion which I most intensely feel for continued existence hereafter.[24]

Existence and duration are essentially incomprehensible things: "The mind of man delights in truth in the abstract, and is perpetually

23. *Memoirs*, 2:380–81.
24. Adams, *Memoirs*, 7:459, 7:140.

seeking falsehood in the concrete."[25] Matter undergoes change but is never destroyed; why is not the same true of mind?

In reading Isaac Watt's *The Improvement of the Human Mind*, and his discourse on the education of children, Adams was troubled by how the dissenting English clergyman exempted the faith experience from communicable knowledge. Watts insisted strongly on the distinction between things *above reason*, which, as mysteries of religion, may and ought to be believed, and things contrary to reason, which he says must be false. Adams doubted whether such a distinction could sustain any religious creed. Regarding Christianity, Adams noted, "The Trinity, the Divinity of Christ, the whole doctrine of atonement . . . the immaculate conception of Jesus, and a devil maintaining war against Omnipotence, appear . . . as contrary to reason." What Adams described as "the *Real Presence* of the Eucharist," as typical of religion in general, speaks to the *wants* of human nature—"an appetite which must be indulged, since without its gratification human existence would be a burden rather than a blessing." Reason can serve as a restraint or guard upon religious zeal, as well as upon bodily necessities and irrational passions. It would be at the expense of considerable presumption, he thought, for the reason of imperfect man "to set itself up as the umpire of our faith." He would not repudiate a doctrine simply because reason could not vouchsafe its authority. Even the reasonable man must "appeal to a higher tribunal," not as a substitute for reason, but as an objective reminder of how the human spirit breaks and remakes the harmonies and unities of nature.[26] Neither religion nor philosophy alone comprehended man in a dimension sufficiently high or deep to do full justice to his capacity for both good and evil.

Watts's *argumentum ex absurdo* is conclusive only with regard to phenomena of a finite nature; "excellent for mathematics and geometry, but incompetent for infinity." Adams looked to the doctrine of transubstantiation to make his refutation. The empirical absurdity of this dogma proclaimed by the Roman Catholic Church is not, ipso facto, a proof of error; its weakness stems from a tendency "to enslave

25. Ibid., 139–40.
26. *Memoirs*, 2:356; Isaac Watts, *The Improvement of the Human Mind*.

the human mind, to subject it to the arbitrary dominion of the priest-hood—weak, corrupt, and fallible men like ourselves." Adams saw a normative connection between religious freedom and political liberty.

> Could I once bring myself to believe that by a special power from heaven a priest can turn a wafer into a God, and a cup of wine into the blood of my Redeemer, the next and natural step would be to believe that my eternal weal or woe depended upon the fiat of the same priest—that the keys to heaven were in his hands to . . . unlock at his pleasure and that the happiness or misery of my existence in the world to come depended upon the chance of propitiating not the Deity, but His master.[27]

Admittedly, the doctrine is countenanced by *the letter* of Christ's words: Matthew 26:26; Mark 14:22; Luke 22:19; and John 6:26–66. Yet these words, when spoken by Christ, shocked his disciples so much that many no longer walked with him, though he told them, by way of explanation, that "his words were spirit." This acknowledgment was enough to settle the matter in Adams's mind.

Adams sought proofs of human immortality from the ancient phi-losophers and gospel of Christ. "It is," Cicero says in the first *Tusculan*, "a tacit judgment of Nature herself, and the greatest argument in favor of the immortality of souls, that all men take a deep interest in that which will happen after death." Adams pointed to the judgment of Statius in his Synephebi: "He plants trees for the benefit of another century; for what purpose, if the next century were not something to him? The diligent husbandman, then, shall plant trees upon which his own eyes shall never see a berry; and shall not a great man plant laws, institutions, a commonwealth?" Adams treasured Cicero and the con-tempt of death that moved him to record the heroic deeds of states-manship. Indeed, God had given to man both reason and passion to check, or, as Francis Bacon said, "to mate the fear of death." The articles of Christian faith lead men to long for death even if they dare not hasten to it. Adams was troubled, however, by a certain hollowness in the Stoic defense of man's immortal soul; he could not keep from

---

27. *Memoirs*, 2:357.

acknowledging his own inveterate "love of life and the horror of dissolution." He was reminded of a shrewd saying of Sappho's, mentioned in a note to D'Olivet's translation, that death was an evil, inasmuch as none of the gods have ever chosen to die. A much more faithful account of man's agonizing predicament at the end of his life was given by Shakespeare in his *Measure for Measure.*

> Ay, but to die, and go we know not where;
> To lie in cold obstruction and to rot;
> This sensible warm motion to become
> A kneaded clod; and the delighted spirit
> To bathe in fiery floods, or to reside
> In thrilling region of thick-ribbed ice;
> To be imprison'd in the viewless winds,
> And blown with restless violence round about
> The pendent world; or to be worse than worst
> Of those that lawless and incertain thought
> Imagine howling: 'tis too horrible'!
> The weariest and most loathed worldly life
> That age, ache, penury and imprisonment
> Can lay on nature is a paradise
> To what we fear of death.[28]

Both death and immortality are "topics never unsuitable nor exhaustible to a teacher of religion and morality." Adams studied the mix of ancient and religious inspiration at the core of Pope's "Dying Christian to His Soul." Adams complained that this ode was composed of five half-ludicrous Latin lines, a curious compound of words spoken by the Emperor Hadrian at the moment of his death, Sappho's lyric ode, and the exclamation by St. Paul in the fifteenth chapter of Corinthians: "Oh, death, where is thy sting? O grave, where is thy victory?" From these materials, and at the request of Sir Richard Steele, Pope transformed the cheerful dying spirit (Hadrian's *Animula vagula*) into two or three stanzas of music. In comparing the verse with the lines of Hadrian, Adams saw "the effect of Christian doctrines upon the idea

---

28. Cicero, *Tusculan Disputations*, Vol. 1 in *The Basic Works of Cicero*, ed. Moses Hadas, 78; *Memoirs*, 7:234; *Measure for Measure*, act. 3, sc. 1.

of death." Pope contends that there is nothing trifling or lighthearted in the lines of Hadrian; however, the poet's Latin verse convinced Adams that "his imagination leads his judgment astray." Both Greek and Roman philosophers taught that death was to be met with indifference, "and Hadrian attempted to carry this doctrine into practice by joking at his own death while in its agonies." However, the thought of what was to become of his soul was grave and serious. The character of Hadrian's lines "is a singular mixture of levity and sadness," the spirit of which to Adams appeared lost in Pope's translation. Adams recorded his own literal translation of the passage:

> Animula, vagula, blandula,
> Hospes comesque corporis,
> Quae nunc abibis in loca?
> Pallidula, rigida, nudula,
> Nec (ut soles) dabis joca!
>
> (Dear, fluttering, flattering little soul,
> Partner and inmate of this clay,
> Oh, whither art thou now to stroll?
> Pale, shivering, naked little droll,
> No more thy wonted jokes to play!)

Pope claims that the diminutives are epithets not of levity, but of endearment. Adams argued that they are significant of both; the representation of them with the rhyme of "*loca*" and "*joca*," in Latin verses of that age, "decisively marks the merriment of affected indifference." Pope made the cheerful dying spirit a *Christian*, "and cheerful death then became the moment of triumphant exultation, and the song is . . . the song of an angel."[29]

On September 11, 1811, John Quincy Adams began a series of religious essays addressed to his son, George Washington Adams. The complete eleven-letter collection is instructive regarding Adams's outlook on issues ranging from Christian pedagogy to the religious foundations of civil society. He counseled his son to read the Bible with the same purpose imparted to him through his father's teaching—i.e., not

---

29. *Memoirs*, 6:78–79.

only for advancement in wisdom and virtue, but also in order to prove a useful citizen to his country and a respectable member of society. Adams's own self-analysis revealed that this desire "is indeed very imperfectly successful"; like the Apostle Paul, "I find a law in my members, warring against the laws of my mind." But even the infirmities of human nature do not exempt man from his "duty to aim at perfection." Man, deploring his frailties, must "pray Almighty God . . . to strengthen [his] good desires, and subdue [his] propensities to evil." Mere meditation is vacuous unless it aims at some special object in view; useful thoughts often arise in the mind and pass away without being remembered or applied to any good purpose. Part of the realization of virtue entails honestly confronting the manner in which self-love conceals human weaknesses, "either in attempting to disguise them to us under false and delusive colors, or in seeking out excuses and apologies to reconcile them to our minds." Adams's theology did not look to a universe where the revolutions of fate and ungovernable fortune leave embattled man without any promise of redemption and progress. "Heaven," Adams reflected, "has given to every human being the power of controlling his passions, and if he neglects or loses it, the fault is his own, and he must be answerable for it. Was it pleasure? Why did I indulge it? Was it dissipation? This is the most inexcusable of all; for it must have been occasioned by my own thoughtlessness or irresolution. It is of no use to discover our own faults and infirmities, unless the discovery prompts us to amendment."[30]

Knowing the difference between right and wrong is impossible without a recognition of duties to one's God, to one's fellow creatures, and to oneself. Adams recorded Christ's answer to the Pharisees in Matthew 22:34: "Thou shalt love the Lord thy God, with all thy heart, and with all thy soul, and with all thy mind, and with all thy strength, and thy neighbor as thyself." About these two commandments, Christ (as interpreted by Adams) expressly says, "Hang all the law and the prophets"; in other words, the whole purpose of divine revelation is to inculcate these obligations upon the minds of men. It is worth noting that

30. John Quincy Adams, *The Bible and Its Teachings,* 9–15.

Adams emphasized duties to *oneself*, distinct from those to God and other living beings. The reason this obligation is not accentuated, along with the other two, is because the teachings of Christ "consider self-love so implanted in the heart of every man . . . that it requires no commandment to establish its influence over the heart." But from the love of God, and the love of our neighbor, "result duties to ourselves as well as to them, and they are all learned in equal perfection by our searching the Scriptures." On the one hand, the Bible tells of the creation of the world and the history of mankind. On the other hand, it teaches "a system of religion, and of morality, which we may examine upon its merits, independent of the sanction it receives from being the Word of God."[31]

Considering the Bible from the standpoint of divine revelation, Adams looked past metaphysical subtleties for its practical use to mankind. Revealed religion embodies three points of doctrine that constitute the foundation of all morality. The first is the existence of God; the second is the immortality of the human soul; and the third is a future state of rewards and punishments. To surrender these articles of faith leaves the conscience of man with "no other law than that of the tiger or the shark." The laws of man alone "cannot make him wise, virtuous, or happy." Adams conceded that it is possible to embrace these ethical axioms "without believing that the Bible is Divine revelation." Reasonable men, he thought, cannot help but acknowledge that neither they, nor the world they inhabit, can exist without paying homage to a creative agency transcending human society. Similarly, "there is also a [human] consciousness that the thinking part of our nature is not material, but spiritual—that is, it is not subject to the laws of matter, not perishable with it." Hence arises Adams's belief in man's immortal soul: "and pursuing this train of thought which the visible creation and observation upon ourselves suggest, we must soon discover that the Creator must also be the Governor of the universe; that His wisdom . . . must be without bounds—that he is a righteous God . . . that mankind are bound by the laws of righteousness, and are

31. Ibid., 18–20.

accountable to him . . . according to their good or evil deeds. The completion of Divine justice [however] must be reserved for another life."[32]

Human reason may be able to capture an obscure glimpse of these sacred truths (or, in Adams's words, "it is so impossible for natural reason to disbelieve them"), but reason alone is not capable of discovering them in all their clearness. Pope's *Universal Prayer* is a tribute to the idea of God at the center of religion throughout the ages.

> Father of all! in every age,
> In every clime adored—
> By saint, by savage, and by sage—
> Jehovah, Jove, or Lord.[33]

The Zoroastrians of Persia worshiped Ormazd (also called "Ahura Mazda"), the source of light, creator of the world, and the embodiment of good. The religion of Pharaonic Egypt encompassed a multitude of different gods, as well as a belief in animistic spirits within "not only oxen, crocodiles, dogs and cats, but even garlics and onions." Virtually all the Greek philosophers meditated on the nature of the gods; "but scarcely any of them reflected enough to imagine that there was one God . . . the creator of the world." Cicero assembled the philosophers' opinions on the nature of the gods, and "pronounced them more like the dreams of madmen than the sober judgment of wise men." Yet even the great Roman statesman started his inquiry with the revealing question: "Whether justice could exist upon earth unless founded upon piety?" In the first book of Ovid's *Metamorphoses*, there is an account of the change of chaos in the world. Before the sea and the earth and the sky that surrounds all things (Ovid says), "there was a thing called *chaos*, and some one of the gods (he does not know which), separated from each other the elements of this chaos, and turned them into a world." But something more was needed, even after "God, or kindlier Nature, settled all argument," and separated Heaven from earth:

32. Ibid., 23–24.
33. Pope, *Collected Poems*, 216.

> . . . a finer being
> More capable of mind, a sage, a ruler,
> So Man was born, it may be, in God's image,
> Or Earth, perhaps, so newly separated
> From the old fire of Heaven, still retained
> Some seed of the celestial force which fashioned
> Gods out of living clay and running water,
> All other animals look downward; Man,
> Alone, erect, can raise his face toward Heaven.[34]

These examples, cited by Adams, were as far as reason could go; however, the first words of the Bible are "In the beginning God created heaven and the earth."

Adams found the source of all human virtue and happiness in the first verse of the Book of Genesis; "because when we have . . . attained the conception of a Being, who by the mere act of his will created the world, it would follow . . . that man . . . was also created by him, and must hold his felicity and virtue on the condition of obedience to his will." The first chapters of the Bible are an account of the manner in which the world was made; of the condition on which happiness and immortality were "bestowed upon our first parents"; of their transgression; and of the punishment inflicted upon them, as well as the promise of redemption from it by "the seed of the woman." The details of these miracles did not delay Adams much in thought.

> There have always been, where the holy scriptures have been known, petty witlings and self-conceited reasoners who cavil at some of the particular details of this narration. Even serious inquirers after truth have . . . been perplexed to believe that there should have been evening and morning before the existence of the sun; that a man should be made of clay and a woman from the rib of a man; that they should be forbidden to eat an apple; and for disobedience to that injunction, be with all their posterity doomed to death; that a serpent

---

34. Adams, *The Bible and Its Teaching*, 26; Cicero, *Tusculan Disputations*, in *The Basic Works of Cicero*, 1:67–68; Cicero, *On the Nature of the Gods*, trans. Hubert Poteat, 179; Ovid, *Metamorphoses*, trans. Rolfe Humphries, 4–5.

should speak and beguile a woman; and that eating an apple could give the knowledge of good and evil.[35]

Although the creation language is figurative and allegorical, it symbolizes an experience of transcendence through which man and society achieve meaning in the cosmos. This idea of the transcendent power of the Supreme Being is "essentially connected with that by which the whole duty of man is summed up: obedience to his will." Once an individual assumes the idea of a single God, whose will is the law of moral obligation among men, then piety "becomes the first of human duties; and not a doubt can . . . remain that fidelity and associations of human piety and justice, repose upon no other foundation."[36]

Adams refers to Longinus, the Greek rhetorician and Platonic philosopher, who quotes the third verse of the first chapter of Genesis as an example of the sublime: "And God said let there be light, and there was light." The sublimity herein finds striking expression in the image of transcendent power presented to the mind. Adams quarreled with Longinus's example, arguing that the excerpt "only exhibits the effects of that transcendent power which the first verse declares in announcing God as the creator of the world." The true sublimity, then, is the idea of God given to man. To such a God the heart of man must yield "with cheerfulness the tribute of homage which it could never pay to the numerous gods . . . of the Grecian philosophers and sages."[37]

Adams, like many others of his generation, saw no conflict between the Christian counsel of human perfectibility and man's consistent betrayal of the ethical law. Christ commanded his disciples to aim at absolute perfection, and this perfection consisted in self-subjugation and brotherly love. Similarly, "the moral philosophy . . . of the Stoics resembles the Christian doctrine in . . . requiring the total subjugation of the passions; and this part of the Stoic principles was adopted by the academies." This obligation is addressed by Cicero in the fifth of his *Tusculan Disputations*.

35. Adams, *The Bible and Its Teaching*, 28–29.
36. Ibid., 31–32.
37. Dionysius Longinus, *On the Sublime*, 32–33; Adams, *The Bible and Its Teachings*, 32–33.

As for that tranquility, greatly longed for and pursued—and by that I mean the freedom from anxiety on which the happy life depends—how can any one have it who is or may be attended by a multitude of evils? How will he be able to be lofty and erect, and to treat as trivial everything which can befall a human being, such as we claim the wise man is, unless he considers everything which can affect him to be within himself? When Philip (the II of Macedon) . . . threatened to prevent the Spartans from doing everything they were trying to do, they asked whether he would even prevent them from dying—won't it be much easier to find our ideal individual with such spirit than a whole community? Again, if self-restraint, which controls all distur-bances, is added to the courage of which I speak, what can he lack for living happily whom courage rescues from anxiety and fear, and self-restraint calls away from bad desires and does not allow to exult with excessive rapture? I would demonstrate that these are produced by Virtue.[38]

Adams answered the objection "that this theory [or obligation to pursue the Good] is not adapted to the infirmities of human nature; that it is not made for a being so constituted as man." Admittedly, the weakness of man's nature "is too strongly tested by all human experi-ence, as well as by the whole tenor of the Scriptures." That degree of weakness, however, must be measured by the efforts to overcome it, and not by indulgence to it. Absolute impotence follows once sinful man admits "weakness as an argument to forbear exertion." Only the most inconclusive reasoning could infer "that because perfection is not to be absolutely obtained, it is therefore not to be sought." Human excellence is at best an approximation of perfection; the degree of individual moral achievement will be in exact proportion to the degree of self-control man exercises over himself. According to the Stoics, all vice is resolvable into folly; according to "Christian principle it is the effect of weakness." Moreover, those Christians counted as the most steadfast in their faith are often the very ones most tempted by the passions of others. Because kindness and benevolence "comprise the whole system of Christian duties," there is "great danger of falling into errors and vice" when the individual lacks the "energy to resist the

---

38. Cicero, *Disputations 2 & 5*, trans. and ed., A. E. Douglas, 103.

example or enticement of others." On this point, Adams claimed that "the true character of Christian morality appears . . . to have been misunderstood by some of its ablest . . . defenders."[39]

As an example of this tendency, Adams cited *A View of the Evidences of Christianity* by the English theologian William Paley, who answered the unbelievers of his day. Adams took issue with a passage from the chapter on the morality of the gospel.

> There are two opposite descriptions of character, under which man-kind may . . . be classified: the one possesses vigor, firmness, resolution, is active and daring, quick in its sensibilities, jealous of its fame, . . . inflexible of it purposes, violent in its resentment; the other meek, yielding, complying, forgiving, not prompt to act, but willing to suffer . . . under rudeness and insults . . . where others would demand satisfaction. . . . The former of these characters is . . . the favorite of the world; it is the character of the great men—there is a dignity in which it commands respect. The latter is poor-spirited, tame, and abject. Yet, so it has happened, that with the founder of Christianity, the latter is the subject of his commendation, his precepts, his example, and that the former is so in no part of his composition.[40]

Adams did not accept Dr. Paley's account either as an accurate delineation of character or as a correct representation of Christian principles. Christ pronounced distinct blessings upon the "poor in spirit" (not to be confused with the "poor-spirited") and upon the meek. Where, Adams asked, is there evidence from the gospel that Christ countenanced by "commendation, by precept or example, the tame and abject?" Dr. Paley's Christian "is one of those drivellers, who, to use a vulgar phrase, can never say no, to anybody."[41]

Never once did Christ recede from his authoritative station as "that of a Lord and Master"; he preserved it in washing the feet of his disciples; he preserved it in answer to the officer who struck him for this deportment before the high priest; he preserved it in the agony of

39. Adams, *The Bible and Its Teachings*, 100–102.
40. William Paley, *A View of the Evidences of Christianity*, 2:30–32.
41. Adams and Hackett, *The Bible and Its Teachings*, 104.

his exclamation on the cross, "Father, forgive them, for they know not what they do." He said to his disciples, "Learn of me, for I am meek and lowly of heart"; but where did he ever say to them, "Learn of me, for I am tame and abject?" Nothing, Adams alleged, was more unmistakable in the precepts of Christ than the principle of stubborn resistance against the impulses of others to evil. He called upon his disciples to renounce everything that is considered enjoyment upon earth, "to take up their cross," and to suffer ill-treatment, persecution, and death for his sake. What else is the book of the "Acts of the Apostles" than an inventory of the faithfulness with which the chosen ministers carried these injunctions into practice? Only those of a bold and intrepid spirit could be entrusted with the commission to "teach all nations." The true Christian, Adams wrote, is the *Justum et tenacem propositi virum* of Horace ("the man who is just and steady to his purpose"). These qualities of heroic character—along with those of meekness, lowliness of heart, and brotherly love—are what constitute "that moral perfection of which Christ gave an example in his own life, and to which he commands his disciples to aspire."[42]

In his religious opinions, Adams looked for support "in the text of the scriptures [rather] than in the glosses of disputes or commentators." He found that the partisans to the Unitarian controversy were more adept in "combating the doctrines of their adversaries than in maintaining their own." Duty compelled him to draw conclusions from the operations of his own mind and in light of "such evidence as perhaps too busy a life has allowed me to obtain." As a result, there was no denomination of Christians with which he could not share the fruits of fellowship. For Adams, the single most important contribution of religion is "its influence upon . . . conduct; and upon the conduct of mankind, the question of Trinity or Unity, or of the single or double personal nature of Christ, has or ought to have no bearing whatsoever."[43] He knew himself to be a frequent sinner before God, forever in need of admonishment for his failings and exhortations to be virtuous. Religious liberty for *all* Americans, as well as religious

42. Ibid., 107–8.
43. JQA to George Sullivan, January 20, 1821, 7:90–91.

salvation for the opinions of others, are the only doctrines that Adams judged "essential to all" and universal in scope.

With the passage of time, Adams increasingly grew weary of the internecine feuds among religious factions in American society: "It is the doom of the Christian Church to be always distracted with controversy, and where religion is most in honor, there the perversity of the human heart breeds the sharpest conflicts of the brain." Adams cited the example of Andover Theological Seminary in New England, where Calvinists and Unitarians battled each other over the Atonement, the Divinity of Christ, and the Trinity. These debates had subsided by the mid-nineteenth century, but "other wandering of minds takes the place of that, and equally lets the wolf into the fold." In 1840, Adams noticed a young man, named Ralph Waldo Emerson (a former classmate of his son George's), who started a new doctrine of transcendentalism and declared "all the old revelations superannuated and worn out." The movement toward liberalism and social transformation in New England transcendentalism nurtured a deadly "alliance of atheism and hypocrisy." Adams described "this spirit of hurly-burly innovations" in the following manner:

> The characteristic of the age is to unsettle all established opinions, and to put into perpetual question all the foundations of human society. We are to argue pro and con whether parricide be a crime or virtue; whether property be by the law of nature or the mere creature of conventional law; whether the contract of marriage constitutes an obligation of duty restrictive of promiscuous social intercourse; in short, whether justice or force is at the root of all social institutions. . . . . Religion is sapped and undermined by this fraudulent philosophy; the laboring classes are instigated to hatred and violence against the proprietors; and the elements of a civil war of extermination are stimulated into deadly conflict with one another.[44]

In addition to the Transcendentalists, "[William Lloyd] Garrison . . . and the abolitionists, [Orestes] Brownson and the [Jean Paul] Marat democrats, phrenology and animal magnetism, all come in, furnishing . . . some plausible rascality as an ingredient for the bubbling cauldron

---

44. *Memoirs*, 10:345, 10:350.

of religion and politics." In the midst of this intellectual tumult, Adams found solace in a sermon, "on the virtue of quietness," by the English theologian Isaac Barrow. Prudence and moderation have their own moral vindication, even among the zealous partisans of justice.

> Especially, we should not make ourselves parties in any faction where both sides are eager and passionate, for them even they who have the juster cause are wont to do unjust things in which it is hard for any man engaged not to have [a] share—at least not to undergo the imputation of them. It is wisdom . . . in such cases, to hold off, and to retain a kind of indifferency; to meddle with them is (as the Wise Man saith) to take a dog by the ears; which he that doth, can hardly take care enough of his fingers.[45]

III.

The "philosophical examination of the foundations of civil society . . . and of the rights and duties of men" was, according to Adams, one of the profound consequences of the Protestant Reformation. Under the hierarchy of the Church of Rome, human government was treated as a divine institution. Temporal powers were ordained by God; and the monarch, at the head of the nation, was the Lord's anointed. The moral impulse behind the Protestant Reformation was a repudiation of the ecclesiastical position "that implicit belief and obedience was due to the commandments of men." The controversy at first was confined to the extent and limitations of human authority in matters of religion. The Roman Pontiff claimed the right, and exercised the power, of granting or selling indulgences for the commission of sins. This deceit, "striking at the root of all morality," prompted Martin Luther to champion the standard of human freedom against the right of the Bishop of Rome to peddle insurance for human virtue. The issue raised by Martin Luther "involved the whole theory of the *rights* of the individual man, paramount to all human authority." Moreover, the Reformation raised the question of *right* between the subject and the sover-

45. Isaac Barrow, *Theological Works*, 1:605.

eign. While the struggle for individual liberty first applied to ecclesiastical power, little time passed before the political theory of divine right was no longer a sufficient commission for kings to reign and to decree justice. In Adams's words:

> In Germany, the controversy was confined to the extent and limitations of ecclesiastical power. In France, the progress of the reformation was arrested by the apostasy of Henry of Navarre. From the cell of an Augustine monk . . . issued forth the freedom of the soul from spiritual tyranny. From Saint Stephen's Chapel and the electric spark of mind in an English House of Commons, went forth civil and political freedom, to penetrate into the prison where the body of man was confined, and to lead him forth to the light of day, as the angel of the Lord in a blaze of supernatural light raised up Peter in the dungeon of Herod, smote him on the side, while the chains fell off from his hands, and led him out to preach to the nations the blessed gospel of peace and love.[46]

The "talisman of *human rights*" dissolved the spell of political as well as ecclesiastical power. The Calvinists of Geneva, and the Puritans of England, contested the right of kings to prescribe articles of faith to their people, "and this question necessarily drew after it the general questions of the origin of all human government." The controversy gave rise to the civil wars in seventeenth-century Britain, as well as to the contending parties of Royalists and Republicans (or of Cavaliers and Roundheads). In search of the first principles of government, Thomas Hobbes assumed that the state of nature between man and man was a state of war—"whence it followed that government originated in *conquest*." Natural man, the man with whom the lawmakers must deal, is not a God-seeker, but a power-seeker, and he can find no lasting contentment because no one can ever be secure in the enjoyment of power. The *summum bonum*, according to Hobbes, does not exist within the life of this world: "The felicity of this life, consisteth not in the repose of mind satisfied. For there is no such *finis ultimus*,

---

46. John Quincy Adams, *The Social Compact, Exemplified in the Constitution of the Commonwealth of Massachusetts; with Remarks on the Theories of Divine Right of Hobbes and of Filmer, and the Counter-theories of Sidney, Locke, Montesquieu, and Rousseau, Concerning the Origin and Nature of Government*, 21–22.

utmost aim . . . as it is spoken in the books of the old moral philosophers." These reflections lead Hobbes to his famous conclusion that man is caught up in the ceaseless pursuit of power:

> So that in the first place, I put for a general inclination of all mankind, a perpetual and restless desire of power after power, that ceaseth only in death. And the cause of this, is not always that a man hopes for a more intensive delight, than he has already attained to; or that he cannot be content with a moderate power; but because he cannot assure the power and means to live well, which he hath present, without the acquisition of more. And from hence it is, that kings, whose power is greatest, turn their endeavours to the assuring it at home by laws, or abroad by wars: and when that is done, there succeedeth a new desire; in some, of fame from new conquest; in others, of ease and sensual pleasure; in others, of admiration, or being flattered for excellence in some art, or other ability of the mind.[47]

Adams countered the moral cynicism of Hobbes by citing the rejoinder of Jean Jacques Rousseau. According to the latter, a people subjected to conquest are right in submitting to the government, as long as they cannot help themselves; "but that submission is not peace, and that the first moment of power to resist, confers upon them the right to cast off the yoke."[48] In Book 1 of the *Social Contract*, Rousseau offers his classic critique of the might-makes-right position.

> Force is a physical power; I do not see what kind of morality can result from its effects. . . . If force makes it necessary to obey, it is no longer necessary to obey out of a sense of duty; if a person is no longer forced to obey, he is no longer obligated to do so. . . . Obey the powers that be. If that means yield to force, the precept is good but superfluous; I answer that it will never be violated. All power comes from God, I admit, but every illness comes from him as well. Is this to say that calling a doctor is forbidden? If a thief surprises me in a corner of the woods, I am forced to give him my purse, but am I, in

---

47. Ibid., 23; Thomas Hobbes, *Leviathan*, ed. Michael Oakeshott, 63; Dante Germino, *Machiavelli to Marx*, 98.

48. Adams, *The Social Compact*, p. 23.

conscience, obligated to give it to him when I could hide it? . . . Let us
agree . . . that we are obligated to obey only legitimate powers.[49]

Along similar lines, Adams argued that Hobbes's theory contradicts
the teachings of Christ. Hobbes severs "the Gordian knot with the
sword, extinguishes the rights of man, and makes force the cornerstone of all human government." Furthermore, this leaves open the
possibility of justifying slavery as conformable to the law of nature.
The traces of political absolutism in Hobbes are akin to John Falstaff's
law in Shakespeare's *Henry IV*. When speaking of Justice Shallow, he
exclaims, "If the young dace be a bait for the old pike, I see no reason
in the law of nature but I may snap at him."[50]

"The greatest liberty in the world (if it be duly considered)," wrote
Sir Robert Filmer in *Patriarcha*, "is for a people to live under a monarch . . . [since] all other shows or pretexts of liberty are but several
degrees of slavery." Filmer's royalist tract, first published in 1680, reflected the struggle between King Charles I and Parliament, which
terminated in the overthrow of the monarchy and the death of King
Charles upon the scaffold. His *Patriarcha*, Adams claimed, "was the
theory of government upon which the *cause* of the House of Stuart was
sustained." Filmer derived the origin of human government from the
scriptures of the Old Testament—from the grant of the earth to Adam,
and afterward to Noah. The core of Filmer's argument was the concept
of patriarchy. "I see not," he wrote, "how the children of Adam, or of
any man else, can be free from subjection to their parents. And this
subordination of children is the fountain of all regal authority, by the
ordination of God himself." As Adam had the power of a "Father, King
and Lord over his family," so kings possessed unlimited dominion over
their people. No moral or political alternative existed within the fabric
of nature. Mixed government was "a mere impossibility or contradiction," the people a "headless multitude."[51]

49. *Rousseau's Political Writings*, ed. Allan Ritter, 87–88. See Romans 13:1 and Paul's
discussion of the secular government of Rome.

50. *The Complete Works of William Shakespeare*, 524.

51. Adams, *The Social Compact*, 25–26; *Patriarcha and Other Political Works of Sir
Robert Filmer*, ed. Peter Laslett, 55, 57, 93, 94, 188.

Adams acknowledged that Filmer's theory was "far more plausible though not more sound than that of Hobbes." In fact, Adams's own view of the social contract drew upon a similar religious inspiration in stipulating the rights and obligations of men and nations:

> that by the nature of man and the laws of God, the social compact which constitutes the body politic, or . . . the sovereign state, must be formed by an association of families, as well as of individuals;—that the government of each family, as a community, must be regulated by one will—that of the father—and that God did by *covenant* give the renovated earth to Noah and his *family*, and the land of Canaan, with the promise of blessings to be shared by *all* the *families* of the earth, to Abraham and *his seed*; a promise, the accomplishment of which was not to *commence*, till after the lapse of many generations, and which cannot be consummated till after the lapse of many more.[52]

Filmer's crucial error, Adams suggested, was in assuming that the natural authority of the father over the child, as well as that of the husband over the wife, is either permanent or unlimited. Adams argued that the laws of nature and of God confer rights upon every human being at birth, and that these liberties cannot be taken away by any other individual or combination of individuals. Both parental and spousal authority "must be under the limitation of right and wrong"; in addition, Filmer's theory of patriarchy failed to recognize "that all despotic power over human beings is exercised in *defiance* of the laws of nature and of God"—all examples of Sir John Falstaff's law of nature between the young dace and the old pike. The union of the sexes is necessary for the preservation and continuance of the species, "but this union . . . must be formed by mutual consent and without exercise of authority on either side." Its only law is the law of love; and

> Love, free as air, at sight of human ties,
> Spreads his light wings and in a moment flies.[53]

52. Adams, *The Social Compact*, 24.
53. Ibid.

While the nuptial tie of nature must be formed by mutual consent, the sacred vows achieve permanence only "by the mutual pledge of *faith*, that is by covenant or compact."[54]

The relation of authority to will in the family compact formed the basis of Adams's critique of democracy and self-government. His analysis begins with basic assumptions about the nature of government and political rule. First, government is the "exercise of power directing or controlling the will of human beings." Of all the governments that have ever existed, the most important, as well as the most difficult to achieve, is self-government. Second, man is a social being; he is gregarious and cannot exist alone. Conjugal relations, a union of two different constitutions, are "subject to different modifications of the law of nature, and . . . to different applications of the principle of self-government." According to Adams, the nuptial union superinduces the law of family government to the law of self-government. Each of the four family members (husband and wife, father and mother—son and daughter, brother and sister) "has selfish passions which must be governed, some of which are in harmony with those of the other three, and others discordant with those of one or more of the rest." The full scope of family relations—conjugal, parental, filial, and fraternal—partakes in "rights and duties to the enjoyment and obligation of which, self government is not adequate." A common government, subject to the control of one will, constitutes the law of family government. The will of the husband, "neither unlimited nor even absolute [in its] authority," forms the basis of the family compact. The characteristic difference in the physical and moral nature of the two sexes is captured in the beautiful imagery of Milton's *Paradise Lost*.

> She, as a veil, down to the slender waist
> Her unadorned golden tresses wore
> Dishevell'd, but in wanton ringlets wav'd
> As the vine curls her tendrils, which *implied*
> *Subjection*, but required with gentle sway,
> And by her yielded, by him best received.

54. Ibid.

> Yielded with coy submission, modest pride,
> And sweet, reluctant, amorous delay.[55]

Adams, relying on a priori standards to account for the social conditions of his age, explained the inferior position of women in the family
as a result of the first woman's "disobedience [in the Garden of Eden]
to the divine command."

The social compact at the core of the body politic is formed "by an
association not merely of individuals, but of families." Admittedly, the
Massachusetts state constitution describes the social compact as "a
voluntary association of individuals," whereby "the whole people covenants with each citizen, and each citizen with the whole people." The
actual pledge, however, is made by the father, who acts as a sponsor for
all others—wife, unmarried daughters, minor sons, and his posterity—for the duration of the compact. Adams equated the social compact with a constitution of government, and the act of adherence to it
consisted of assisting in its formulation or of assenting to it in the
electoral process. The family and family compact, basic components of
the social order, antedate the social compact and the body politic.
Under such circumstances, then, the social compact could not create
the social order, which was antecedent to it; the contract merely created the government necessary for the maintenance of safety and stability in a social order that was growing more complicated. Accordingly, the covenants of the social compact must, "by the laws of nature,
be made by a portion of the people for the whole—by that portion of
the people capable of contracting for the whole." Since the compact
was formed by a voluntary association, it presupposed "not only the
capacity but the *will* to contract."[56]

Adams objected to Rousseau's argument that the social contract
"can be formed only by a *unanimous* consent, because the rule itself,
that a majority of votes shall prevail, can only be established by agreement, that is, by compact." For Rousseau, democracy meant direct or
participatory democracy and, as such, required the active exercise of

---

55. Ibid., 11, 12, 25; John Milton, *Paradise Lost and Other Poems*, 173–74.
56. Adams, *The Social Compact*, 9, 13.

political virtue by citizens who are simultaneously both the subjects and objects of the political association. Legitimate political authority can emerge only in accordance with the principles of a properly constructed social contract. Rousseau summarized the task of the lawgiver as follows: "To find a form of association which may defend and protect with the whole force of the community the person and property of every associate, and by means of which each, coalescing with all, may nevertheless obey only himself, and remain as free as before. Such is the fundamental problem of which the social contract furnishes the solution." To the extent that one's rights have been given over to the community as a whole rather than to any of its members in particular, no individual is, thereby, subordinate to the will of another. Inasmuch as each associate transfers all rights originally possessed, no one retains any unique privilege, and each citizen becomes the moral and political equal of every other. With reference to the English parliamentary system, Rousseau wrote:

> Sovereignty cannot be represented for the same reason that it cannot be alienated; it consists in the general will and the will cannot be represented. . . . The deputies of the people, then, are not and cannot be its representatives; they are only its commissioners and can conclude nothing definitely. Every law which the People in person have not ratified is invalid; it is not law. The English people thinks that it is free, but it is greatly mistaken, for it is so only during the election of Parliament; as soon as they are elected, it is enslaved and counts for nothing.[57]

In objecting to Rousseau's concept of the indivisible sovereignty of the people, Adams returned to the threefold classification of government in Aristotle's *Politics*. The word *democracy* is a compound of two Greek words—*demos* (people) and *kratos* (government). The original meaning of the concept, as practiced by the Athenians, was government of the people. Aristotle defined it "as one of the three simple forms of Government, and is . . . itself a good form of government, but having a tendency to degenerate into . . . ochlocracy." As Aristotle explains in Book 4,

57. Jean-Jacques Rousseau, *The Social Contract*, trans. Charles M. Sherover, 23, 161.

Demagogues arise in states where the laws are not sovereign. The people . . . becomes an autocrat—a single composite autocrat made up of many members, with the many playing the sovereign, not as individuals, but collectively. . . . It grows despotic; flatterers come to be held in honour; it becomes analogous to the tyrannical form of single-person government. . . . Once the people are sovereign in all matters, *they* are sovereign themselves over its decisions; the multitude follows their guidance. . . . Where the laws are not sovereign, there is no constitution. Law should be sovereign on every issue, and the magistrates and the citizen body should only decide about details.[58]

Aristocracy is "also according to Aristotle a good Government, but its tendency is to degenerate into *oligarchy* . . . and the few in all such cases must necessarily be the rich, who . . . settle it as a maxim that the ruling power of a state is *Property*." The third of Aristotle's legitimate governments is "Monarchy, the Government of one, according to the Laws, and its degeneracy is despotism, or the Government of one, according to his will—arbitrary power."[59]

The "theory of *good* Government" that Adams "imbibed from childhood" was learned through the instruction of his father. Drawing on Aristotle's concept of the mean, as well as his father's defense of the balance principle, John Quincy Adams argued that a just arrangement for political rule must be a compound of three elements. He recalled the ancient constitution of the *polity*, which Aristotle defined as a form of middle-class rule that avoids the extreme divisions between rich and poor. Government is instituted, Adams suggested, "for the protection both of persons and of property, to secure alike the rights of persons and the rights of things." Insofar as the earth was given by God to mankind in common, "the distribution of property . . . is left to be settled . . . by physical force or by agreement, compact, covenant." If democracy fails to include property under the rubric of natural rights, then it is apt to "degenerate into ochlocracy and Lynch Law, burning down convents and hanging abolitionists or gamblers, without Judge or Jury, without fear of God to restrain, and without remorse to

58. "Letters of John Adams and John Quincy Adams, 1776–1838," 246; *The Politics of Aristotle*, 168–69.
59. "Letters of John Adams and John Quincy Adams," 246.

punish." Aristotle's definition of aristocracy as "Government *of the best* [is] as entitled to all the attributes of virtue" as a democracy of numbers. Adams sided with Burke's defense of virtual representation in his "Speech to the Electors of Bristol":

> Certainly, gentlemen, it ought to be the happiness and glory of a representative to live in the strictest union, the closest correspondence, and the most unreserved communication with his constituents. Their wishes ought to have great weight with him. . . . But his unbiased opinion, his mature judgment, his enlightened conscience, he ought not to sacrifice to you, to any man, or to any set of men living. These he does not derive from your pleasure; no, nor from the law and the Constitution. They are a trust from Providence, for the abuse of which he is deeply answerable. Your representative owes you, not his industry only, but his judgment; and he betrays instead of serving you, if he sacrifices it to your opinion.[60]

Though largely ignored by twentieth-century political thinkers, the political writings of Algernon Sidney shed revealing light on the essence of republicanism in England and America throughout the seventeenth and eighteenth centuries. Born in 1622, he came into active life at the very moment of the struggle "between the Democracy and the Monarchy of England." Sidney's *Discourses on Government*, as Adams noted, were written for the avowed purpose of refuting the doctrines of Filmer. The defenders of the Stuarts asserted that "the best governments are to be found in monarchy, and in no other form of government." Sidney countered that only in a republic was "publick safety . . . provided, Liberty and Propriety secured, Justice administered, Virtue encouraged, Vice suppressed, and the true interest of the Nation advanced." Contrary to the claim that absolute monarchy was founded on the laws of God or nature, Sidney argued for a political system based on consent and subject to revision in light of the changing needs of its members. He stated, "God in Goodness and Mercy to Mankind, hath with an equal hand given to all the benefit of Liberty, with some measure of understanding of how to employ it." The key moral ques-

---

60. R. G. Mulgan, *Aristotle's Political Theory*, 111–12; Edmund Burke, *Selected Writings and Speeches*, 186–87.

tion facing seventeenth-century Englishmen, according to one of Sidney's biographers, was not "What are God's comprehensive plans for mankind?" but rather "What is the nature of man's liberty, why is it valuable, and what form of government most adequately protects and advances it?" Adams referred to the offense given to Charles II by two Latin lines Sidney inscribed upon the album of the royal library at Copenhagen:

> Manus haec inimica tyrannis
> Ense petit placidam sub liberate quietam.
>
> (This hand, the rule of tyrants to oppose
> Seeks with the sword fair freedom's soft repose.)[61]

The second of these lines was adopted, as the motto to the arms of the state, by the founders of the Commonwealth of Massachusetts.

While once walking with Jeremy Bentham through Hyde Park and Kensington Gardens, Adams debated the English utilitarian thinker on the spirit of democratic reform in British politics. The immediate issue was the notice taken of Bentham's *Catechism of Reform* in the House of Commons in 1817. Adams intimated that the "real object of the Radical Reformers [in Parliament] was revolution," and that they would be "satisfied with nothing less than democratic ascendancy." Detailing the "alarming state of the country and the constitution," Bentham protested, "To the democratical, to the universal interest, *give* . . . that ascendancy which by the confederated, partial, and sinister interest has been so deplorably abused." Adams wondered how Bentham could "reconcile that [argument] with the sound theory of the British Constitution," which the American "conceived to be a balance between the monarchical, aristocratical, and democratical branches, forbidding the ascendancy of either of them." Bentham, by saluting the dubious tradition of "Mother Goose" or "Mother Blackstone," ridiculed the idea of the balance. In Bentham's mind, the balance principle was but another defense for monarchy, aristocracy, and the status quo.

---

61. Filmer *Patriarcha*, 86; Algernon Sidney, *Discourses on Government*, 351; Alan Craig Houston, *Algernon Sidney and the Republican Heritage in England and America*, 102; Adams, *The Social Compact*, 25–27.

Balance! balance! Politicians upon roses—to whom, to save the toil of thinking—on questions most wide in extent, and most high in importance—an allusion—an emblem . . . so as it has been accepted by others, is accepted as conclusive evidence—what ye mean by this your *balance?* Know ye not, that in a machine . . . when forces *balance* each other, the machine is at a stand? Well, and in the machine of government, immobility—the perpetual absence of all motion—is that the thing which is wanted? Know ye not that . . . as in the case of the body *natural,* so in the case of the body *politic,* when motion ceases, the body dies?[62]

Bentham's position raised the question of "how . . . the ascendancy of the popular part [could] be established without subverting the whole." He informed Adams that the ascendancy of one part did not necessarily imply the destruction of the others; after all, in religious affairs, Protestant ascendancy was established by law while the Roman Catholic religion was tolerated. As for the predominance of one branch of government over another, that already existed in the present state of things. The combination of the Crown and the aristocracy "overpowered . . . democracy to such a degree that the popular check upon them was a mere name." Adams told Bentham that "this [was] neither demonstrated nor necessary to the cause of reform"; that the only legitimate basis of reform was "restoring democracy to its equal share of power . . . without substituting the other in its stead." Bentham retorted that democratic ascendancy need not entail the erosion of the monarchy or the aristocracy. He invoked the norm of *uti possidetis* (that which you have, continue to have)—a common basis for negotiation in international law—as a principle of municipal government.

In Adams's account of the exchange, Bentham would touch none of the privileges of the peerage, and none of the prerogatives of the Crown, except that of creating new peers at its pleasure. His aim, "if it be possible, [is] a participation in the same benefit to *democracy*—to the *subject-many*—to the poor, suffering and starving people." Adams thought that these reforms could be accomplished only by violating the rule of *uti possidetis*; ultimately, any redistribution of political

62. *The Works of Jeremy Bentham,* ed. John Bowring, 3:446, 450.

power "must take franchises or property from somebody." Did Bentham really think, for example, that the House of Commons "would feel themselves restrained from encroachments upon their co-ordinate, but not coequal, authority by his international principle of the *uti possidetis?*" Bentham at one point conceded that the consequences of radical reform might plunge England into a civil war. Adams opposed the wide-ranging egalitarian appeal to popular sentiment as the only acceptable way to liberate the oppressed "from that absolute despotism under which they are sinking."[63]

Adams admitted that there was one form of democracy in which he was a firm believer—"the democracy of Jesus and his Apostles." This was the message addressed to all men in the Sermon on the Mount, in the twelfth chapter of the first Epistle to the Romans, in the thirteen, fourteenth, and fifteenth chapters of the first Epistle to the Corinthians. St. Paul alluded to the obligations among men whose faith brings them into a covenant before the eyes of God:

> I bid every one among you to think of himself more highly than he ought to think, but to think with sober judgment, each according to the measure of faith which God has assigned him. For as in one body we have many members, and all the members do not have the same function, so we, though many, are one body in Christ. . . . Having gifts that differ according to the grace given to us, let us use them. . . .
> Let love be genuine; hate what is evil, hold fast to what is good; love one another with brotherly affection; outdo one another in showing honor.[64]

Skeptical of any democracy "not unbedded in a profound sense of moral and religious obligation," Adams favored "a democracy of duties always correlative to the democracy of rights."[65]

The radical democracies of Paine, Marat, and Robespierre epitomized "a Government for wild beasts and not for men." The democracy ushered in by the French Revolution abandons "proportionate" for "absolute" equality; it awards the same honor and the same stand-

63. *Writings*, May 22, 1817, 3:536–39.
64. Romans 12:3–9.
65. "Letters of John Adams and John Quincy Adams," 249.

ing to each citizen. Absolute democracy is based on the recognition of one contribution, and one only—that of "freedom"; and that achievement is by no means the highest or weightiest. Not content with the freedom that means a voice for all in the body politic, democracy *en masse* adds a freedom (or license) that means the absence of control, the surrender of moral discipline, and the haphazard life of random desires. Democracy, Adams wrote, "has no forefathers, it looks to no posterity; it is swallowed up in the present, and thinks of nothing but itself." To withstand multitudes, however, "is the only unerring test of decisive character." This personal strength requires wisdom as well as virtue. Stubborn adherence to principle "is wise only so far as the principle is important and as the adherence to it may be productive of practical good."[66]

IV.

Adams's religious beliefs did not diminish his enthusiasm for the study of science. Nor did he view science as entirely separate from the study of man, his mind, and morality. In the history of mankind, astronomical observation was counted among the first objects in the pursuit of knowledge. Adams cited the first chapter of Genesis, "God said, Let there be lights in the firmament of the heavens to divide the day from the night; and let them be for signs, and for seasons, and for days, and for years." He alluded to a "common chain, which unites, as with links of adamant, the circle of sciences, and the liberal arts." Moreover, the people of America did "not sufficiently estimate the importance of patronizing and promoting science as a principle of political action." The benefits of science pointed to education for the public good. "Knowledge is the attribute of [man's] nature which . . . enables him to improve his condition upon earth, and to prepare him for the enjoyment of a happier existence hereafter." Scientific knowledge enables man to discover his own nature as midway between earth and heaven; "as created for higher and more durable ends than the countless tribes

66. *Memoirs*, 8:433, 9:58.

of beings which people the earth, the ocean, and the air, alternately instinct with life, and melting into vapor, or mouldering into dust." To furnish the means of acquiring knowledge is, therefore, one of the chief virtues conferred upon mankind. The earth was given to man for cultivation, in order to better himself and others. The purpose of the newly created Smithsonian Institution was "the diffusion of knowledge among men." Adams eulogized James Smithson in the following terms: "Whoever increases his knowledge multiplies the uses to which he is enabled to turn the gift of his Creator to his own benefit, and partakes in . . . that goodness which is the highest attribute of Omnipotence itself."[67]

Even as a young man, Adams's investigation into the causes of natural phenomena produced a high degree of skepticism that rejected large generalizations and a priori affirmations. In contrast to the dogma of religious fundamentalists, his belief in an infinite universe precluded the acceptance of man as its center. Once preoccupied with the volatile theme of "nothing," Adams expressed the anxiety of a world caught between its old faiths and the insights which science was making possible.

> In the physical world, what are sensual gratifications, what is the earth, and all it contains, what is life itself?—nothing. In the moral world, what is honour, what is honesty, what is religion?—nothing. In the political world, what is liberty, what is power and grandeur?—nothing. The universe is an atom, and its creator is all in all. Of him, except that he exists, we know nothing, and consequently our knowledge is nothing. Perhaps the greatest truth of all is, that for this half hour I have been doing nothing.[68]

Adams, much like Locke, saw no essential contradiction between his empiricism and his natural law doctrine. In this respect, Adams was vulnerable to Hume's criticism that tentative judgments to which the investigator aspires cannot be transformed into objective truth. His

67. Quincy, *Memoir of the Life of John Quincy Adams*, 265, 306; Adams, *Cincinnati Oration*, 34, 38; *Memoirs*, 11:441.
68. John Quincy Adams, *Life in a New England Town: 1787, 1788; Diary of John Quincy Adams*, 79.

search for scientific knowledge was carried on within a metaphysical framework he did not question. As one historian has written, "His search for theoretical activity placed a surprising reliance upon the capacity of the rational mind to arrive at truth through discussion, a truth discoverable through the logical inspection of principles." Man's reason was his immortal part, and its best use must be in the inquiry into relations between unseen causes and observable effects, with the heavens the proper object of initial inquiry.[69]

With respect to the realm of philosophical values, as apart from science, Adams was less given to questioning the reasons for things than his father, with whom he discussed the issue. John Quincy Adams spoke of never having "much relish for the speculations of the first philosophy"; his mind was not one that took delight "in reasoning high upon 'Fix'd fate, free will, and foreknowledge absolute.'" He had learned much of inestimable value from his father, including the courage to state his convictions frankly as an independent man and devoted son.

> In that respect I resemble your eels in vinegar, and your mites in cheese, more than you do. . . . I venture to suggest that this inquiry into the why and wherefore of all things is precisely that which constitutes the difference between your transcendental philosophers and the eels and mites. . . . [And] although you have been all your life doing as you would be done by, yet your theory and your practice do not always coincide. Your great example does not strengthen all your laws. . . . Now my theory is more like your practice, and my practice more like your theory.[70]

Adams's preference for practical ethics notwithstanding, he conceded that "it is only by such researches that the mind of man can arrive at the idea of a God." Indeed, reasoning upon the why and wherefore of things supplies "the foundation of all morality."[71]

Adams believed in the "genuine doctrines of Christianity in their application to the pursuit of happiness." In addition, he cited the "So-

69. Lipsky, *John Quincy Adams, His Theory and Ideas*, 73, 80–81; Adams, *Cincinnati Oration*, 16–17.

70. JQA to John Adams, October 29, 1816, 6:111–12.

71. Ibid.

cratic and Ciceronian moral philosophy as the most exalted system of human conduct ever presented to the world." This synthesis of classical and Christian dimensions is broadly compatible with the moral-legal precepts shaping the Founders' faith in a constitution grounded in principles of "higher law."

> Its tenets were beyond the ordinary level of human infirmity; and so are those of Christianity. It made the essence of virtue to consist in self-subjugation; and so does Christianity. It gave out a theory of perfection to the aim of man, and made the endeavor to attain it duty; so does Christianity. The perfect example . . . was not given, as by Christ; not even Socrates. Yet he, and Cicero . . . did attain an eminence of practical virtue.[72]

It was among the obligations of statesmen, Adams believed, to "aim in so far as their abilities extend towards the moral purification of their country from besetting sins." This should be accomplished, in the first instance, "by setting the example of private morality"; and, in the second, "by promoting the cause in every way that they can lawfully act on others."[73] For Adams, natural religion was not the product of a spontaneous understanding in the heart, but was a learned body of principles in the keeping of society and brought to each generation by the forces of civic education.

In Adams's political theory, the Creator had made man a social being, had blended his happiness with that of his fellow man, and government was a necessary instrumentality for the effectuation of this liaison. Yet he differed from the general spirit of his day, which was manifested in either a conservative desire for a government only strong enough to keep the enemies of social order in harness, or a more radical—and Jacksonian—opposition to strong government, except insofar as it must be used to keep the economic oligarchy from tyranny. Civil society merely reflected the prevailing concepts of character and virtue among its members. Government did represent "a restraint upon human action, and as such, a restraint upon Liberty." The consti-

---

72. *Memoirs*, 2:462.
73. JQA to James Lloyd, October 1, 1822, 7:312–13.

tutional framers were "aware that to induce the People to impose upon themselves such binding ligaments, motives were not less cogent than those from which the basis of human association were . . . necessary." A theory of rights, therefore, is inconceivable without a corresponding conception of obligations. A passage from Adams's first State of the Union address is worth quoting at length.

> The great object of the institution of civil government is the improvement of the condition of those who are parties to the social compact, and no government . . . can accomplish the lawful ends of its institution but in proportion as it improves the condition of those over whom it is established. . . . But moral, political, and intellectual improvement are duties assigned by the Author of Our Existence to social no less than individual man. For the fulfillment of these duties governments are invested with power, and for the attainment of the end . . . the exercise of delegated power is a duty as sacred . . . as the usurpation of powers not granted is criminal and odious.[74]

By no means, however, was Adams's tribute a ceremony of national self-congratulation. He believed that the doctrine of internal improvement had *more* than an American application. He was, for example, filled with admiration for Peter the Great as the genius who had built St. Petersburg according to a magnificent plan. Peter applied his energies through government, and the capital was suited to the leadership that was reorienting Russia in a new direction. As secretary of state, Adams admonished the Colombians to think little of Colombia as a center of empire but to give due regard to the bounties of nature. "God to thee has done his part—do thine." No negative suspicion of government limited his conception of what men could accomplish through its agency. He enjoined men of all lands to apply their skills through government to the task of internal improvement. He believed that the people would desire that which was good if they could see it; he believed that national resources should be used wisely, not for private speculation, but as the source from which the nation could promote its advancement in philosophy, literature, and the arts. Government should

74. Adams, *The Lives of James Madison and James Monroe*, 34–35; John Quincy Adams, "First Annual Message," 1:243–44.

be held accountable to the people, but only to the best interests of that people, not to its commonplace or base desires. Harsh in his judgment of others, Adams was even more uncharitable about his own foibles. Adams was forever tormented by the thought of what he *should* have been, destroyed by a nation and a superintending Providence unable or unwilling to heed his vision of national grandeur.

> If my intellectual powers had been such as have been sometimes committed by the Creator of men to single individuals of the species, my diary would have been, next to the Holy Scriptures, the most . . . valuable book ever written by human hands, and I should have been one of the greatest benefactors of my country and of mankind. I would, by the irresistible power of . . . Almighty God, have banished war and slavery from the face of the earth forever. But the conceptive power of mind was not conferred upon me by my Maker, and I have not improved the scanty portion of His gifts as I might and ought to have done.[75]

75. National Archives, Records of the Department of State, *Diplomatic Instructions,* All Countries, 9:297–98; Adams, *Degradation of Democratic Dogma,* 34–35.

THREE

Adams's Realism and the Role of Domestic Ideals in Foreign Affairs

T he celebration of a new world order, one compatible with the presidential vision of a new American century, is anything but new as a symbol of the diplomatic tradition of the United States. From the Monroe Doctrine to Woodrow Wilson's Fourteen Points and Franklin Roosevelt's Four Freedoms, external threats to national security have been answered with worldwide appeals that mirror the internal purposes of the American nation. The virtues of prudence and restraint at the center of Washington's Farewell Address were inspired by the faith of a people dedicated to "the benign influence of good Laws under a Free Government." Observing good faith and justice toward all nations entails an inward responsibility: "Can it be, that Providence has not connected the permanent felicity of a Nation with its virtue?"[1] Linking external commitments to domestic vitality is essential for a debtor nation that is seeking in the 1990s to rescue its own economic liberty, in addition to fighting for the political rights of victims of tyranny in distant lands.

Adams's worldview—relating domestic ideals to the nature of international politics—cannot be understood apart from the priorities assigned to domestic and foreign policy in classical and modern political

1. *Messages and Papers of the Presidents, 1789–1897,* 1:213 ff.

114

philosophy. For Adams and theorists of republican rule, these intellectual traditions posed two essential questions: 1) whether internal or external affairs should have primacy in calculating the national interest; and 2) whether expansion and foreign involvement are compatible with republican principles of government. These questions led Adams to reflect on democratic purposes in politics and diplomacy. His national vision coincided with Madison's description of America as a "workshop of liberty," an approach to the national purpose that blends idealism with realism, conservative methods with revolutionary purposes. A democratic government must accomplish two tasks: on the one hand, it must pursue policies that maximize the chances for success; on the other hand, it must secure the approval of its people for these foreign policies. The need to perform these two tasks simultaneously poses a dilemma for democratic government; for the conditions under which popular support can be obtained for a foreign policy are not necessarily identical with the conditions under which such a policy can be successfully pursued. Popular foreign policy is not necessarily good foreign policy.[2]

I.

The seed of the great foreign policy debates between "idealists" and "realists" in American history was planted as early as the Federal Convention of 1787. Charles Pinckney's presentation in the convention, Louis Hartz suggested, surpassed on a number of points Madison's masterpiece in *Federalist* #10. Neither the virtues of the ancients nor the views of the moderns prevailed in America, Pinckney informed his colleagues. Americans were "not only very different from the inhabitants of any State we are acquainted with in the modern world," but their achievement was "distinct from either the people of Greece or Rome, or any State we are acquainted with among the ancients." Could the "orders introduced by the institution of Solon" be found in the United States? Could the "military habits & manners of

2. Hans J. Morgenthau, *A New Foreign Policy for the United States*, 150–51.

Sparta be resembled to our habits & manners?" America's domestic purpose—extending to its citizens the blessings of civil and religious liberty—"is the great end of Republican Establishments." Pinckney, speaking for the Anti-Federalists, objected to any conception of the national interest where "reason of state" sacrificed the respectability of a people for a campaign of "conquest or superiority among other powers." Hamilton disputed Pinckney's ideal distinction and argued that domestic tranquility could not be contemplated in a vacuum, that no tranquility was likely if the government "did not possess sufficient stability and strength to make us respectable abroad."[3] Foreign policy played a far-from-negligible role in the Founders' debates on a proper frame of government.

A similar exchange took place between Madison and Patrick Henry in the Ratifying Convention of Virginia. An aging Henry struck a surprisingly modern note:

> The American spirit has fled from hence: it has gone to regions where it has never been expected; it has gone to the people of France, in search of a . . . strong, energetic government. Shall we imitate the example of those nations who have gone from a simple to a splendid government? Are those nations more worthy of imitation? . . . If we admit this consolidated government, it will be because we like a great, splendid one. Some way . . . we must be a great and mighty empire; we must have an army, and a navy, and a number of things. When the American spirit was in its youth, the language of America was different: liberty, sir, was . . . the primary object.[4]

Madison responded: "I agree with the . . . gentleman that national splendor and glory, are not our objects." Henry failed, however, to "distinguish between what will render us happy and secure at home, and what will render us respectable abroad." Madison believed that being free and happy at home could only enhance the power of the nation's prestige. What is worth noting here is that Madison and Henry

---

3. Louis Hartz, *The Liberal Tradition in America*, 84; Max Farrand, *The Records of the Federal Convention of 1787* 1:401–2, 4:28ff., 466–67.

4. Jonathan Elliot, ed. *The Debates in the Several State Conventions on the Adoption of the Federal Constitution*, 3:53.

had philosophical differences about the prerequisites for domestic security and happiness; yet they could still speak with a common voice about the evil of expansionism for republics. John Dickinson, writing as "Pennsylvania Farmer," was troubled by the "*thirst of empire*," a vice that "must be fatal to republican forms of government."[5]

Pinckney's reservations about political relations between the Greek states notwithstanding, Thucydides explained Athens's defeat as largely the result of an internal failure in democratic government and statesmanship. Thucydides' *History of the Peloponnesian War*, no less than the observations of Plato and Aristotle, prompted American thinkers to reflect upon the priorities assigned to the internal and external needs of states. At the same time, the Founders drew upon the insights of modern thinkers: Machiavelli, Francis Bacon, James Harrington, Algernon Sidney, and Montesquieu. Both classical and modern positions, as they relate to the foreign policy goals of the new republic, bring a greater diversity of thought to bear upon the facile distinction between "power politics" and "moral choice" in defining the national interest.

When Thucydides speaks of the causes of war—particularly Sparta's fear of Athens's increasing power—he seems to have little patience for the philosopher's commitment to the self-sufficiency of the polis. For example, he could have written about the liberation of the Greek cities from Athenian tyranny, basing his judgment on the premise that there is a good common to all Greek cities that should limit the ambitions of each belligerent. This line of reasoning would vindicate Aristotle's description of a perfectly good city that has no "foreign relations" whatever. When Plato and Aristotle defended the *bios theoretikos* against the ambition to rule, they expressed a theory of politics that looked to the primacy of internal policy. Leo Strauss described Plato's theory of justice as

> the unconditional primacy of internal policy. . . . For this theory says: there is no happiness for men without justice; justice means attending

---

5. Ibid., 135; John Dickinson, "Letters of Fabius," in P. L. Ford, ed., *Pamphlets on the Constitution of the United States*, 202.

to one's own business, bringing oneself into the right disposition with regard to the transcendent unchanging norm, to which the soul is akin, and not meddling into other people's affairs; and justice in the State is not different from justice in the individual, except that the State is self-sufficient and can thus practice justice—attending to his own business—incomparably more perfectly than can the individual who is not self-sufficient. Accordingly, for the properly constituted State, its self-assertion against other States is an accidental result of its proper constitution and not its main object.[6]

Similarly, in Book 7 of the *Politics*, Aristotle found it possible to conceive of "a state living somewhere or other by itself and in isolation. . . . It will obviously have a good constitution; but the scheme of its constitution will have no regard to war, or to the conquest of enemies, who, upon our hypothesis, will not exist."[7]

The connection between foreign policy and the geographic, economic, and social conditions of a country can be seen clearly in the case of Athens, whose politics received a more complete treatment at the hands of Thucydides than those of Sparta. A good example is furnished by the rather clear division of Athenian opinion on foreign policy, which followed class and party lines generally. This division of opinion was in evidence as early as the Athenian victory over the Persian forces at Salamis. The aristocracy, supported by rural elements, was the main carrier of resistance against the invader, whereas the demos inclined toward an intra-Hellenic expansionism at the expense of Sparta. In order to challenge Sparta's leadership by means of naval superiority, the Athenians had to make themselves into islanders permanently by abandoning their city and withdrawing to their ships. The propertyless demos, without much to lose, was quite willing to put itself on such a footing. The well-to-do and the peasants were less eager to abandon their property to seizure and destruction by the enemy. Objective economic and sociological interests launched the democratic masses to the forefront of Athenian political life.

Athenian foreign policy was compromised by the frequency with

6. Leo Strauss, *The Political Philosophy of Hobbes*, 101.
7. *The Politics of Aristotle*, 286.

which democratic leaders were subjected to punishment or censure out of jealousy or unfounded suspicion. Themistocles was ostracized by the masses in 471. Similarly, repeated invasions led democratic forces to try, convict, and sentence Pericles. The Athenian statesman responded to his accusers with revealing candor.

> When the whole state is on the right course, it is a better thing for each separate individual than when private interests are satisfied but the state as a whole is going downhill. However well off a man may be in his private life, he will still be involved in the general ruin if his country is destroyed; whereas, so long as the state itself is secure, individuals have a much greater chance of recovering from their private misfortunes. Therefore, since a state can support individuals in their suffering, but no one person can bear the load that rests upon the state, is it not right for us all to rally to her defence? . . . What has happened is this: you took my advice when you were still untouched by misfortune, and repented of your action when things went badly with you; it is because your own resolution is weak that my policy appears to you to be mistaken.[8]

The Sicilian expedition offers an illustration of the rash sentiments that preempted the open-mindedness and self-criticism necessary for such a grandiose enterprise. Thucydides acknowledges that the debate was so dominated by emotions that it was not safe for those opposing it to express their views lest they be suspected of a lack of patriotism. In Book 6, he writes,

> There was a passion for the enterprise which affected everyone alike. The older men thought they would either conquer the places against which they were sailing or . . . with such a large force could come to no harm; the young had a longing for the sights of distant places, and were confident they would return safely; the general masses and the average soldier . . . saw the prospect of getting pay . . . and of adding to the empire. . . . The result of this excessive enthusiasm of the majority was that the few who . . . were opposed to the expedition were afraid of being thought unpatriotic if they voted against it, and therefore kept quiet.[9]

8. Thucydides, *The Peloponnesian War*, 2:60–61.
9. Ibid., 6:24.

This campaign required the services of an outstanding leader who could rely upon sustained support. Yet the recall of Alcibiades, shortly after the expedition set out, was based on spurious reasons. Although he was formally charged with participation in sacrilegious endeavors, the real concern for his recall appears to have been an intrigue instigated by demagogues who did not relish the prospect of a hero's welcome for him if he returned as the conqueror of Sicily.

> It was found that . . . nearly all the stone Hermae in . . . Athens had their faces disfigured. . . . No one knew who had done this, but large rewards were offered by the state in order to find out who . . . knew of any other sacrilegious act that had taken place. . . . The whole affair . . . was taken very seriously, as it was regarded as an omen for the expedition, and . . . as evidence of a revolutionary conspiracy to overthrow democracy. . . . One of those accused was Alcibiades, and this . . . was taken up by those who disliked him most because . . . he stood in the way of their keeping a firm hold themselves of their leadership of the people. . . . They . . . exaggerated the whole thing . . . saying that the affair of . . . the defacement of the Hermae were all part of a plot to overthrow the democracy.[10]

The difficulties arising from the ill-advised change in command were further aggravated by the failure of Athens to give needed support to the forces abroad.

> Such a policy . . . led to a number of mistakes, amongst which was the Sicilian expedition, though in this case the mistake was not so much an error of judgment with regard to the opposition to be expected as a failure on the part of those who were at home to give proper support to their forces overseas. Because they were so busy with their own personal intrigues for securing the leadership of the people, they allowed this expedition to lose its impetus, and by quarrelling among themselves began to bring confusion into the policy of the state.[11]

Even with the failure of the mission, however, disaster could have been avoided. The main body of the forces might still have been saved by a last-minute withdrawal. Nicias, guided by the fickleness of the demos,

10. Ibid., 6:28–29.
11. Ibid., 2:65.

decided against withdrawal out of fear of execution at the hands of his countrymen, who would attribute his failure to dishonorable motives. Nicias was "prepared to agree that their [military] affairs were in a bad way, but did not want the fact of their weakness to be . . . reported to the enemy that the Athenians . . . were openly voting in favour of the withdrawal." The Athenian generals could see the facts as they were and reach a decision about them without having to depend on the reports of hostile critics; "but this was not the case with the voters of Athens, whose judgments would be swayed by any clever speech designed to create prejudice." Nicias also believed that most of the soldiers in Sicily "who were now crying so loudly about their desperate position, would, as soon as they got to Athens . . . change their tune and . . . say that the generals had been bribed to betray them and return."[12]

These examples point to the difficulties in policy making under the direct control of the demos, limited only by self-imposed restraints and checks resulting from factional strife. Athens's defeat by Sparta followed largely from an inability to keep its own house in order. Overextension and dissipation of power, a propensity to impulsive decisions in situations requiring circumspection, and distrust of its leaders stand out as the immediate cause of the city's decline. In addition, the intellectual and moral ambivalence of the masses was exacerbated by the factional hatred dividing the citizenry. This, as much as Sparta's virtue, decided the war. Pericles had seen the need for self-restraint, but his warning was ignored by his successors. The Athenian legacy in politics and diplomacy was not just the costs of imperialism but also the inability of defective institutions to apply the restraints that prudence demanded.

Different strands in modern political thought present the challenge of relating natural law to the increasingly empirical study of political power. While the classical philosophers defended the importance of internal policy, Machiavelli elevated the conduct of foreign policy to a normative plane. The Italian state system created its own patterns and demands that transformed the interest of the state (*raigon di stato*) by

12. Ibid., 7:48.

reference to the interstate environment. The founder of a new polity "will have to consider whether he wishes to have her expand in power and dominion like Rome, or whether he intends to confine her within narrow limits." Whether Machiavelli was sincere or merely paying lip service to ethics, he acknowledged that a republic designed for self-preservation rather than aggrandizement "would be the best political existence, and would insure to any state real tranquility." A republic built upon conquest would lead the people "to organize her as Rome was." Another alternative would be for the legislator to "organize her like Sparta and Venice; but as expansion is the poison of such republics, he must by every means . . . prevent her from making conquests, for such acquisitions for a feeble republic always prove their ruin."[13]

One problem in relating normative precepts to empirical patterns of state conduct is the tendency of international theorists to move little beyond the seventeenth- and eighteenth-century philosophy of natural rights. By equating the state of nature (and the equal right of each individual to self-preservation) with international society, Hobbes created the basis for a simplistic and one-sided approach to foreign affairs. Hobbes's juridical line of reasoning endowed every independent "sovereign" entity with "equal" rights. The doctrine of the sovereign equality of states was taken up by John Locke, Samuel Pufendorf, and the main body of international law. In the *Camillus* essays, Hamilton paraphrased Vattel in defining the voluntary law of nations as "a system of rules resulting from the equality and independence of nations, and which . . . attributes equal validity, as to external effects, to the measures or conduct of one as of another, without regard to the intrinsic justice of those measures or that conduct." Vattel put succinctly the nonpolitical aspect of the equality of states in the following terms: "Strength or weakness . . . counts for nothing. A dwarf is as much a man as a giant is; a small republic is no less a sovereign State than the most powerful kingdom."[14]

The emphasis that a legalistic approach to foreign policy places on

13. Niccolò Machiavelli, *The Prince and the Discourses*, 128.
14. Hedley Bull, "Hobbes and the International Anarchy," 724–29; *The Works of Alexander Hamilton*, ed. Henry Cabot Lodge, 5:422; Vattel, *The Law of Nations*, 3:5a, 7.

the norm of equality pays insufficient attention to the empirical science of international politics that flourished between the time of Machiavelli and the French Revolution. American statesmen drew upon this empirical heritage—a science of politics that treated external *and* internal duties as essential to the general welfare—in philosophical debates over the meaning of virtue and self-interest in republican government. John Adams wrote in 1776, "As Politiks . . . is the Science of human Happiness and human Happiness is clearly best promoted by Virtue, what thorough Politician can hesitate who has a new Government to build whether to prefer a Commonwealth or a Monarchy?" Yet it was not always to the Christian virtues of brotherly love, or to the Hellenic identity of virtue with highest wisdom, that American statesmen turned for inspiration. The early phase of modern political thought—from Machiavelli and Montesquieu to Mably and Rousseau—was distinguished by an uneasy fusion of the ancient ideal of public spiritedness with an ateleological view of human nature that denied genuine highmindedness to man. These republican writers regarded virtue as a passion for public good. A republic of men impelled by zeal for the common good could be sustained only by manipulating the passions; the private passions had to be put in the straightjacket of "virtue" and social equality. Montesquieu testified to this new conception by saying

> The less we are able to satisfy our private passions, the more we abandon ourselves to those of a general nature. How comes it that monks are so fond of their order? It is owing to the very cause that renders the order insupportable. Their rule debars them from all those things by which the ordinary passions are fed; there remains . . . only this passion for the very rule that torments them. The more austere it is . . . the more it curbs their inclinations, the more force it gives to the only passion left them.[15]

Important differences remained among modern thinkers regarding the need for either consolidation or expansion as the norm for republics.

James Harrington knew of Machiavelli's division of commonwealths "into such as are for *preservation* . . . and such as are for *encrease*." Both

---

15. Gerald Stourzh, *Alexander Hamilton and the Idea of Republican Government*, 64–75; Montesquieu, *The Spirit of Laws*, 20–22; 40–42; 132–33.

Algernon Sidney and Machiavelli combined a belief in the primacy of foreign policy with measured confidence in large territories for republics. Sidney's *Discourses on Government* took note of Machiavelli's typology of regimes and recognized the political impact that would accompany the maritime power of an expanding Britain. At stake was whether it is "better to constitute a commonwealth for war, or for trade; and of such as intend for war, whether those are the most to be praised who prepare for defence only, or those who design by conquest to enlarge their dominions." Sidney was unequivocal; both war and conquest take priority.

> Those only can be safe who are strong, and that no people was ever well defended, but those who fought for themselves; the best judges of these matters have . . . given the preference to those constitutions that principally intend war, and make use of trade as assisting to that end; and think it better to aim at conquest . . . since he that loses all, if he be overcome, fights upon very unequal terms; and if he obtain the victory, gains no advantage, than for the present to repel the danger.[16]

The vigorous conduct of foreign policy overshadowed more familiar distinctions. "This does not less concern monarchies than commonwealths; not the absolute less than the mixed: all of them have been prosperous or miserable . . . as they were better or worse armed, disciplined, or conducted."[17]

Machiavelli knew that states were compelled "to many acts to which reason will not influence them." Since "human things are kept in a perpetual movement, and can never remain stable," so it is also the case that states will either rise or decline. He saw no precise middle course between consolidation and expansion; ultimately, he thought, "it is proper in the organization of a republic to select the most honorable course and to constitute her so that, even if necessity should oblige her to expand, she may . . . be able to preserve her acquisitions." The classical notion of undisturbed tranquility for a republic may "enervate . . . or provoke internal dissensions, which . . . will be apt to prove her

16. Zoltan Haraszti, *John Adams and the Prophets of Progress*, 34–35; Stourzh, *Alexander Hamilton and the Idea of Republican Government*, 136.

17. Stourzh, *Idea of Republican Government*, 136.

ruin." Under these circumstances, drastic means are required to promote civic virtue. A design "to keep the state rich, but the citizens poor"—Machiavelli's often-repeated advice in the *Discourses*—was reflected in the laws of Lycurgus. The Spartan legislator made it easier for the citizens to live in union by establishing equality in fortunes and inequality in conditions; "for an equal poverty prevailed there, and the people were . . . less ambitious, as the offices of the government were given to a few citizens . . . ; and the nobles in the exercise of their functions did not treat the people sufficiently ill to excite in them the desire of exercising them themselves."[18]

The realism of Machiavelli and Sidney created a predisposition not only against the rhetoric of Thomas Paine and Patrick Henry, but also against the high authority of Montesquieu. In fact, Montesquieu spoke of another "particular view" by which each state comes to the same "general end."

> Increase of dominion was the view of Rome; war, of Sparta; religion, of the Jewish laws; commerce, that of Marseilles; public tranquility, that of the laws of China; navigation, the laws of Rhodes; natural liberty, that of the policy of the Savages; in general, the pleasure of the prince . . . that of monarchies, the prince's and the kingdom's glory; the independence of individuals is the end aimed at by the laws of Poland, thence results the oppression of the whole.
>
> One nation [England] there is also in the world that has for the direct end of its constitution political liberty.[19]

Montesquieu's hope to obtain by the supervision of the passions what classical philosophers upheld as the highest achievement of reason was reflected in his foreign policy preferences. He presented noteworthy modifications of both ancient and early modern trends in political thought. Unlike Aristotle, his ideal republic was built upon individual austerity and passionate love for the common good. Unlike Machiavelli, he rejected Roman expansion in favor of Spartan stability. Sparta's long duration as a republic was the result of "it[s] having continued

18. Machiavelli, *The Prince and the Discourses*, 126–30.
19. Montesquieu, *The Spirit of the Laws*, 150–51.

in the same extent of territory after all its wars." By affirming the Spartan alternative of defensive wars, "peace" as a principle only denoted the absence of wars of expansion. Less sanguine than either Machiavelli or Sidney about avoiding the evils that had led to Rome's fall, Montesquieu believed that overextension brought about the decay of republican virtue. Large republics bring "men of large fortunes, and consequently of less moderation." According to Montesquieu, "Interests are divided; an ambitious person soon becomes sensible that he may be happy, great, and glorious, by oppressing his fellow citizens; and that he might raise himself to grandeur on the ruins of his country."[20]

Montesquieu's liberal theory of international commerce accentuated Americans' concern with the peacefulness of republics. The eighteenth century brought increasing awareness that the center of gravity in international politics had shifted from the possession of military force to the calculus of sea and commercial power. In *Federalist #12*, Hamilton argued that "the property of commerce is now perceived . . . by all enlightened statesmen to be the most useful . . . source of national wealth; and has . . . become a primary object of their political cares." Again in *Federalist #30*, Hamilton adds that money is "considered as the vital principle of the body politic; as that which sustains its life and motion, and enables it to perform its most essential functions." He took as his inspiration (especially in *Federalist #6*) a treatise on international politics by the Abbé Mably. The essay documented two memorable events that produced political revolutions—the conquest of America by Spain and the Portuguese exploration of the East Indies.

> Princes were in a hurry to favor luxury and commerce which might render their courts more brilliant and . . . augment the revenues of their customs. Navigation spread to all the seas; trading posts were established in all parts of the world; colonies were founded. It was necessary to devote to . . . commerce a prodigious number of men who would have been soldiers. . . . Money became the sinews of war and of politics; and a nation that desired to be a conquering one, had to become a commercial one in order to entertain armies.[21]

---

20. Ibid., 176–77.
21. Cooke, ed. *The Federalist*, 73, 188. Stourzh, *Idea of Republican Government*, 142.

The revolution in the composition of national power led Montesquieu, like David Hume, to describe the "ideal type" of modern commercial policy, to isolate extraneous factors like princely love of splendor or the need to finance wars of expansion from the natural laws of
commercial interaction. Trade, Montesquieu stipulated, "has some relation to forms of government!" In monarchies, trade satisfies "the
pride, the pleasure, and the capricious whims of the nation." In republics, trade is "commonly founded on economy. Their merchants, having an eye to all the nations . . . bring from one what is wanted by
another." Since the enterprises of merchants "are always . . . connected
with the affairs of the public," a rational commercial policy would
facilitate free trade and an international division of labor (although not
excluding colonial monopolies). The expectation here, shared by some
of the American Founders, was that economic interdependence was
likely to diminish arbitrariness and violence among nations. John Winthrop, writing as "Agrippa" from Massachusetts, paraphrased Montesquieu in making a case for the interdependence of peace, trade, and
republican government.

> The argument against republicks, as it derived from the Greek and
> Roman states, is unfair. . . . We find . . . in practice, that limited
> monarchy is more friendly to commerce, because more friendly to
> the rights of the subject, than an absolute government; and that it is
> more liable to be disturbed than a republick, because less friendly to
> trade and the rights of individuals. . . .
> In a republick, we ought to guard . . . against the predominance of
> any particular interest. It is the object of government to protect them
> all. When commerce is left to take its own course, the advantage of
> every class will be nearly equal.[22]

By the mid–1780s, American hopes for a new beginning at home
and abroad had been keenly disappointed. The imposition by France
of a commercial system of monopoly and exclusion prompted John
Adams to react with bitterness: "We shall be obliged to imitate their
wisdom in practice, and exclude from the United States . . . those

---

22. Montesquieu, *The Spirit of the Laws*, 318–19; Paul L. Ford, ed. *Essays on the
Constitution of the United States*, 94, 109.

foreign goods which would be hurtful to the United States and their manufactories [and] make the balance of trade to be against them. . . ." For Adams, it was a question of "whether one nation who should abolish it [i.e., monopolies], while the rest maintain it, would not be ruined by their liberality." He regarded national pride as "the bulwark of defense to all nations." The irrationality of monarchies and the reasonableness of republics gave way to a new debate about defense versus opulence. Even Adam Smith, in the *Wealth of Nations,* issued an important caveat to any scheme of free trade: "As defense . . . is of much more importance than opulence, the act of navigation is, perhaps, the wisest of all the commercial regulations of England."[23] In other words, the logic of sea power could lead to a supremacy more enduring than any conquest of land, which was vulnerable to the vagaries of both dynastic changes and weak economies.

Hamilton and Madison relied upon Montesquieu extensively, particularly in their analyses of a "confederate republic" and the separation of powers doctrine; however, their defense of federalism relied upon a newer, different, understanding of individual and republican virtue. Public-spiritedness or virtue, from Machiavelli to Montesquieu, was thought to be possible in society only with general frugality and the "mediocrity of fortunes." A second stage of modern political theory asserted the primacy of the passions for self-preservation *and* self-enrichment. Hobbes, on the first page of his *Leviathan,* wrote that "the *wealth* and the *riches* of all particular members, are the *strength* of the commonwealth." In writing "Of Commerce," Hume laid out what was called the "modern policy":

> Ancient policy was violent and contrary to the more natural and usual course of things. It is well known with what peculiar laws Sparta was governed and what a prodigy that republic is justly esteemed. . . . Were the testimony of history less positive and circumstantial, such a government would appear a mere philosophical whim . . . and impossible ever to be reduced to practice. . . .
> And the less natural any set of principles are which support a

23. Adams, *Works,* 8:298–99; Haraszti, *John Adams and the Prophets of Progress,* 143; Adam Smith, *An Inquiry into . . . the Wealth of Nations,* 431.

particular society, the more difficulty will a legislator meet with in raising and cultivating them. It is his best policy to comply with the common bent of mankind and give it all the improvements of which it is susceptible. . . . That policy is violent which aggrandizes the public by the poverty of individuals.[24]

Madison's indebtedness to Hume is evident in *Federalist* #10: "Theoretic politicians who have patronized this species of [republican] government, have erroneously supposed that by reducing mankind to a perfect equality in their political rights, they would be . . . equalized and assimilated in their possessions, their opinions, and their passions." Hamilton, praising Hume as "a very ingenious and sensible writer," told the New York Ratifying Convention: "Look through the rich and the poor of the community; the learned and the ignorant. Where does virtue predominate? The difference . . . consists, not in the quantity but the kind of vices . . . and here the advantage of character belongs to the wealthy. Their vices are probably more favorable to the prosperity of the state, than those of the indigent; and partake less of moral depravity."[25]

The lessons of human nature as revealed in history provided Hamilton with the ammunition to destroy Pinckney's arguments about the peaceful nature of republican government. A man would have to "be far gone in Utopian speculations," Hamilton charged, to expect "a continuation of harmony between a number of independent unconnected sovereignties, situated in the same neighbourhood." He moved on to assess the sources of conflict among nations. There are some that have "a general and almost constant operation" on the vigilant statesman. Hamilton included here "the love of power or the desire of preeminence . . . the jealousy of power, or the desire of equality and safety." Other causes may be "more circumscribed, though an equally operative influence, within their spheres: Such are the rivalships . . . of

24. Hobbes, *Leviathan*, 19; Charles W. Hendel, ed. *David Hume's Political Essays*, 133–34.

25. Douglass Adair, "'That Politics May Be Reduced to a Science': David Hume, James Madison, and the Tenth *Federalist*," 343–60; *The Papers of Alexander Hamilton*, 5:43.

commerce between . . . nations." In a final thrust at the doctrine that free governments reduced arbitrariness in foreign affairs, Hamilton took exception with those "visionary, or designing men, who stand ready to advocate the . . . perpetual peace between the States":

> Have republics in practice been less addicted to war than monarchies? Are not the former administered by *men* as well as the latter? . . . Are not popular assemblies frequently subject to the impulses of rage, resentment, jealousy, avarice, and other irregular and violent propensities? Is it not well known that their determinations are often governed by a few individuals in whom they place confidence, and are . . . liable to be tinctured by the passions and views of those individuals?[26]

The Founders' quest for the limits of republican government took much of its meaning from the conflicting claims of ancient and modern ways of thought, especially the ideas of those thinkers who made a last attempt to bridge the gap between antiquity and modernity. A number of limitations must be noted in relating philosophical models to the pragmatic requirement of workability in politics. First, there was no clear agreement on the substance of liberty and how political opportunities would be distributed over an expansive republic. Second, the theoretical issues were rarely debated apart from the problems of persuasion inherent in a democracy—the need for simplifying issues less than clear even to the most learned. For many, public or republican virtue became "morality," pure and simple. Finally, consider Washington's heroic claim in June 1783: "The foundation of our Empire was . . . laid . . . at an Epocha when the rights of mankind were better understood . . . than at any former period; the researches of the human mind after social happiness . . . have been carried . . . by the labours of Philosophers, Sages, and Legislators, [and] are laid open for . . . the Establishment of our forms of Government."[27]

"Philosopher," as written here, was a word evoking optimism and hopes of the high tide of Enlightenment on both sides of the Atlantic. By 1792, events in France led many to equate "philosophy" with the

26. Cooke, ed. *The Federalist*, 28–29; 31–36.

27. Adair, "'That Politics May Be Reduced to a Science,'" 343.

guillotine, atheism, and the reign of terror. So a commitment to the moderns by no means eased the task of statesmanship. A nation had to be built upon the double premise of the actual selfishness of men and the principle that the sense of the majority ought to prevail.

II.

Adams's realism reflected the classical preoccupation with the internal strength produced by a virtuous citizenry as well as the modern presumption about the primacy of foreign policy. There was never a greater champion of America's commitment to human rights. Yet, in foreign affairs, the nature of that commitment derives partly from obligations to ourselves as much as from obligations to others. Adams realized that American support for revolutionary movements abroad "opened an extensive field of speculation to the philosopher and to the politician." The Monroe administration was challenged to define America's obligation to recognize and intervene in behalf of Latin American independence. Speaker of the House Henry Clay, in 1821, recommended that the United States countenance the patriots' cause "by all means short of actual war"; "it would give additional tone, and hope and confidence, to the friends of liberty throughout the world." Finally, he proposed that "a sort of counterpoise to the Holy Alliance should be formed in the two Americas, in favor of national independence and liberty, to operate by the force of example, and moral influence."[28]

In his *Memoirs*, Secretary of State Adams recorded the reservations and convictions he voiced in a long exchange with Clay on the limits of American power in the domestic affairs of these nations.

> I have never doubted [he said to Clay] that the final issue of their [the revolted provinces] present struggle will be their entire independence of Spain. It is equally clear that it is our true policy and duty to take no part in the contest. . . . So far as they are contending for independence, I wish well to their cause; but I have not yet seen . . . any prospect that they will establish free or liberal institutions of govern-

---

28. Arthur Whitaker, *U.S. and Latin American Independence*, 344–63.

ment. . . . Arbitrary power, military and ecclesiastical, is stamped upon their education, upon their habits, and upon all their institutions. . . . I have little expectation of any beneficial result to this country from any future connection with them, political or commercial.[29]

Admittedly, the United States acquired some responsibility to the Spanish colonies since their cause drew upon "the practical illustration given in the . . . establishment of our Union to the doctrine that voluntary agreement is the only legitimate source of authority among men, and that all just government is a compact." To a cause reposing upon the sovereignty of the people, "the sentiments of the government of the United States have been in perfect harmony with those of their people." Adams spoke of America's duties in the following terms:

> *Civil, political, commercial,* and *religious* liberty, are but various modifications of one great principle founded in the unalienable rights of human nature, and before the universal application of which, the colonial domination of Europe over the American hemisphere has fallen. . . . Civil liberty *can* be established on no foundation of human reason which will not at the same time demonstrate the *right* to religious freedom. . . . To promote this event by all the moral influence which we can exercise by our example, is among the duties which devolve upon us in the formation of our future relations with our southern neighbors.[30]

Moreover, enlightened self-interest did not rule out significant moral gains for America and the world. Adams argued for the achievement of liberal principles of commercial relations and exchange, with the aim of opening South American ports to the commerce of the world by relaxing imperial restrictions. He described the policy of the United States with regard to South America as based upon the two principles of "entire and unqualified reciprocity" and permanent most-favored-nation treatment, which were necessary to the realization of South American independence. In negotiating treaties of commerce, a nation

29. Adams, *Memoirs*, 5:324–25.
30. JQA to Richard C. Anderson, May 27, 1823, 7:466–67.

should seek to satisfy its own interests but should also be willing "to concede liberally to that which is adapted to the interest of the other."[31]

Adams cautioned, however, that the independence of the Spanish colonies "proceeded from other causes, and has been achieved upon principles, in many respects different from our own." In America's revolution, "the principle of the social compact was, from the beginning, in immediate issue." Independence was "declared in defence of our *liberties*, and the attempt to make the yoke a yoke of oppression was the cause and justification for casting it off." The independence of the Spanish colonies, by way of comparison, was forced upon the inhabitants by the temporary subjugation of Spain herself as a foreign power. Despite Adams's hopes, he saw "no spirit of freedom pervading any portion of the population, no common principle of reason to form an union of mind: no means of combining force for exertions of resistance to power." Being on terms of peace with Spain, and having "relative duties to all the parties," the United States was bound to consider the struggle for independence "as a case of civil war to which their national obligations prescribed to them to remain neutral."[32]

"The United States," Adams advised, "could not recognize the independence of the colonies as existing *de facto*, without trespassing on their duties to Spain, by assuming as decided that which was precisely the question of the war." President Monroe, as Adams explained in a letter of instruction to the American minister in Colombia, "considered the question of recognition, both in a moral and political view as merely a question of the proper *time*." He would also insist that Spain "had no right upon the strength of this principle to maintain the pretension, after she was manifestly disabled from maintaining the contest, and . . . to deprive the independents of their rights to demand the acknowledgments of others." To fix upon "the precise *time* when the duty to respect the prior sovereign right of Spain should cease . . . became in the first instance a proper subject of consultation with other powers having relations of interest to themselves with the newly opened

31. See National Archives, Records of the Department of State, *Diplomatic Instructions*, All Countries, 7:241; Adams, "Third Annual Message," 380.
32. JQA to Richard Anderson, May 27, 1823, 7:442–43.

countries, as well as influence in the general affairs of Europe."[33] This was a clear statement on the limits of American unilateralism and how "the moral influence which we can exercise" was inseparable from those methods through which American interests interacted with the European balance of power.

To Adams's mind, the national interest was not simply a question of purpose, objective, or doctrine; it also was a question of "how" as much as "what." From this angle, Adams was preoccupied with the style or conduct of American foreign policy, rather than any hierarchy of predetermined goals. George F. Kennan, who studied Adams's career, commented that "manner of execution is always a factor in diplomacy of no less importance than concept." Harshly judging America's diplomatic dilettantism in foreign affairs, Kennan lamented, "Objectives were normally vainglorious, unreal . . . even pathetic—little likely to be realized. . . . But methods were another matter. These were real. It was out of their immediate effects that the quality of life was really molded. In war as in peace I found myself concerned less with what people thought they were striving for than with the manner in which they strove for it."[34] For Kennan and Adams, good form in outward behavior "becomes a value in itself, with its own validity and effectiveness, and perhaps—human nature being what it is—the greatest value of them all." A similar position was taken by the French statesman Callières, who documented the personal qualities of the good negotiator. On the one hand, a "man who has entered public employ must consider that his public duty is to act and not to remain too long closeted in his study; his chief work must be to learn what goes on among the living rather than what went on among the dead." On the other hand, the diplomat must possess "that penetration which enables him to discover the thoughts of men and to know by the least movement of their countenances what passions are stirring within, for such movements are often betrayed even by the most practiced negotiator."[35]

33. Ibid., 444–46.
34. George F. Kennan, *Memoirs, 1925–1950*, 199.
35. Barton Gellman, *Contending with Kennan: Toward a Philosophy of American Power*, 31; Francois de Callières, *On the Manner of Negotiating with Princes*, 18–19.

Adams distinguished between the procedures and goals of American diplomacy in 1822 and 1823, when he urged President Monroe to moderate his open endorsement of the Greek independence movement. The revolutionary tide had slowly gathered strength until, by 1821, it posed an immediate threat to Ottoman rule. Sultan Mahmud II retaliated with such violence that he aroused anti-Turkish sentiment throughout western Europe and the United States. The outbreak of the Greek revolution in 1821 raised again the role of human rights in American foreign policy. "The mention of Greece fills the mind with the most exalted sentiments and arouses in our bosoms the best feelings of which our nature is susceptible," said President Monroe in his annual message of 1822. In the first draft of the Monroe Doctrine, the president proposed to reprove the French invasion of Spain, to acknowledge the independence of Greece, and to ask Congress for a diplomatic mission to Athens! Albert Gallatin proposed to lend the Greek government a fleet; William Cullen Bryant wrote *The Greek Partisan*; and Daniel Webster declared that he preferred the Greeks to "the inhabitants of the Andes, and the dwellers in the borders of the Vermilion sea." In his speech before Congress, Webster answered for America "when the first blast of the trumpet of liberty rang along the Ionian seas, and through the Peloponnesus." Webster continued,

> The Greeks, contending with ruthless oppressors, turn their eyes to us, and invoke us, by their ancestors, by their slaughtered wives and children, by their own blood poured out like water, by the hecatombs of dead they have heaped up . . . to heaven; they invoke, they implore from us some cheering sound, some look of sympathy, some token of compassionate regard. They look to us as the great Republic of the earth—and they ask us, by our common faith, whether we can forget that they are struggling, as we once struggled, for what we now so happily enjoy?[36]

Not only did the moralism of Webster promise trouble with the Ottoman Empire, but it also threatened American shipping in the

36. Morison and Commager, *The Growth of the American Republic*, 1:458–59; Seward, *Life of John Quincy Adams*, 124.

flourishing opium trade. "This is no small item," Thomas H. Perkins wrote, under the pseudonym of "A Merchant," in a Boston newspaper. "Shall we then go on a crusade in favor of the Greeks and hazard the liberty of our citizens and a valuable trade?" Webster's congressional resolution in favor of Greece was also assailed by John Randolph, who had reservations about America making commitments to either Greeks or Latin Americans.

> Not satisfied with attempting to support the Greeks, our world, like that of Pyrrhus or Alexander, is not sufficient for us. We must have yet another world for exploits: we are to operate in a country [Chile] distant from us eighty degrees of latitude, and only accessible by a circumnavigation of the globe, and to subdue which we must cover the Pacific with our ships, and the Andes with our soldiers. . . . Why . . . these projects of ambition surpass those of Bonaparte himself.[37]

Other participants in this debate worried less about over-commitment than about an environment that would sap America's foreign policy resolve in the face of foreign threats. Henry Clay chided his more timid colleagues, asking whether it was "a wise way of preparing for this awful event to talk to this nation of its incompetency to resist European aggression?" Robert Walsh seconded Clay's position and suggested "alarms have been sounded which would have come with more propriety from members of the public councils of a Republic like St. Marino, than from any American representative."[38]

The issue of recognizing and aiding the cause of the Greeks was taken up at a cabinet meeting on August 15, 1823. In addition to Gallatin, who recommended assisting with a "naval force" (one frigate, one corvette, and one schooner), both Secretary of War John C. Calhoun and Attorney General William Wirt were inclined to speak of yet another great war of revolution against tyranny. Adams believed his colleagues susceptible to "two sources of eloquence at these cabinet meetings—one with reference to sentiment, and the other to action."

37. *National Gazette,* January 28, 1824; Richard N. Current, *Daniel Webster and the Rise of National Conservatism,* 43.
38. *National Gazette,* January 27, 1824.

In this instance, championing the Greek cause "is all sentiment, and the standard of this is the prevailing popular feeling." As for a course of action, "they are seldom agreed," and the meeting was "dismissed, leaving it precisely where it was, nothing determined, and nothing practical proposed by either of them." Having little patience "for the enthusiasm which evaporates in words," Secretary Adams told Monroe, "I thought not quite so lightly of a war with Turkey." He informed the president that the unamended version of his historic message "would have an air of open defiance to all Europe, and I should not be surprised if the first answer to it from Spain and France, and even Russia should be to break off diplomatic intercourse with us. . . . The aspect of things is portentous; but if we must come to an issue with Europe, let us keep it off as long as possible. Let us by all means carry the opinion of the nation with us, and the opinion of the world." Even if the Holy Alliance were determined to take issue with the United States, Adams warned that "it should be our policy to meet, and not to make it." The United States "had objects of distress to relieve at home," while intervening in behalf of the Greeks would "be a breach of neutrality, and therefore improper."[39]

III.

As ethicist, Adams wrote at length about the moral purposes of government and how American ideals are anchored "upon the adamantine rock of human rights." All the "moral ligatures of friendship and neighborhood" spread through "to the broader and more complicated relations of countryman and fellow-citizen; terminating only with the circumference of the globe . . . in the coextensive charities incident to the common nature of man." Adams rejected any state-centered morality as inimical to "the sacred bonds of the social union"; to each of these relations, "different degrees of sympathy are allotted by the ordinances of nature." Yet the "tie which binds us to our country, is not

39. Adams, *Memoirs,* 6:195–96; *The Diary of John Quincy Adams, 1794–1845,* 300, 323.

more holy in the sight of God, but it is more deeply-seated in our nature, more . . . endearing, than that looser link which merely connects us with our fellow mortal man."[40]

In an address delivered to the citizens of Washington on July 4, 1821, Adams answered certain British publications on the theme "What has America done for mankind?" He was especially annoyed by the suggestion of the *Edinburgh Review*, in May 1820, that the United States should align with liberals in Great Britain by supporting the principles of reform and liberty in Spain, France, and Italy. The relevant passages deserve to be quoted at length.

> It is impossible [said the *Edinburgh Review*] to look to the state of the Old World without seeing . . . that there is a greater and more momentous contest impending, than [has] even before agitated human society. In Germany—in Spain—in France—in Italy, the principles of Reform and Liberty are visibly arraying themselves for a final struggle with the principles of Established abuse,—Legitimacy, or Tyranny,—or whatever else it is called, by its friends or enemies. . . . We conceive, that much will depend on the part that is taken by America. . . . It is as an associate or successor in the noble office of patronizing and protecting general liberty, that we now call upon America . . . to unite herself . . . with the liberal and enlightened part of the English nation, at a season when their joint efforts will in all probability be little enough to crown the good cause with success. . . . [America's] *influence*, as well as her example, will be wanted in the crisis which seems to be approaching.[41]

Accepting the challenge of British liberals, Adams justified colonial revolutions for independence, whether in North or South America, without rushing, armed, to their support. His intention was to demonstrate *"from the political and physical nature of man that colonial establishments cannot fulfill the great objects of government in the just purpose of civil society."* This premise, Adams observed in a letter to Edward Everett, ought to be evaluated for "its bearing upon the system of

40. Adams, *Fourth of July Oration*, 13–14.
41. *Edinburgh Review* 66 (1820), 403–5.

political morality, and upon the future improvement of the human character."[42]

Reflecting on his address, Adams listed the normative precepts joining the principles of American self-government with the obligation to enhance the worldwide prospects of freedom and liberty:

> 1. It places on a new and solid ground the *right* of our struggle for independence, considering the intolerable oppressions which provoked our fathers to revolt only as its proximate causes, themselves proof of the viciousness of the system from which they resulted.
>
> 2. It settles the justice of the . . . struggle of South America for independence, and prepares for an acknowledgment upon the principle of public law of that independence, whenever it shall be sufficiently established by the fact.
>
> 3. It looks forward . . . to the downfall of the British Empire in India as an event which must . . . ensue at no very distant period of time.
>
> 4. It anticipates a great question in the national policy of the Union which may be nearer at hand than most of our countrymen are aware of: Whether we . . . shall annex to our federative government a great system of colonial establishments?
>
> 5. It points to a principle proving that such establishments are incompatible with the essential character of our political institutions.
>
> 6. It leads to the conclusion that . . . colonial establishments are but mighty engines of *wrong*, and that in the progress of social improvement it will be the duty of the human family to abolish them, as they are now endeavoring to abolish the slave trade.[43]

The 1821 address laid out "a principle of *duty*," by which American leaders were admonished that "direct interference in foreign wars, even wars for freedom" would "change the very foundations of our government from *liberty* to *power*." Adams did not believe that "this question of political morality transcendently important to the future destiny of this country [had] even been presented before." The merits of his life's work, either as a literary man or politician, consisted "in the application of moral philosophy to business, in the . . . reference direct or

42. JQA to Edward Everett, January 31, 1822, 7:197–202.
43. Ibid.

indirect of all narrative, argument, and inference, to the standard of *right* and *wrong.*" Adams suffered few illusions about how moral choices are endlessly twisted by the ideological trappings of power.

> Erroneous moral principle is the most fruitful of all the sources of human calamity and vice. The leaders of nations . . . are generally but accomplished sophists, trained to make the worse appear the better reason. The intercourse of private life is full of sophistical palterings and human law itself, with deference to Hooker be it said, . . . is too often but a system of formal sophistry substituted for eternal truth and justice. Yet so congenial are truth and justice to the human mind, that it is always vehemently moved by a . . . forcible appeal to them, and of appeals to them direct or implied, explicit or deductive, the whole substance of my public writings is composed.[44]

On his nation's duty to mankind, Adams thought "our answer should be this: America, with the same voice which she spoke herself into existence as a nation, proclaimed to mankind the inextinguishable rights of human nature, and the only lawful foundations of government." It was "not by the contrivance of agents of destruction, that America wishes to commend her inventive genius to the gratitude of aftertimes." Nor was the American purpose "the glory of Roman ambition; nor Tu regere *Imperio* populos—her momento to her sons." Adams found an unmistakable moral lesson for American power in world affairs: "Her glory is not *dominion*, but *liberty*. Her march is the march of the mind. She has a spear and a shield: but the motto upon her shield is, *Freedom, Independence, Peace.* This has been her Declaration: this has been, as far as her necessary intercourse with the rest of mankind would permit, her practice."[45]

Adams, then, drew a sharp line between intervention and sympathy in behalf of those fighting for freedom. "Whenever the standard of freedom and independence, has been or shall be unfurled, there will [America's] heart, her benedictions, and her prayers be." Similarly, respect for the independence of other nations dictated that the United States abstain "from interference in the concerns of others, even when

44. Ibid.
45. Adams, *Fourth of July Oration*, 29–31.

the conflict has been for principles to which she clings. . . ." Prudence placed limitations upon the presumption of American moral omnipotence. Universal principles alone did not entitle America to venture "abroad, in search of monsters to destroy." Here, Adams reflected the counsel of Edmund Burke: "Nothing is so fatal to a nation as an extreme of self-partiality, and the total want of consideration of what others will naturally hope or fear."[46] Adams was a principled realist who recognized that universal norms cannot be applied to the actions of states in their abstract formulation, but that they must be filtered through the concrete circumstances of time and place. The individual may embrace an ethic of self-sacrifice in defense of a moral principle, such as liberty or honor. *Fiat justitia pereat mundus* (Let justice be done, even if the world perish). The state, however, can claim no such right in the name of those who are in its care, for successful political action is itself inspired by the moral principle of national survival.

46. Edmund Burke, "Remarks on the Policy of the Allies with Respect to France," 4:447.

F O U R

American Nationhood
and the Duty to Posterity

*J*ohn Quincy Adams, like his father's generation before him, saw
America as the expression of certain objective truths to which
both the cosmic order and human society were thought to owe
their existence. That order was conceived in both religious and secular
terms. The religious order ran the gamut from English High Church
through Puritanism to Quakerism, and the rational order was received
through the teachings of the Romans, Locke, and the French En-
cyclopedists. Certain transcendent purposes were deemed essential for
the workings of democracy. The Founding Fathers were practical philosophers whose views on democratic government and foreign policy
were based on a clear-cut conception of the nature of man, the state,
and the world. Edward S. Corwin, one of America's leading constitutional theorists, argued that these early American leaders succeeded in
formulating principles of transcendental justice in terms of personal
and private rights. The principles of natural law, he wrote, "were made
by no human hands; indeed, if they did not antedate deity itself, they
still express its nature as to bind and control it." These laws are eternal
and immutable. In relation to such principles, "human laws are, when
entitled to obedience . . . merely a record or transcript, and their
enactment an act not of will or power, but one of discovery and
declaration." Although there are different schools of natural law and

natural rights, there are fundamental principles common to all of them: that, in Cicero's words, "law is the bond of civil society," and that all men, governors as well as governed, are under, never above, laws; that these laws can be refined through rational discussion; and that the highest laws are those upon which all rational men of good will, when fully informed, will tend to agree.[1]

What Sir Ernest Barker described as the "traditions of civility," a consensus on first and last things, was put by Walter Lippmann into the framework of a general public philosophy.

> The rational faculty of man was conceived as producing a common conception of law and order which possessed a universal validity. . . . It was a set of ideas which lived and moved in the Middle Ages; and St. Thomas Aquinas cherished the idea of a sovereign law of nature imprinted on the heart and nature of man, to which kings and legislators must everywhere bow. . . . Spoken through the mouth of Locke, [they justified] the English Revolution of 1688, and . . . served to inspire the American Revolution of 1776. . . . They were ideas of the proper conduct of states and governments in the area of internal affairs. They were the ideas of the natural rights of man—of liberty, political and civic, with sovereignty residing essentially in the nation, and . . . of a general fraternity which tended in practice to be sadly restricted within the nation, but which could, on occasion, be extended by decree to protect all nations struggling for freedom.[2]

At times of great stress and revolution, some of these endangered traditions were committed to writing, as in the Magna Carta and the Declaration of Independence. For the guidance of lawyers and jurists, large portions were described—as in Lord Coke's examination of the common law. The public philosophy was, in part, expounded in the British Bill of Rights of 1689. It was recreated in the first ten amendments to the Constitution of the United States. As Lippmann observed, however, the largest part of the public philosophy was never

---

1. Morgenthau, *The Purpose of American Politics*, 17–18; Edward S. Corwin, *The "Higher Law" Background of American Constitutional Law*, 4–5; Walter Lippmann, *The Public Philosophy*, 123.

2. Sir Ernest Barker, *Traditions of Civility*, 10–12; Lippmann, *The Public Philosophy*, 76–77.

explicitly stated. The wisdom of a great society over centuries can never be encapsulated in a solitary document or a series of documents. Yet the traditions of civility and higher law "permeated the peoples of the West and provided a standard of public and private action which promoted, facilitated and protected the institutions of freedom and the growth of democracy."[3]

I.

John Quincy Adams was the leading son of that generation of Americans whose sacrifice in defense of independence and liberty was immortalized as a celebration of self-evident truths about the unalienable rights of man's political existence. Adams, a youthful witness to the fall of the first patriots at Bunker Hill, was inspired as much by the passions that accompany tragic loss as by the exuberance that instills a righteous defense of noble causes. Intervening years of public service and notorious political battles did not lessen the vigor with which he urged his countrymen to renew their national purpose. Yet his experience and his education taught him that the politician is little more than an inglorious ideologue when the limits of all human attainment are not acknowledged. The powers of speech, "the special prerogative of man, as a member of the animal creation, are not unlimited"; indeed, the power of reason, "though looking before and after, is bounded in its vision by an horizon; and Eloquence herself best performs her appropriate office by silence upon exhausted topics."[4] Upon the bonds of national union, Adams seldom exhibited either reticence or quiescence in seizing a moral vantage point from which to measure his nation's glory.

Adams readily admitted that the American experiment in self-government is "susceptible of being considered under a great variety of points of view." While the contemplation of its causes "must . . . ever remain the same," the estimation "of its consequences varies from year

---

3. Lippmann, *The Public Philosophy*, 78.
4. John Quincy Adams, *Quincy Oration, 1831*, 5.

to year." Addressing the citizens of Quincy in 1831, on the fifty-fifth anniversary of the Declaration of Independence, Adams reminded his audience that man is both a creature and creator of history. A speaker, on the first anniversary of the Declaration, "had a far different theme from him who now, after the lapse of nearly two generations . . . is called upon to review the progress of [its] principles . . . as their influence has expanded on the mind of civilized man." Adams believed that the test of all principle is time; "that which when first announced as truth, may be treated by the . . . unanimous voice of mankind as pernicious paradox or hateful heresy, [but] when scrutinized . . . and felt in practical results, may become an axiom of knowledge, or an article of uncontroverted faith." Adams cited the example of the astronomer,

> who in his nightly visitation of the heavens perceives a ray of light before unobserved, [yet he] discovers no new phenomenon in nature. He is only the first to discern the beam which has glowed from the creation of the world. After-observations and the calculations of science will disclose whether it proceeded from a star fixed in the firmament from the birth of time, from a planet revolving around the central luminary of our system, or from a comet, "shaking from its horrid hair, pestilence and war."[5]

The Declaration of Independence, a "manifesto to the world," was the work of "delegates of thirteen distinct, but UNITED colonies of Great Britain, in the name and behalf of their people." It was a united declaration. Their union preceded their independence. The language of the document states, "We the Representatives of the *United* States of America, in General Congress assembled, do, in the name and authority of the good people of these Colonies, solemnly publish and declare that these *United Colonies*, are, and of right ought to be, free and independent States." This affirmation was the act of one people. The colonies are not named, and their number is not designated. Moreover, no indication is provided as to "which of the colonies any one of the fifty-six delegates by whom it was signed had been deputed." The signers "announced their constituents to the world as one people, and

5. Ibid., 6.

unitedly declared the Colonies to which they . . . belonged, united, free and independent states." The Declaration was much more than a proclamation to the world that the colonies had ceased to be a colonial dependency of Britain; these united people, Adams said, "had bound themselves, before God, to a primitive social compact of union, freedom and independence."[6]

The motive for the Declaration was avowed to be a decent respect for the opinions of mankind; its purpose was to declare the causes that led the people of the English colonies to separate themselves from Britain. The causes of separation enumerated by the colonists were followed by "their assumption of the separate and equal station to which the laws of nature and of nature's God entitle them among the powers of the earth." Preliminary to indexing the "history of repeated injuries and usurpations" under George III, Jefferson paid tribute to the self-evident character of universal human rights. The first movement of the American Revolutionists began with an appeal to natural law "for their *right* to assume the attributes of sovereign power as an independent nation."

> The causes of their *necessary* separation . . . alleged in the Declaration, are all founded on the same laws of nature and of nature's God—and hence as preliminary to the enumeration of the causes of separation, they set forth as self-evident truths, the rights of individual man . . . to life, to liberty, to the pursuit of happiness. That all men are created *equal*. That to *secure* the rights of life, liberty and the pursuits of happiness, governments are instituted among men, deriving their *just* powers from the *consent* of the governed.[7]

Natural law "presupposes the existence of a God, the moral ruler of the universe, and a rule of right and wrong, of just and unjust binding upon man; preceding all institutions of human society and of government."[8] Government, then, is instituted to secure these rights of nature

6. John Quincy Adams, *July 4, 1793 Oration*, 12–13; *Quincy Oration, 1831*, 6–7.
7. John Quincy Adams, "The Nature of Federal Government," 79; John Quincy Adams, *The Jubilee of the Constitution*, 13.
8. Adams, *Jubilee of the Constitution*, 14.

and may be altered or abolished whenever any form of government becomes destructive of these ends.

The Declaration acknowledged that the united colonies were free and independent states, "but not that any one of them was a free and independent state, separate from the rest." Adams defended the case for a federal union by citing the analogous language contained in the state constitution for the Commonwealth of Massachusetts. Here it is declared that the body politic is formed by a voluntary association of individuals; "that it is a social compact, by which the whole people covenants with each citizen, and each citizen with the whole people, that all shall be governed by . . . laws, for the common good." Likewise, the body politic of the United States was formed "by the voluntary association of the people of the United Colonies." The Declaration was a "social compact, by which the whole people covenanted with each citizen of the United Colonies, and [where] the United Colonies were, and of right ought to be, free and independent states." In such a compact, union was as vital as freedom or independence. From the moment of signing, no state could, without violation of that primitive contract, secede or separate from the rest. Each was pledged to all, and all were pledged to each "by a concert of souls, without limitation of time, in the presence of Almighty God, and proclaimed to all mankind." Adams pointed out that the colonies were not declared sovereign states; in fact, the term *sovereign* is not to be found in the Declaration. Far removed "was it from the contemplation of those who composed . . . it, to constitute either the aggregate community, or any one of its members, with . . . uncontrollable despotic power." This united sovereignty could not be reconciled with the absolute sovereignty of the separate states.

> That were to make
> Strange contradiction, which to God himself
> Impossible is held, as argument
> Of weakness, not of power.[9]

These were united, free, and independent states. All three properties were equally essential to their existence. Without union, "the covenant

9. *The Portable Milton*, ed. Douglas Bush, 492–93.

contains no pledge of freedom or independence; without freedom, none of independence or union; without independence, none of union or freedom."[10]

Adams had little patience for those who protested that the philosophy embodied in the Declaration "deals too much in abstractions." Rather this was precisely its characteristic excellence, for upon those universal norms resided the justice of the nation's cause. Without them, the American Revolution would have been but one more successful rebellion.

> The Divinity that stirs within the soul of man is abstraction. The Creator of the universe is a spirit, and all spiritual nature is abstraction. Happy would it be, could we answer with equal confidence another objection, not to the Declaration, but to the consistency of the people by whom it was proclaimed! Thrice happy, could the appeal to the Supreme Judge of the World for rectitude of intention . . . have been [if] accompanied with an appeal equally bold to our own social institutions to illustrate the self-evident truths which are declared.[11]

The Declaration, then, was not an announcement of liberty "newly acquired, nor was it a form of government." Colonial Americans were already free, and their forms of government were various. The people of the colonies, speaking through their representatives, constituted themselves one moral person before the face of their fellow man. According to Adams, "Frederick I, of Brandenburg, constituted himself King of Prussia by putting a crown upon his own head. Napoleon Bonaparte invested his brows with the iron crown of Lombardy, and declared himself King of Italy. The Declaration of Independence was the crown with which the people of United America, rising . . . as one man, encircled their brows, and there it remains." The Founders recognized the "laws of nations, as they were observed and practiced among Christian communities"; they considered the state of nature between nations as a state of peace, and, as a necessary consequence, that the

10. John Quincy Adams, *Newburyport Oration, 1837*, 24–25; *Quincy Oration, 1831*, 17–18.

11. Adams, *Quincy Oration, 1831*, 19.

new confederacy was at peace with all other nations, Great Britain excepted.[12]

Adams wrote on several occasions about the significance of America's revolutionary mission as it grew out of, and in some respects departed from, the heritage of civil and political liberties of the British nation. America's struggle was for "chartered rights—for English liberties—for the causes of Algernon Sidney and John Hampden—for trial by jury—the Habeas Corpus and Magna Charta." The civil wars of Britain in the seventeenth century "had been the result of a long and sanguinary conflict between the primary principles of human authority and human freedom." During the Hundred Years' War (1337–1453) with France, England became "the theatre of desolating civil wars upon a question in the theory of government, as insignificant to the people of the realm, as if it had been upon the merits of the badges respectively assumed by the parties to the strife." The question between the Houses of York and Lancaster—antagonists in the Wars of the Roses (1455–1485)—was "whether upon the death of a King of England, childless, the right to the crown devolved upon the son of a brother, previously deceased, but who had been next to himself by birth, or to his surviving younger brother." In this crisis, the British people "had abstracted from the personal qualities of the pretenders to the crown, no more interest than in the dissensions in the kingdom of Lilliput on the question [of] whether an egg should be broken at the big or at the little end." Yet the subsequent revolutions by which the House of Hanover supplanted that of the House of Stuart "were of a very different character."[13]

The English Civil War, culminating in the regicide of Charles I in 1649, was not about who had the right *to* the throne, but what were the rights *of* the throne. The matter could not be resolved without a reckoning of "the lawful extent of power" in the crown; the extent of obligation "upon the people to yield obedience to him"; the extent to which the people's "right and duty to defend themselves" can be sub-

12. Ibid., 20; Quincy, *Life of John Quincy Adams*, 336–39; *Newburyport Oration, 1837*, 17.

13. Adams, *Quincy Oration, 1831*, 8.

stantiated against royal encroachments; and the extent to which "just and lawful" remedies may be produced against abuses of royal authority. Adams believed that the issue of ultimate political authority in the British political system involved the struggle between right and might, between liberty and power. Philosophers and moralists alike have identified few other issues for which "war becomes the most imperious of human obligations, and the field of battle the sublimest theatre of heroic martyrdom and patriotic achievement." James II was exiled to France in 1688, and the British nation construed his flight as a voluntary abdication of power. This he had done *"by breaking the original contract between king and the people."* With the accession to the throne in 1689 of William III and Mary II, "it had been settled . . . that the supreme powers of government, under their political constitution, were possessed and exercised by virtue of an original contract with the people."[14]

The charters of the thirteen colonies were also original contracts between the king and the people to whom they had been granted. By both long usage and common consent, this right became an acknowledged attribute of colonizing power; and in Great Britain, this was "a royal prerogative in which the Parliament had no agency." Adams alluded to an English chancellor of the exchequer, Charles Townshend, who "undertook to perform by an act of Parliament, that which he did not dare to attempt by the mere authority of the king." Legal experts "ascertained, since the days of John Hampden and ship-money, that the royal authority, however competent to the grant of charters, did not extend to the arbitrary levy of money by taxation." The privileges of British subjects extended to the principle that no portion of their property could be confiscated but by an authority in which they were represented. This was also the principle to which American colonists appealed in their resistance against the Stamp and Tea Acts of 1765 and 1773. It was not, Adams said, the burden of the taxes to which they objected; rather, "it was to the inherent servitude of the principle." With the passage of time, the ministers of George III prevailed upon

14. Bernard Schwartz, *The Great Rights of Mankind*, 21–23, 32, 43–44, 170; Adams, *Quincy Oration, 1831*, 10.

Parliament "to repeal the tax but, at the same time, to *declare* their right to make laws for the colonies in all cases whatsoever." The taxation dispute, and the naked issue of power that arose with the Coercive Acts of 1774, brought about a dramatic showdown. "The dye is now cast," wrote George III to Lord North. "The Colonies must either submit or triumph." Dr. Samuel Johnson, in a controversial essay on the split between Britain and her colonies, laid down the principles behind British rule:

> All government is essentially absolute. That in *sovereignty* there are no gradations. That there may be limited royalty; there may be limited consulship; but there can be no limited government. There must in every society be some power or other from which there is no appeal; which admits no restrictions; which pervades the whole mass of the community; regulates and adjusts all subordinations; enacts laws or repeals them; erects or annuls judicatures; extends or contracts privileges; exempts itself from questions or control; and bounded only by physical necessity.[15]

Adams saw in Parliament's declaration of right the semblance of a mere declaration of power. Parliament's claim was founded upon an erroneous first principle of government, one that was still "very far from being eradicated even at this day, in our own . . . country." No better authority could be found to substantiate the power of Parliament than "the great commentator upon the laws of England." In the words of William Blackstone: "There is, and must be, in all forms of government, however they began, or by what right . . . they subsist, a supreme, irresistible, absolute . . . authority, in which the *jura summi imperii* or the rights of sovereignty, reside." In treating the power of Parliament, he adds, "This is the place where that absolute despotic power which must in all governments reside somewhere, is entrusted by the constitution of the British kingdoms." Adams found Blackstone guilty of offering a false definition of sovereignty, as well as an erroneous estimate of the extent of sovereign power.

15. John Quincy Adams, *The New England Confederacy of 1643*, 22–23; *Oration of July 4, 1793*, 10–11; Samuel Johnson, "Taxation No Tyranny," 10:423.

It is not true that there *must* be in all governments an absolute, uncontrolled, irresistible, and despotic power: nor is such power in any manner essential to sovereignty. The direct converse of the proposition is true. Uncontrollable power exists in no government upon earth. The sternist despotisms, in every region and . . . age of the world, are and have been under perpetual control; compelled, as Burke expresses it, to truckle and huckster. Unlimited power belongs not to the nature of man; and rotten will be the foundation of every government leaning upon such a maxim for its support.[16]

In addition, Blackstone's contention was incompatible with principles of natural right. Adams cited the analogous example of defending the right to life. The birth of an infant carries a right to the life, which it has received from the Creator. He acknowledged that ethicists have sometimes denied that this right can be forfeited to human laws, even by the commission of a crime. Without concurring in that sentiment, Adams affirmed that no combination of human beings "has the power . . . not the physical but the moral power, to take a life not so forfeited, unless in self-defence or by the laws of war." No power in government exists to take it without a cause; "none, surely none, in the British Parliament." It mattered little to the substance of the argument that governments have exercised and do exercise this power. The law of nature cited in the Declaration of Independence was a judgment upon the arbitrary and destructive will of men. American statesmen held to the self-evident truth, that the right of life is the first of the unalienable rights of man, and "to *secure,* and not to destroy that [for] which, governments are instituted among men." The sovereignty that arrogates to itself unlimited power "must appeal for its sanction to those illustrious expounders of human rights, Pharaoh of Egypt, and Herod the Great of Judea."[17]

John Selden, during the Petition of Right debate in the House of Commons in 1628, elaborated the ancient maxim in a way the American founders would later approve when he asserted: "*Salus populi suprema lex, et libertas popula summa salus populi*" (the welfare of the

16. Bernard Bailyn, *The Ideological Origins of the American Revolution*, 201–2; Adams, *Quincy Oration, 1831*, 12.
17. Adams, *Quincy Oration, 1831*, 13–14.

people is the supreme law, and the liberty of the people the greatest welfare of the people).[18] Statesmanship consisted in bringing man-made law into harmony with natural law. Reason must be left free to test the validity of all political policies, to set aside superstition, and to measure the artful contrivances of princes and courtiers. Only a political structure based on consent and agreement could leave reason free to correct the errors of the past and open the way for a bright new future.

Even after the promulgation of the Stamp Act, the independence of the colonies from Great Britain "was neither pretended nor contemplated by the great body of the people." In their emigration from Europe, the early American settlers reflected on the rights to which they would be entitled in the land of their new habituation, in addition to the obligations by which they would be bound to the land of their nativity.

> The first of the reasons assigned by the parties to the New England Confederacy for their *consociation*, is . . . to advance the kingdom of . . . Christ *and* to enjoy the liberties of the Gospel in *purity, with peace.* This purpose was twofold and necessarily imported a system of national policy—the propagation of the Gospel bearing upon their relations with the natives of the country—and the enjoyment of their religious liberties, resulting from their domestic relations among themselves, and their dependent condition on their sovereign and their country beyond the seas.[19]

Even David Hume, "the Atheist Jacobite, at once their reviler and their eulogist, acknowledges [the Puritans] to have been the . . . exclusive founders of all the freedom of the British islands." The reciprocal influence of liberty and obligation did not contravene the relations "between a parent state and her colonies . . . founded upon the laws of nature and nations, modified by the civil institution of the colonizing state." History teaches that the administration of human affairs often nurtures a "reluctance at recurring to the first principles of government." Practical men are "apt to entertain the opinion that they have

---

18. Sandoz, *A Government of Laws*, 197.
19. Adams, *New England Confederacy*, 43.

little influence upon the conduct of nations, and theoretic men are often wild and fanciful in their application of [those principles]." Yet the passage of time made it unlikely that the sentiment of local patriotism among the original inhabitants would sustain grateful allegiance to a sovereign beyond the seas, changing in succession from a "Stuart to a Commonwealth, from a Commonwealth back to a Stuart, then to a William of Orange, to the wife of a Prince of Denmark, and finally to a family . . . of Germany." Adams cited the Scottish poet Robert Burns, who in colloquy with himself exclaimed, "This is my own, my native land." But to what land would this exclamation have applied "upon the lips of Carver and Bradford, of Endicott and Winthrop?" America's colonial dependence, "suffered to enjoy the rights of Englishmen," was truncated when—in violation of those rights—Parliament "declared its own right to make laws for them in all cases . . . and undertook to give effect to this declaration by taxation." Americans were subjected to "a dependence [on] parchments and of proclamations, unsanctioned by the laws of nature [and] disavowed by the dictates of reason."[20]

II.

The Articles of Confederation were an abortive experiment created through the cooperation of Congress with the state legislatures, "without recurrence to the fountain of power, the people." This error "prostituted the faith and energy of the nation in peace" and became "a source of impotence in . . . the relations of the country with foreign powers." Unable to enact necessary taxes, generate revenue, or regulate commerce and industry, this confederal system "disabled the nation from the performance of its engagements to others, and from the means of exacting the fulfillment of theirs in return." The Second Article provides, "Each state retains its sovereignty, freedom and independence, and every power, jurisdiction and right, which is not by this confederation expressly delegated to the United States, in Congress

20. John Quincy Adams and Charles Francis Adams, *The Life of John Adams* 17–18; *Quincy Oration, 1831*, 15–16.

assembled." Adams saw in this provision a departure from both the language and guiding principles of the Declaration. Where, he asked, did each state get the sovereignty that it retains? The delegates at the Continental Congress in 1776 declared the "United Colonies" free and independent states. Not sovereign states—but the people alone—were the rightful source of all legitimate government. Certainly the people of each colony had not conferred sovereignty on each free and independent state, "nor could they . . . declare it, because each was already bound in union with all the rest; a union formed *de facto*, by the spontaneous revolutionary movement of the whole people, and organized by the meeting of the first Congress in 1774." Adams likened the articles—ratified on March 1, 1781—to "the statue of Pygmalion before its animation,—beautiful and lifeless." He wrote, "The articles of confederation [are] stamped with the features of contention; beginning with niggardly reservations of corporate rights, and [also] in the grant of powers, seeming to have fallen into the frame of mind described by the sentimental traveller, bargaining for a post chaise, and viewing his conventionist with an eye as if he was going with him to fight a duel!"[21]

The primary cause for these misfortunes, Adams suggested, lies in the same mistaken estimate of sovereignty that the British Parliament had made in undertaking to levy taxes upon the colonies. This "political sophism," finding an identity between sovereign and despotic power, had as "its offspring . . . the doctrine of nullification—i.e., the sovereign power of any one state of the confederacy to nullify any act of the whole twenty-four states [as of 1831], which the . . . state shall please to consider as unconstitutional." Adams later saw in nullification an effort to organize insurrection against the laws of the United States; "to interpose the arm of state sovereignty between rebellion and the halter; and to rescue the traitor from the gibbet." His break with the Federalist party was facilitated by his belief that members of that party had laid plans for a rebellion by state authority against the government of the nation. Learning that William Plumer, senator from New Hampshire,

21. Adams, *Jubilee of the Constitution*, 19–20; Adams, *Newburyport Oration, 1837*, 40–41, 43.

intended to write a history of the United States, he encouraged him to teach the doctrine of the indissolubility of the union. Although a state could not be punished for treason, "nullification cases herself in the complete steel of sovereign power." Three decades prior to the Civil War, when "the paroxysm of this fever [had] hitherto proved not extensively contagious," Adams recoiled in the warning of Francis Bacon, "not to measure the discontentments in the body politic by this"—that is, "whether they be just or unjust; nor yet by this, whether the griefs whereupon they rise, be great or small—neither to be secure, because they have been often or long, without ensuing peril. Not every fume or vapor turns indeed to a storm, but from vapors and exhortations imperceptibly gathered, the tempest of dissolution does come at last."[22]

Adams turned to a biblical parable to illumine the threat of disunion and war, a disturbing omen on the struggle between state sovereignty and national unity.

> The event of a conflict in arms, between the Union and one of its members . . . would be but an alternative of calamity to all. In the holy records of antiquity, we have two examples of a confederation ruptured by the severance of its members, one of which resulted, after three desperate battles, in the extermination of the seceding tribe. And the victorious people, instead of exulting in shouts of triumph, came to the house of God, and . . . lifted up their voices, and wept sore, and said, —Oh Lord God of Israel *why* is this come to pass in Israel, that there should be today one tribe lacking in Israel? The other was a successful example of resistance against tyrannical taxation, and severed forever the confederacy, the fragments forming separate kingdoms; and from that day their history presents an unbroken series of disastrous alliances, revolts, and rebellions, until both parts of the confederacy sunk into tributary servitude to the nations around them; till the countrymen of David and Solomon hung their harps upon the willows of Babylon, and were totally lost

22. Quincy, *Life of John Quincy Adams*, 181; JQA to Ezekiel Bacon, November 17, 1808, 3:250–51; JQA to Nahum Parker, December 5, 1808, 3:257; JQA to John Adams, July 13, 1812, 4:369–70; JQA to William Plumer, August 16, 1809, 3:340–41; Adams, *Quincy Oration, 1831*, 23.

amidst the multitudes of Chaldean and Assyrian monarchies, "the most despised portion of their slaves."[23]

This alliance of states, from 1781 to 1787, was an attempt "to preserve their sovereignty entire; reluctant to confer power, because power might be abused; and also because they perceived that every grant of power to the confederate body could be made only by the relinquishment of their own." The articles gave liberty to sectionalism. In fact, they symbolize Blackstone's fatal fallacy of unlimited sovereignty. These, Adams said, were errors not of intention, nor even of judgment, so much as of inexperience. The idea of recurring to the people of the union for a constitution "does not appear to have presented itself then to any mind." The result was humiliation and the appearance of great turmoil out of which finally came a "a national Constitution" made by the people "in their original character,"[24] a Constitution to consummate the work begun by the Declaration.

The provisions of the Tenth Amendment to the Constitution testify to the supreme foundation of political authority, "anything in the constitution or laws of any State to the contrary notwithstanding." The amendment declares that the powers not delegated to the United States by the Constitution, nor prohibited by it to the states, are reserved to the states respectively, or to the people. There are powers of government, then, reserved to the people, which never have been delegated either to the United States or to the separate states. Neither the United States nor the states themselves "possess any powers, not delegated to them by the people—by the people of the whole Union to the United States—by the people of each State to that State." Therefore, it followed that the people of each state were incompetent to delegate to the state, any power already delegated by the people of the whole union to the United States. In vain did Adams "search all the Constitutions past or present of the states, for a power to nullify any act of the United States in Congress assembled." The pretence to grant such a power, "under the cabalistic denomination of *sovereignty*, would have been

23. Quincy, *Life of John Quincy Adams*, 250–51.
24. "Publicola No. 4," *Writings*, 1:79–80.

null and void." Nullification had been the vital disease of confederacies from the day when Philip of Macedon obtained a seat among the Amphyctions of Greece.[25]

The Declaration of Independence and the Constitution were founded upon one and the same theory of government, a theory "expounded in the writings of Locke, but . . . never . . . adopted by a great nation in practice." And, language being imperfect, the "extent of powers conferred . . . must in a very great degree depend upon the construction which it [the Constitution] received." There was an authoritative constitutional law that antedated the constitutional document, as, for example, the law upholding the right of petition, which the Constitution confirmed but did not create. While the higher law theory underlying American government commanded bipartisan affirmation, the practitioners of that theory were far from united on how that law shaped the institutions and machinery of a federal system. Alexander Hamilton and Thomas Jefferson were the leading champions of two widely different theories of government. Jefferson, drawn "to the search and contemplation of abstract rights," objected to the initial draft of the basic document "for its supposed tendency to monarchy, and for its omission of a Declaration of Rights." Hamilton, "prompted by a natural temper aspiring to military renown," believed a more energetic national government was necessary; his federalism was wed "to the doctrine of implied powers . . . and to a liberal construction of all grants of power in the Constitution."[26]

The fight for ratification posed difficult questions, "not only in politics but in morals, and questions not less controvertible of constitutional power were . . . involved." The Constitution balanced, one against the other, the fundamental rights of man, the sovereignty of the people, the rule of right and wrong, and responsibility to the supreme ruler of the Universe for the rightful use of power. In suggesting that the Constitution provided a national government complicated with a federation, Adams paid tribute to his father for helping to

25. Adams, *Quincy Oration, 1831*, 26, 34.

26. *Congressional Globe*, 27th Cong., 2nd sess., January 28, 1842, 192; Adams, *Parties in the United States*, 10–11; *Jubilee of the Constitution*, 40–41, 107–8.

establish "the *balance* . . . as the great and fundamental principle of the American Constitution." A charter of limited powers, it set the government of the United States off from those other governments constitutionally enabled to act "gubernativamente." Moreover, on the basis of sound interpretations by Chief Justice John Marshall, the Constitution restrained "the corporate action of States claiming to be Sovereign and Independent." Since the powers under the Constitution were derived from the people, with a Lockean emphasis Adams insisted that they could not be delegated by the government to the states. Thus there existed a great moral bond between the people and the moral entity, the nation, which they had created, a moral bond that could be maintained only by the "heart" and not by "constraint."[27]

Adams joined Jefferson in expressing regret that the Bill of Rights had not been written into the original Constitution; he also asserted that the defect had not been fully remedied by the first ten articles of amendment. Including a provision for personal liberties "would have marked in a more emphatic manner [than the preamble's "We the people of the United States"] the return from the derivative sovereignty of the states, to the constituent sovereignty of the people for the basis of the federal Union." This remedy might have "prevented many delicate and dangerous questions of conflicting jurisdictions" between different levels of government; in addition, it would have supplied an "informing principle" of civil liberties. For example, Adams held that the repressive power of government should be applied only against "actual transgression," that the freedom of the individual or group not be curtailed until it threatens immediately the social order. In a letter to Hyde de Neuville in 1817, Adams wrote, "From the nature of . . . the laws of this [United States] country you will be aware that the repressive powers of the government, in their application to the freedom of individuals, are limited to cases of actual transgression, and do not extend to projects which, however exceptionable in their character, have not matured at least into an attempt or a commencement of execution." Personal liberty was formed upon a right inhering in every

27. JQA to John Adams, 1811, 4:120–21; *Jubilee of the Constitution*, 45, 54; *Lives of James Madison and James Monroe*, 34; Lipsky, *John Quincy Adams*, 215–17.

individual as his own—*Jus Suum*, and not created by government. The defense of such personal liberty—the personal liberty of sailors attacked by "press gangs"—was the cause of the War of 1812. The "sparing delegation and cautious distribution of power" in the American system and "the securities and hedges with which personal civil, political and religious liberty [were] surrounded" served as nowhere else in the world, Adams thought, to protect the individual's possession of such liberty.[28]

Adams doubted "whether a single constitution has been formed in Europe or in South America, without some violence, some admixture of conflicting force in its confection." In ancient mythology, the god of boundaries was the only deity who could not be assuaged by a blood sacrifice; he, too, was the only god who refused to yield his place, even to Jupiter (the supreme God of the ancient Romans). In analogous fashion, Adams conceived of America as the "land-mark, bloodless and immoveable . . . between freedom and force." The ordinary proclamation of righteous principles he knew to be an insufficient safeguard for the liberties enshrined in a republican polity. After all, "myriad constitutions . . . decorated by the ornamental rights of man . . . have passed into the memory of things beyond the flood; leaving the principles behind—blood-stained and defaced—monuments . . . of their own mutilation." The measure of America's success would be seen by the extent to which the traditions of civic virtue would enable public servants to abide by the norms of accountability and lawful rule that such principles presume. While "much good has already been affected by the solemn proclamation of our principles, much more [may come] by the illustration of our example."[29]

Adams turned his attention to the republican virtue of the statesman in order to substantiate an organic connection between human nature and the defense of constitutional rule. The ethical character of the statesman is defined by two qualities, "both developed in his

28. JQA to Hyde de Neuville, September 24, 1817, 2:190; *Jubilee of the Constitution*, 45–46; JQA to James Lloyd, October 1, 1822, 7:311–12; Lipsky, *John Quincy Adams*, 164–65.

29. Adams, *Quincy Oration, 1831*, 33, 38.

intercourse with his fellow creatures and . . . belonging to the immortal part of his nature." These entail broadly the spirit of command and the spirit of meekness. Their ideal combination in perfection was exhibited in the mortal life of Christ; the supernatural character of his earthly example was "a model to teach mortal man . . . what sublime elevation his nature is capable of ascending." They had also been displayed by the preceding legislator of the children of Israel:

> That shepherd, who first taught the chosen seed
> In the beginning, how the heavens and earth
> Rose out of Chaos . . . [30]

These two realms of human action—the dialectic between nature and spirit, necessity and freedom—"belong rather to the moral than the intellectual nature of man." In order to save command and self-assertion from arrogance, and to save meekness and self-sacrifice from weakness, man must be regulated by a profound sense of responsibility to a higher power. This responsibility imposed a duty on the republican statesman to save democratic freedom from mindless mass indulgence, to give expression to objective standards of political conduct that reconcile the will of the majority with the rights of the minority. In the words of one leading political philosopher,

> Liberalism holds certain truths to be self-evident which no majority has the right to abrogate and from which . . . the legitimacy of majority rule derives. . . . It is on this absolute and transcendent foundation that the philosophy of genuine democracy rests, and it is within this immutable framework that the processes of genuine democracy take place. The pluralism of these processes is subordinated to, and oriented toward, those absolute truths.[31]

Adams pointed to important conceptual distinctions in calling for objective political standards to regulate the performance of republican and even democratic institutions. He meant "by democratic, a government the administration of which must always be rendered comfort-

---

30. Adams, *Jubilee of the Constitution*, 51–52.
31. Morgenthau, *The Purpose of American Politics*, 252; Adams, *Jubilee of the Constitution*, 53.

able to that predominating public opinion." America's government was not based upon the virtues or power of any one man—or "upon that *honour* which Montesquieu lays down as the . . . principle of monarchy," or "upon that *fear* which he pronounces [as] the basis of despotism"—but rather "upon that *virtue* which he . . . proclaims as a fundamental principle of republican government." Although conceding that the Constitution "was republican and democratic," Adams learned from Thucydides and Aristotle that democracy was the most unstable and short-lived form of rule. If virtue—the virtue of the people—was the foundation for republican government, then "the stability and duration of the government must depend upon the stability and duration of the virtue by which it is sustained." Virtue did not consist of one single substantive ideal or doctrine; on the contrary, it rested upon self-evident truths, rational and moral, from which society derived whatever truth was to be found in its thought and action. The relativism of majority rule—denying the existence of absolute, transcendent truth independent of the majority will—tends toward the immanent absolutism of a tyrannical majority, while the pluralism of genuine democracy assumes as its corollary the existence of such truth limiting the will of the majority. What Adams characterized as the "moral platform" of the Constitution was nothing other than those virtues that enable man to rely upon objective standards of universal validity to protect individual freedom while upholding the general welfare. The administration of republican government "must . . . be always pliable to the fluctuating varieties of public opinion"; at the same time, however, the stability of constitutional rule depends upon the "duration in the hearts and minds of the people of that *virtue*, or in other words, of those principles proclaimed in the Declaration . . . and embodied in the Constitution of the United States."[32]

III.

Among the most powerful sentiments operating "upon the human heart, and . . . honorable to the human character, are those of venera-

---

32. Adams, *Quincy Oration, 1831,* 54.

tion for our forefathers, and of love for our posterity." John Quincy Adams described them as the connecting links between the selfish and social passions. The precepts of Christianity, for example, establish the happiness of the individual on the basis of "innumerable and imperceptible ties" that bind man's destiny with that of his contemporaries; "by the power of filial reverence and parental affection, individual existence is extended beyond the limits of individual life, and the happiness of every age is chained in mutual dependence upon that of every other." Respect for ancestors "excites in the breast of man, interest in their history, attachment to their characters, concern for their errors, involuntary pride in their virtues." Posterity stimulates man to virtue by imitation of their example, and "fills him with the tenderest solicitude for their welfare." Man, Adams thought, was not made for himself alone; he was also made for his country by the obligations of the social compact. Under the influence of these principles, "existence sees him spurn her bounded reign." The voice of history redeems his physical nature from the subjection of time and place. No longer a "puny insect shivering at a breeze," the human soul "is the glory of creation—form'd to occupy all time and all extent: bounded during his residence upon earth, only by the boundaries of the world, and destined to life and immortality in brighter regions, when the fabric of nature itself shall dissolve and perish."[33]

Tacitus, in *Vita Agricolae*, records the battle address of the barbarian chieftain who, driven to a remote part of Britain, defended his country against the Roman invasion. Galgacus concludes the exhortation to his followers by a solemn appeal to these irresistible feelings—"*Proinde ituri in aciem, et majores vestros et posteros cogitate*" (Think of your forefathers and of your posterity). Celebrations of posterity are a pledge of respect we bear to the memory of our ancestors and "are . . . testimonials of our gratitude, and schools of virtue to our children." Cultivation of these sentiments—the formation of moral character—in civic education is less innocent pleasure and more "incumbent duty."[34]

33. John Quincy Adams, *Plymouth Oration*, 5–6.
34. Ibid., 28.

From the first discovery of the Western Hemisphere by Columbus, until the settlement of Virginia, most of the expeditions to the New World "were . . . instigated by personal interests—Avarice and ambition had turned their souls to that pitch of exaltation." Selfish passions were the parents of their heroism, "that ardor of enterprise and stubbornness of pursuit, which set all danger at defiance and chain the violence of nature at their feet." It remained for the first settlers of New England "to trample down obstructions equally formidable . . . under the single inspiration of conscience." Alluding to the history of the Plymouth settlers, Adams explained the execution of that instrument of government by which they formed themselves into a body politic. The process was the result of "circumstances and discussions" that transpired both before and after the first landing upon the American coast. Plymouth Colony stood out as a rare instance in human history "of that positive, original social compact, which speculative philosophers have imagined as the only legitimate source of government." Here was an example of that unanimous and personal assent "by all the individuals of the community, to the association by which they became a nation." The compact was a convincing "demonstration that the nature of civil government, abstracted from the political institutions of their native country, had been an object of their serious meditation." After twelve years of exile from England, the followers of John Robinson and William Brewster were "led to reflect upon the relative rights and duties of allegiance and subjection."[35]

The odyssey of the English Pilgrims from 1608 until 1620, particularly the intellectual ferment to which they were exposed in relocating to Amsterdam and Leyden, testified to the pursuit of order and liberty in the political existence of a free people. During this period, and after their separation from the crown of Spain, the people of the United Province witnessed a deadly struggle between two parties. "The contest embraced within its compass not only theological doctrines, but political principles, and *Maurice* and *Barnevelt* were the temporal leaders of the same rival factions, of which *Episcopius* and *Polyander*, were

35. Adams and Adams, *The Life of John Adams*, 20–21; Adams, *Boston Oration of July 4, 1793*, 12–13.

the ecclesiastical champions." That fundamental principles were deeply embedded in these dissensions was "evident from the immortal work of *Grotius*, upon the rights of war and peace, which . . . originated from them." Not only was Grotius "a most distinguished actor and sufferer in those important scenes of internal convulsion," but his *On the Law of War and Peace* (1625) "was first published very shortly after the departure of our forefathers from Leyden." Adams also cited passages from William Bradford's *Of Plymouth Plantation* (e.g., his account of how "Mr. *Robinson* more than once appeared . . . as a public disputant against *Episcopius*") to illustrate that "the whole English church at Leyden took a zealous interest in the religious part of the controversy."[36]

Although the Puritans wisely avoided entanglement in the political contentions of the upheaval, "the theoretic principles . . . could not fail to arrest their attention, and must have assisted them to form accurate ideas concerning the origin and extent of authority among men, independent of positive institutions." For Adams, the importance of these circumstances had to be weighed in the context of the state of opinions then prevalent in Britain. The whole substance of human authority was centered in the simple doctrine of royal prerogative, the origin of which was always traced in theory to divine institution. Only twenty years later, and for a half century thereafter, "the subject . . . became one of the principle topics of controversy between the ablest and most enlightened men in the nation." The instrument of voluntary association "executed on board the *Mayflower*, testifies that the parties to it had anticipated the improvement of their nation." In this sense, the social compact was formed "by a foreseeing and directing mind." In his *History of America*, William Robertson, the Irish historian, traced this pervasive mindset back to the Puritan settlers of Plymouth and of Massachusetts Bay.

From the first institution of the Company of Massachusetts Bay, its members seem to have been animated by a spirit of innovation in

36. See, for example, *Bradford's History of Plymouth Plantation, 1606–1646*, ed. William T. Davis; Adams, *Plymouth Oration*, 18–19.

civil policy as well as in religion; and by the habit of rejecting established usages in the one, they were prepared for deviating from them
in another. They . . . applied for a royal charter, in order to give effect
to their . . . acts of a body politic; but the persons whom they sent out
to America . . . considered themselves as individuals, united together
by voluntary association, possessing the natural right of men who
form a society to adopt what mode of government and to enact what
laws they deemed most conducive to general felicity.[37]

The social compact draws attention to the revolutionary sphere of
political action within which institutional safeguards protect and defend the character of public—as opposed to private—freedom.

Even at this point, the difference between the Europeans and the
Americans, whose minds were still influenced by an almost identical
tradition, is conspicuous and important. Americans believed that public freedom consisted in having a share of public business, and that the
activities connected with this business by no means constituted a
burden but gave those who discharged them in public a feeling of
happiness they could acquire nowhere else. Citizens were brought together (in James Harrington's words) by "the world and the public
interest of liberty," and what moved them was "the passion for distinction" that John Adams held to be "more essential and remarkable"
than any other human faculty: "Wherever men, women, or children,
are to be found, whether they be old or young, rich or poor, high or
low, wise or foolish, ignorant or learned, every individual is seen to be
strongly actuated by a desire to be seen, heard, talked of, approved and
respected by the people about him, and within his knowledge." The
virtue of this passion Adams called "emulation"; its vice, the desire to
excel another, he called "ambition" because it "aims at power as a
means of distinction." And, psychologically speaking, these are the
chief virtues and vices of political man. For the thirst and will to
power, regardless of any passion for distinction, though characteristic
of the tyrannical man, is no longer a typically political vice; rather, it
becomes that quality which destroys all political life, its vices no less
than its virtues. Lacking all passion for distinction, the tyrant has no

---

37. John Quincy Adams, *Lives of Celebrated Statesmen*, 12–13.

desire to excel and finds it congenial to rise above the company of all men; conversely, it is the very desire to excel that makes men love the world and enjoy the company of their peers, and drives them into public business.[38]

Another occasion for important reflections was the attempt by the original settlers to establish "that community of goods and of labor which fanciful politicians, from the days of *Plato* to . . . *Rousseau*, have recommended as the fundamental law of a perfect republic." Adams viewed this theory as the byproduct of reasoning most flattering to the human character.

> If industry, frugality, and disinterested integrity, were alike the virtues of all, there would apparently be more of a social spirit, in making all property a common stock, and giving to each individual a proportional title to the wealth of the whole. Such is the basis upon which *Plato* forbids in his republic the division of property. Such is the system upon which *Rousseau* pronounces the first men who enclosed a field with a fence and said *this is mine*, a traitor to the human species.[39]

Adams took exception with this austere idealism and emphasized that "a wiser and more useful philosophy" would treat man "according to the nature in which he was formed." Man's capacity for virtue and self-transcendence cannot be understood at all if a capacity for, and inclination toward, evil in man himself is not presupposed. We are, as Adams knew, in the presence of an anxious being "subject to infirmities, which no wisdom can remedy; to weaknesses which no institution can strengthen; to vices which no legislation can correct." A similar message can be found in Psalms 8:4, "When I consider thy heavens, the work of thy fingers, the moon and the stars, which thou hast ordained; What is man that thou art mindful of him?" The vantage point from which man judges his insignificance is a rather significant vantage point. This fact, according to theologian Reinhold Niebuhr, has not been lost on modern thinkers whose modesty before the cosmic immensity was

---

38. "Discourses on Davila," in *Works of John Adams*, 6:232–33; Hannah Arendt, *On Revolution*, 119–20.

39. Adams, *Plymouth Oration*, 21.

modified considerably by pride in their discovery of this immensity. It
was a modern, the poet Swinburne, who sang triumphantly:

> The seal of his knowledge is sure, the truth and his
> spirit are wed: . . .
> Glory to Man in the highest! For man is the master of
> things,[40]

thereby proving that the advance of human knowledge about the world
does not abate the pride of man. Adams recognized that the creative
and destructive possibilities of human history are inextricably intermingled. The very power which organizes society and establishes justice, also generates injustice by its preponderance of power.

Adams's estimate of the human condition led him to conclude "that
separate property is the natural and indisputable right of separate
exertion—that community of goods without community of toil is
oppressive and unjust." It counteracts the laws of nature, "which prescribe . . . that he only who sows the seed shall reap the harvest."
Communalism, therefore, discourages all energy by destroying its rewards; it also makes the most virtuous and active members of society
the slaves and drudges of the worst. The philosophical error of this
system was "demonstrated by the experiment among our [puritan]
forefathers." To base principles of government upon "too advanta-
geous an estimate of the human character [was] an error of inexperience, the source of which is so amiable, that it is impossible to
censure it with severity." While the early Pilgrims were able to relin-
quish a communal dream "upon discovering its irremediable inef-
ficacy," the excesses of the French Revolution pointed to "the same
mistake, committed in our own age, and upon a larger theatre." Napoleon was the product of a social catastrophe that shredded the whole
social fabric in disregard of moral law. Adams saw clearly that, without
a moral restraint on the portentous anarchy of the French masses, the
result of the revolution would be a "military government, by turns
anarchical and despotic," itself unconfined by moral restraint, even
though clothed with democratic forms. The first Americans "had no

40. Reinhold Niebuhr, *The Nature and Destiny of Man*, 1:3.

pride of vain philosophy to support, no perfidious rage of faction to glut, by persevering in their mistakes until they should be extinguished in torrents of blood."[41]

IV.

John Quincy Adams began a biography of his father's life by documenting the historical and religious traditions that defined his own intellectual heritage, as much as the civic culture of the early New England settlers. There was nothing that so clearly characterized the "Puritan founders . . . as their institutions for the education of youth." It did not escape Adams's attention that many of the prodigious changes heralded by the Reformation began in the universities. "[John] Wickliffe, John Huss, Jerome of Prague, and Luther, all promulgated their doctrines first from the bosom of universities." Moreover, the debate between the Protestant reformers and the Church of Rome was essentially a struggle between liberty and power; "between submission to the dictates of other men and the free exercise of individual faculties." Universities were centers of Christianity, "the original ideal of which may . . . have been adopted from the schools of the Grecian sophists and philosophers, but which were essential improvements upon them." Against the authority of Rome, "founded upon the abstract principle of power," the Reformation, "in all its modifications, was founded upon the principle of liberty." Even the Bishop of Rome, as the successor of Saint Peter, is "yet compelled to rest upon human reason for the foundation of faith itself." Similarly, the Protestant churches, while acknowledging the Scriptures alone as the rule of faith, universally recur to human authority for prescribing bounds to that freedom.

> It was in universities only that this . . . question between liberty and power could be debated . . . in all its bearings upon human agency. It enters into the profoundest recesses of metaphysical science; it mingles itself with the most important principles of morals. Now the . . . metaphysics of the universities were formed from the school of Aris-

41. John Quincy Adams, *Eulogy on Lafayette,* 16–17; JQA to Abigail Adams, May 12, 1814, 5:43; JQA to John Adams, September 21, 1797, 2:215–16.

totle . . . [he being] perhaps . . . the acutest intellect that ever appeared in the form of man. In that school, it was not difficult to find a syllogism . . . to demolish all human authority usurping the power to prescribe articles of religious faith, but not to erect a substitute for human authority in the mind of every individual.[42]

The principal achievement of the Reformation, then, was to substitute one form of human authority for another. The followers of "Luther, of Calvin, of John Knox, and of [Thomas] Cranmer, while renouncing . . . the supremacy of the Romish Church and the Pope, terminated their labors in the establishment of other supremacies in its stead." The community of Puritans saw that, among all the Protestant reformers, the Church of England departed least from the principles, and retained most of the practices, of the Church of Rome. The king substituted for the pope as head of the Church; the Parliament, in regulating the faith of the people, performed the office of the ecclesiastical councils. Adams cited numerous examples of how, in England, the progress of the Reformation was entangled with both state affairs and the personal caprices of the monarch. Henry VIII, while earning the pious gratitude of Pope Leo X (son of Lorenzo de Medici) for his censure of Luther, "quickly learned from his angelic doctor, Thomas Aquinas, that the infallibility of the Pope could not legitimate his marriage with his brother's widow." Mary, the daughter of Catherine of Aragon, "restored the papal authority in all its despotism; and Elizabeth, the daughter of Anne Boleyn, restored again the Protestant supremacy upon the ruin of the triple tiara." The principles of Elizabeth were "not less arbitrary than those of her father." Her Stuart successors, James I and Charles I, continued to countenance the Reformation just so far as its progress "contributed to the . . . extension of their own temporal power, and to resist . . . every step . . . to restore to its pristine purity and simplicity the religion of the meek and lowly Jesus." But even this "half way reformation," connected with the government of the state and the passions of individuals, still leaned "for its support from human reason upon the learning and intellect of the schools."[43]

42. Adams and Adams, *The Life of John Adams*, 18–19.
43. Ibid., 21–22.

When Henry VIII had exhausted the resources of his temporal power to enlist the aid of the pope in dissolving his marriage with Catherine, his last resort to authority was to the opinions of the universities. Although the academies of learning were sometimes warped by temporal interests and sordid passions, their glory resided in "the studies to which they afford access." Men of learning found little solace "by the expulsion of Locke," or "by the application of the scourge to . . . Milton, yet there it was that Milton and Locke drew the nutriment which made them the pride and glory of their country." For Adams and his Puritan ancestors, the English universities were the "cradles of the New England colonies; and the Reformation was their nursing mother."

> [While] the successive kings and queens of England, with their syco-phant Parliaments . . . could shape and mold the reformation of the law, according to the standard of their politics and . . . vices, they could not so control the march of the mind in the universities. From the moment when the spell of human authority was broken, the right of private judgment resumed its functions; and when the student had been told that the only standard of faith was in the Scriptures, to prescribe creeds upon him under pains and penalties, however reasonable it might appear in White Hall [or] in St. Stephen's Chapel . . . was but inconsistency . . . and tyranny at Cambridge and even at Oxford.[44]

The unavoidable consequence of exercising private judgment is the diversity of faith. Human nature was so constituted, "that in everything relating to religion, different minds reasoning upon the same facts come to different conclusions."[45]

The seminal principle of the New England colonies, therefore, was religious controversy. Adams thought it impossible to set aside all human authority in the formation of religious belief. Faith itself, as defined by St. Paul, is "the substance of things hoped for, the evidence of things not seen." Without an express revelation from heaven, however, the formation of this hope—as well as the belief in the existence

44. Ibid., 24.
45. Ibid.

of this evidence—"come not from the internal operations of the mind, but by tradition from others, by the authority of instruction." To deny human authority in religious matters is tantamount to asserting an abstract principle to which human practice cannot conform. Equally impractical is the imposition of unrestricted control, either secular or spiritual, over the exercise of the faculties of the human mind. In this connection, the younger Adams recalled his father's ranking at Harvard in 1751, placing fourteenth out of a class of twenty-four. At the time, the arrangement of class members was based upon family rank; it was not until the graduating class of 1773 that an alphabetical order was introduced in assigning the names and places of the members of each class. Adams saluted the innovation as an important demonstration of the rising ascendancy of republican principles in the country.

> Orders and degrees
> Jar not with liberty, but well consist.

These were the words of Milton, "who, in all his works, displays a profound and anxious sense of the importance of just subordination."[46]

For John Quincy Adams, the glory of the American Founders was "the gentle temper of Christian kindness—the rigorous observance of reciprocal justice—the unconquerable soul of conscious integrity." Their accomplishment was not in the clarion of conquest, or "colossal statues upon pedestals of human bones, to provoke and insult the tardy hand of heavenly retribution." Worldly fame had "been parsimonious of her favors to the memory of those generous champions," who exhibited "the better fortitude of patience and heroic martyrdom." Such hubris was "that common crier, whose existence is only known by the assemblage of multitudes—That pander of wealth and greatness so eager to haunt the palaces of fortune, and so fastidious to the houseless dignity of virtue—that parasite of pride, ever scornful to meekness, and ever obsequious to insolent power—that heedless trumpeter, whose ears are deaf to modest merit, and whose eyes are blind to bloodless distant excellence." Two principal objectives may guide other genera-

46. Ibid., 17.

tions of American statesmen: to "emulate those qualities of their minds which we . . . find deserving of our admiration"; and to "recognize with candor those features which forbid approbation or even require censure."[47] Adams's realism underscored the importance of taking to our hearts both their frailties and their perfections either as warning or as example.

Adams seldom wavered in his confidence that nature's God intended a progressive improvement in the condition of man. His faith did not permit him to believe that such a transcendent purpose would be disappointed, even if his confidence in God was not always matched by trust in his countrymen. He wished to avoid any delusion of national vanity in holding to the presumption that "our own country and her people have been selected as instruments for preparing . . . much of the good yet in reserve for the welfare . . . of the human race." Adams's tribute to American exceptionalism was a descent into humility, a feeling "of profound gratitude to the God of our Fathers" rather than the complacent certification of national grandeur. He also believed that it was "in the order of the dispensations of Providence to adapt the characters of men to the times in which they live." A life of tranquil ease could hardly define the mission of a new nation, a workshop of liberty, as Madison defined it, through which the great energies of mankind would be displayed. Of the responsibility of the public servant to posterity, Adams wrote,

> Toils and dangers are the trials of the soul. Doomed to the first by his sentence at the fall, man, by submission, converts them into pleasure. . . . To see them in advance . . . to meet them with the composure of unyielding resistance, and to abide with firm resignation the final dispensation of Him who rules the ball,—these are the dictates of philosophy—these are the precepts of religion—these are the principles of . . . patriotism;—these remain when all is lost—and of these is composed the spirit of independence.[48]

He understood that the formulation of the national purpose was often the story of bad theology and absurd metaphysics, of phony

47. Adams, *Plymouth Oration*, 9–12.
48. Adams, *Quincy Oration, 1831*, 39.

theories and vulgar delusions of grandeur. To deny the reality of the national purpose, however, is another matter altogether; it is to fall into the error of logical positivism, which denies the validity of either philosophy or religion because such knowledge is uncertain and subject to abuse. He had little more than contempt for what he termed "political empirics." Yet the heroic symbols and high ideals through which a nation finds meaning are not simply figments of the imagination or artifacts of deception. They express in rational or symbolic terms the reality of an inner experience, which is not less real for not being of the senses. No government, as Madison wrote in *Federalist* #62, "will long be respected without being truly respectable; nor be truly respectable without possessing a certain portion of order and stability." Adams's attachment to American principles, and the moral cement of national union, was echoed by Tobias Smollett in his "Ode To Independence."

> Thy spirit, *Independence*, let me share,
> Lord of the lion heart, and eagle eye!
> Thy steps I follow, with my bosom bare,
> Nor heed the storm that howls along the sky.[49]

Adams used a literary example from Virgil's *Aeneid* to throw into broad relief the political and moral obligations of Americans gathered to celebrate the Jubilee of the Constitution. When the Goddess mother of Æneas supplies the celestial armor with which he is to triumph over his enemy, and thereby lay the foundations for Imperial Rome, he is depicted as gazing with confused delight upon the crested helm that vomits golden fires—

> His hands the fatal sword and corslet hold,
> One keen with temper'd steel—one stiff with gold:
> He shakes the pointed spear, and longs to try
> The plated cuishes on his manly thigh;

---

49. Adams, *Memoirs*, 6:370; Alexander Hamilton, et al., *The Federalist Papers*, 382; *Poetical Works of Johnson, Parnell, Gray and Smollett*, 246.

> But most admires the *shield's* mysterious mould,
> And Roman triumphs rising on the gold—[50]

Adams saw America's dominion rooted in the power of moral restraint rather than in the energies of imperial conquest. The statesmanship of Washington, in contrast to the martial zeal of Æneas, drew strength from its own celestial armor—"a helmet, consisting of the principles of piety, of justice, [and] of honour." Justice encompasses "the whole duty of man in the social institutions of society toward his neighbour." The failings of human nature required that Washington's "spear, studded with the self-evident truths of the Declaration of Independence," be the same "with which he . . . led the armies of his country . . . to the summit of the triumphal arch of independence."[51] Adams hereby affirmed the admixture of persuasion and coercion indispensable for the preservation of individual liberty. His political thought made room for justice and cohesion, each the ultimate guarantor of the other. Only a stable social order could institutionalize justice; only a just social order could avoid disintegration. The statesman's task is not to eschew coercion, but to find the mode of coercion that is least destructive and most redemptive—i.e., most likely to preserve some sense of community within and between nations.

Adams's challenge to his countrymen was no different from the fundamental question posed by the authors of the *Federalist Papers*, "whether societies of men are really capable or not of establishing good government through reflection and choice." Hannah Arendt, one of the few philosophers to give a theoretic interpretation of the problem of the founding of the American republic, noted that "beginning and principle, *principium* and principle, are not only related to each other but are coeval." Drawing on the language of antiquity at the threshold between myth and philosophy, Arendt noticed the philosophical duties of the founding statesman:

> The absolute from which the beginning is to derive its own validity and which must save it . . . from its inherent arbitrariness is the principle which, together with it, makes its appearance in the world.

---

50. *Virgil: The Aeneid*, trans. John Dryden, 247.
51. Adams, *Jubilee of the Constitution*, 80.

> The way the beginner [statesman] starts whatever he intends to do
> lays down the law of action for those who have joined him in order to
> partake in the enterprise to bring about its accomplishment. As such,
> the principle inspires the deeds that are to follow and remains appar-
> ent as long as the action lasts.[52]

A similar inspiration prompted Adams to return to this theme many
years after America achieved independence. Speaking before the citizens of Newburyport in 1837, he suggested that the duties of the future
could not be contemplated apart from the beginning of American
national history. He exhorted his listeners

> to review the principles proclaimed by the founders of your empire;
> to examine what has been their operation upon your own destinies,
> and upon the history of mankind; to scrutinize . . . your condition at
> this day; to compare it with that of your fathers on the day which you
> propose to commemorate [the sixty-first anniversary of the Declara-
> tion of Independence]; and to discern what portion of their princi-
> ples has been retained inviolate,—what portion of them has been
> weakened . . . or abandoned; and what portion of them it is your first
> of duties to retain, to preserve, . . . to transmit to your offspring . . .
> and [to be] transmitted to *their* posterity of unnumbered ages to
> come.[53]

Adams's appeal to civic virtue is couched in the language of classical
politics, of Machiavelli, and of Anglo-Saxon Whiggery. In the *Discourses*, Machiavelli argues that the survival of social order in republics
necessitates bringing them back to their original principles ("ritirarla
spesso verso il su principio"). In Book 3, Machiavelli writes, "It may be
concluded . . . that there is nothing more necessary in a . . . republic
than to restore to it the reputation that it had at its beginnings and to
strive to see that there are either good laws or good men to produce
this effect without . . . resort to external forces." Beginning and principle, as Jürgen Gebhardt explains, are identical in that at the moment of
its founding every society contains a *bontà* "by means of which they

---

52. Cooke, ed. *The Federalist*, 3; Arendt, *On Revolution*, 212–13.
53. Adams, *Newburyport Oration*, 48.

obtain their first growth and reputation."[54] A return to the beginning,
then, means regaining a primary *bontà*, the original content of order
within the founding principles. Article 19 of the Massachusetts state
constitution, for example, reads:

> A frequent recurrence to the fundamental principles of the constitu-
> tion, and a constant adherence to those of piety, justice, moderation,
> temperance, industry, and frugality, are absolutely necessary to pre-
> serve the advantages of liberty, and to maintain a free government.
> The people ought, consequently, to have a particular attention to all
> those principles, in the choice of their officers and representatives,
> and they have a right to require of their lawgivers and magistrates an
> exact and constant observation of them, in the formation of the laws
> necessary for the good administration of the commonwealth.[55]

These principles embrace the civic virtue underlying the formal rules
and institutions of republic government.

Had Adams been permitted to select a name for the party of his
political affiliation, it would have been that of Constitutionalist; "meaning thereby faithful adhesion to the two Constitutions, of the United
States and of the Commonwealth." Both were the work of the people;
one of the Union, the other of the State—"not of the whole people, by
the phantom of universal suffrage, but of the whole people by that
portion of them capable of contracting for the whole." This new experiment in republican government was not "the work . . . of eternal
justice ruling through the people, but of man,—frail, fallen, imperfect
man, following the dictates of his nature and [still] aspiring to perfection." America's constitutional heritage was not to be found in the
politics of democracy, nor of monarchy or aristocracy, "but in a compound of them all, of which democracy is the vital air, too pure in itself
for human respiration, but which, in . . . union with other elements
equally destructive in themselves and less pure, forms the moral and
political atmospheric . . . in which we . . . have our being." But above all

54. *The Portable Machiavelli*, ed. and trans. Peter Bondanella and Mark Musa, 355;
Jürgen Gebhardt, *Americanism, Revolutionary Order and Societal Self-Interpretation in
the American Republic*, 50.
55. John Adams, *Works*, 6:227–28.

else, and even in the heat of party collisions, Adams appealed to a cause embracing and transcending all others

> like the all surrounding orb in the philosophical theory of the learned and ingenious [James] Bowdoin, President of the Convention which formed the Constitution of [the Massachusetts] Commonwealth, which he supposed necessary as a counterbalance to the principle of gravitation, to preserve the system of the material universe from ruin—that cause, before which all party spirit must hide . . . kindling every affection of the heart, and inspiring every faculty of the soul—the cause of *our Country.*[56]

56. Adams, *The Social Compact*, 31–32.

F I V E

Philosophy, Politics,
and Statecraft at the Founding

J ust prior to his twenty-fifth birthday, Adams was catapulted to
the center of the nation's intellectual life with the publication of
his Letters of "Publicola." Eleven of these essays, constituting a
vigorous censure upon Thomas Paine's *Rights of Man*, appeared in the
Columbian Centinel of Boston between June 8 and July 27, 1791. These
papers, inspired by the controversy between Paine and Edmund Burke
concerning the French Revolution, point to Adams's reliance on natural law to illumine the foundations of liberty and defend minority
rights in representative government. As his father had done in his
writings, Adams opposed the extreme views of Paine, while retaining
faith in the American theory of natural rights. Several reasons compel
greater attention to the contours of Adams's early political thought as
an original and farsighted contribution to the heritage of American
statecraft. Adams looked with anticipation to the intellectual foundations upon which French leaders would establish their newly won
liberty. Paine's "encomium upon the National Assembly of France"
called into question American principles of self-governance: consent,
liberty, accountability, human rights, petition, and representation. Finally, Adams recognized that Paine's support for revolutionary principles in domestic affairs would directly touch upon the nation's foreign
obligations. In this connection, Paine was elevating concerns equally

important to all mankind; "and the citizens of the United States are called upon . . . to *rally* around the *standard* of this champion of Revolutions."[1] Precisely how, when, and under what circumstances America was obliged to support revolutionary causes beyond its own borders was a dilemma that Adams wrestled with throughout his career.

I.

Some background details are essential in order to explain the public notice occasioned by the energies of "Publicola." Paine's *Rights of Man*, a response to Burke's *Reflections on the Revolution in France* (1790), appeared in London early in 1791, with a dedication to George Washington. A copy reached John Beckley, clerk of the House of Representatives, and was passed by James Madison to Thomas Jefferson. From him, it reached the printer, with a letter of gratification: "I am extremely pleased to find that it is to be re-printed here, and that something is . . . to be publicly said, against the *political heresies* which have sprung up among us." Writing to John Adams later, Jefferson admitted to "being thunderstruck with seeing it come out at the head of the pamphlet."[2] He hoped it would not attract notice. John Quincy Adams jumped into the fray and was at a loss to determine what Jefferson meant by political heresies. He objected to Paine's treatise as "the canonical truth of political scripture." While Adams expressed no desire to defend the principles of Burke, he averred that Americans

> have not yet established any infallible criterion of *orthodoxy*, either in church or state: their principles in theory, and their habits in practice, are equally averse to that slavery of the mind, which adopts, without examination, any sentiment that has the sanction of a venerable name. *Nullius in verba jurare magistri* is their favorite maxime; and the only political tenet which they would stigmatize with the name of heresy, would be that which should . . . impose an opinion upon their understandings upon the single principle of authority.[3]

1. John Quincy Adams, "Publicola No. 1," *Writings*, 1:65–67.
2. Ibid., 65 n.1.
3. Ibid., 68.

"Nobody doubts here who is the author of Publicola, any more than of Davila," wrote Jefferson to Madison in June 1791. Jefferson was hesitant to accept the disavowal of the Boston editor, that John Adams "has no more concern in the publication of the writings of 'Publicola' than the author of the *Rights of Man* himself." If, he continued, "the equivoque here were not intended, the disavowal is not entirely credited, because not from Mr. Adams himself, and because the stile and sentiments raise so strong a presumption. Besides to produce any effect he must disavow Davila and the *Defence of the American Constitutions*." In July 1791, Madison wrote to Jefferson: "Beckley . . . says . . . that *Publicola* is probably the manufacture of his son out of materials furnished by himself [John Adams], and that the publication is generally as obnoxious in New England as it appears to be in Pennsylvania." Doubting that "the printer would so directly disavow the fact if . . . Adams was himself the writer," Madison found "more of method . . . in the arguments, and much less of clumsiness and heaviness in style" that was the mark of the elder Adams. An exchange of letters on the subject passed between John Adams and Jefferson, but could not entirely do away with a feeling on either side that the publication marked a hostile divergence of political beliefs and a personal participation in furthering newspaper criticisms. Writing two years later, John Adams remarked, "Poor Jay has gone through as fiery an ordeal as I did when I was suspected of a blasphemous doubt of Tom Paine's infallibility, in consequence of *Publicola*'s eloquence and Jefferson's rashness."[4]

The crux of Adams's political debate with Paine grew out of the requirements of human nature—the conditions of individual freedom and just composition of civil authority—that define the legitimate ends of power for republican government. In his "miscellaneous" chapter, Paine observed that "when a man in a long course attempts to steer his course by anything else than some *polar truth or principle*, he is sure to be lost." What Archimedes said of the mechanical powers of levers may be applied to Paine's estimation of modern liberal reason in the service of liberty. "Had we," said he, "a plane to stand upon, we might

---

4. *Writings of James Madison*, 6:56 n.; *Works of John Adams*, 8:504–11; *Writings of Thomas Jefferson*, 5:328; *Writings of George Washington*, 12:37 n.

raise the world." In fact, America's revolution "presented in politics what was only theory in mechanics." America provided a point in the political universe, "where the principles of universal reformation could begin, so also was it best in the natural world." An assemblage of circumstances conspired "not only to give birth, but to add gigantic maturity to its principles." The obligation to defend the natural rights of mankind would spell the end of those aristocratic and sinister impulses that sustained the diplomatic concert underlying the European balance of power. Paine called for a "European Congress to patronize the progress of free governments, and promote the civilization of nations with each other." In Adams's view, the objectionable component in Paine's presentation was not so much "the object which he promised to himself" (i.e., the defense of natural rights) but the "dubious . . . principle on which he wrote." Paine offered "a commentary upon the rights of man inferring questionable deductions from unquestionable principles."[5]

Paine suggested that the British "have neither Liberty nor a Constitution," that the only conceivable method to guarantee these blessings is to "topple down headlong" their present government in imitation of the French model. The nation acts in accord with political right inasmuch as "that which a whole nation chuses to do, it has a right to do." Adams compared Paine's arguments to the natural law principles of Burke's political philosophy. Both disputants developed their respective arguments in response to Doctor Richard Price's sermon, delivered in 1789, "being the anniversary of what is called in England the Revolution." In his *Reflections on the Revolution in France*, Burke wrote, "The political divine proceeds . . . to assert that, by the principles of the Revolution, the people of England . . . acquired three fundamental rights: 1. To choose their own governors; 2. To cashier them for misconduct; and 3. To frame a government for themselves." Burke denied that such rights exist in the corporate body of the people, either in whole or part; moreover, "the people of England utterly disclaim such . . . right[s], and . . . will resist the practical assertion of [them] with

5. *The Life and Works of Thomas Paine*, 6:211, 231–32; "Publicola No. 2," *Writings*, 1:69–70.

their lives and fortunes." Paine, in response, cuts the Gordian knot and "declares the Parliament of 1688 to have been . . . usurpers, censures them for having unwisely sent to Holland for a King, denies the existence of the British Constitution, and invites the people of England to overturn their . . . Government, and to erect another upon the broad basis of national sovereignty." Against the conservatism of Burke, Paine declares,

> Man has not property in man; neither has any generation a property in the generations which are to follow. The Parliament . . . of 1688 . . . had not more right to dispose of the people of the present day, or to bind or to control them *in any shape whatever*, than the Parliament or the people of the present day have to dispose of . . . or control those who are to live a hundred or a thousand years hence. Every generation is, and must be, competent to all the purposes which its occasions require. It is the living, and not the dead, that are to be accommodated.[6]

The people of England had, in common with other nations, a natural and unalienable right to form a constitution of government. Inasmuch as governments are instituted to provide for the common security of the natural rights of every individual, they must be liable to alterations upon becoming incompetent for that purpose. Adams objected, however, that this was on occasion as a whole nation has a right to do whatever it chooses to do. The right of one generation to legislate for its successors achieves legitimacy by the "consent of that posterity . . . bound by their laws." Adams saw no absurdity in the expressions of perpetuity adopted by the Parliament of 1688. Expressions of a similar nature were close at hand in the constitutions of the several states of the union. In defending the integrity of minority rights, the precepts of natural law enabled Adams to contend that the "immutable laws of justice and morality are paramount to all human legislation." His defense of the Higher Law tradition, and rule of law, in American politics deserves to be quoted at length.

> The violation of those laws is certainly within the power, but it is not among the rights of nations. The power of a nation is the collected

---

6. Burke, *Selected Writings and Speeches*, 429–39; *Life and Works of Paine*, 6:16–21; "Publicola No. 2," *Writings*, 1:70–71.

power of all the individuals which compose it. The rights of a nation
are in like manner the collected rights of its individuals; and it must
follow . . . that the powers of a nation are more extensive than its
rights, in the very same proportion with those of individuals. . . . It is
of infinite consequence that the distinction between *power* and *right*
should be fully acknowledged, and admitted as one of the fundamental principles of Legislators.[7]

Along with Burke, Adams stipulated that a whole nation can act only
by representation; the acts of a representative majority in a legislature
are the acts of a whole body. If the majority is unrestrained "by no law
human or divine, and have no other rule but their sovereign will . . . to
direct them," then what protection remains to defend those unalienable rights? Individual liberty becomes "the sport of arbitrary power,
and the hideous form of despotism may lay aside the diadem and
sceptre, only to assume the party-colored garments of democracy."[8]

"A Constitution," says Paine, "is not a thing in name only but in
fact. It has not an ideal, but a real existence; and wherever it cannot be
produced in visible form, there is none." On practical grounds, Adams
doubted that his countryman "would . . . find in all history, a government which will come within this definition." As an issue in philosophy, Paine's assertion reflected those principles embodied in the posi-
tivist doctrine of law. Positivism accepted the breakdown of the great
metaphysical systems of the eighteenth and early nineteenth centuries
and the resulting decadence of metaphysical jurisprudence as an established fact. Adams believed that legal rules refer to ethics and mores for
the determination of their meaning and vice versa. The guiding influence as to the ideals, ends, and interests to be pursued within the social
order emanates from the ethical sphere. From it law and mores receive
the fundamental distinctions between the good and the bad, the ends
to be advanced and the ends to be opposed, the interests to be protected
and the interests to be repudiated. There is, at the foundation of any
legal or constitutional framework, a body of principles that incorporates

7. "Publicola No. 2," 70.
8. "Publicola No. 3," 74.

the seminal ideas of justice and order to be expounded by the rules of law.[9]

These distinctions were uppermost in Adams's mind and led him to insist that "the word [constitution] with an idea affixed to it, had been in use, and commonly understood, for centuries." The Whig writers of the eighteenth century, for example, contended for liberty upon the principles of the English constitution. When the Continental Congress in 1774 declared that "the inhabitants of the English colonies of North America were entitled to rights by the immutable laws of nature, [by] *the principles of the English Constitution*, and [by] the several charters or compacts," they were perfectly understood by all mankind. Paine further argued that "a Constitution is to a Government, what the laws, made afterwards by that Government, are to a court of judicature." This assertion, Adams claimed, was incompatible with the practice of those American states that "expressly adopted [in their constitutions] the whole body of the *common law*, so far as it was applicable to their respective situations." Paine's hue and cry that a constitution must be authenticated only in visible form testifies to, but does not fully explain, the moral force of law as it touches upon man's rational temperament. Adams's outlook was in harmony with Cicero's discussion of natural law.

> Of all the things about which learned men dispute there is none more important than . . . to understand that we are born for justice, and that right is founded not in opinion but in nature. There is . . . a true law, right reason, agreeing with nature and diffused among all, unchanging, everlasting, which calls to duty by commanding, deters from wrong by forbidding. It is not . . . one law at Rome and another at Athens, one law today and another hereafter; but the same law . . . will bind all nations and all times; and there will be one common lord and ruler of all, even God, the framer and proposer of this law.[10]

A constitution embraces a system of fundamental laws by which a people have consented to be governed, "which is always supposed to be

9. Ibid., 73; Hans J. Morgenthau, *Dilemmas of Politics*, 217–22.

10. *The Life and Works of Paine*, 76; E. H. Corwin, *The "Higher Law" Background of American Constitutional Law*, 9–10.

impressed on the mind of every individual, and of which the . . . printed copies are nothing more than the evidence."[11]

Adams asserted that Paine was mistaken in tracing the origin of the British government to the conquest of William of Normandy. "The victory obtained at Hastings not being a victory over *the nation collectively*," wrote Blackstone, "but only over the person of Harold, the only right that the conqueror could pretend to acquire . . . was the right to possess the crown of England, not *to alter the nature of the Government*." According to Adams,

> He [William] obtained the crown of England by popular election, upon the express condition that he would govern the nation according to her ancient laws and customs; he took the same oath at his coronation which had been taken by his predecessors, and by his last will, after bequeathing the province of Normandy to his eldest son Robert, he expressly acknowledged that he did not possess the kingdom of England as an inheritance, and only recommended his son William as his successor.[12]

The principle of being governed by an oral or traditional law prevailed in England eleven hundred years before that invasion. The British constitution consisted "of *principles*, not of *articles*"; in addition, the people of England were bound by a social compact and have "no right to demolish their Government, unless it be clearly incompetent for the purposes for which it was instituted." Adams did not deny to the English the right to cashier their governors if they abuse their position and their constitutional powers. They may, under such extreme duress, form another constitution, which should more permanently secure the natural rights of the whole community. America, he believed, offered a vivid example of a people reconciling their natural rights and liberties with peaceful and purposeful government. The Burkean influence in Adams's thought is unmistakable: "Their principles of religious liberty did not result from an indiscriminate contempt of all religion whatever, and their equal representation in their legislative councils was founded upon an equality really existing among them, and not upon meta-

11. "Publicola No. 3," 74.
12. Blackstone, *Commentaries*, 1:199; "Publicola No. 6," 87–88.

physical speculations of fanciful politicians, vainly contending against the unalterable course of events, and the established order of nature."[13]

The flaw in Paine's thinking, Adams asserted, arose from a "partial adoption of the principle upon which Rousseau founds the social compact." Rousseau described the social compact as "formed by a personal association of individuals, which must be unanimously assented to and which cannot possibly be made by a representative body." Rousseau's social contract amounts to an act of association that "produces a moral and collective body" and, likewise, involves the "total alienation of each associate, and all his rights, to the whole community." What is formed in this association is a "public person, which took formerly the name of *city* and now takes that of *republic* or *body politic*. It is called by its members *State* when it is passive, *Sovereign when in activity*." Rousseau's political association is little more than a modern version of the ancient Greek politeia, or "soul of the polis." His description of it is a reaction to the excessive individualism and atomism of the English contractualists. Suggesting that this "is neither practicable nor even metaphysically true," Adams believed that Rousseau's theory of sovereignty would "turn the whole body of the American constitutions, the pride of man, the glory of the human understanding, into a mass of tyrannical and unfounded usurpations." While Paine does not go quite so far, he does suggest that "a Government, on the principles on which constitutional Governments arising out of society are established, cannot have the right of altering itself. Why not? Because if it had, it would be arbitrary."[14]

Paine's corollary—that a constitutional government has no right of altering itself—also failed to persuade Adams. Nations, in forming a social contract, were free to delegate "the whole of their collective power to ordinary legislatures, in perpetual succession." The people may reserve only the right "of refusing the abuse of those powers; and every other question relative to the reservation of powers to the nation, must be only a question of expediency." In fact, the constitutions of the

13. "Publicola No. 3," 75; "Publicola, No. 8," 97–98.
14. "Publicola No. 3," 76; Jean-Jacques Rousseau, *The Social Contract*, chaps. 6, 7, 8; Lee Cameron MacDonald, *Machiavelli to Burke*, 2:391.

various American states are all alterable in every part by their respective legislatures. In forming a constitution, a nation may reserve only the unalienable right of resistance against tyranny. The British people, Adams believed, had reserved only this right. While the English delegated all their power, "they have no right in their original character to change their form of Government, unless it has become incompetent for the purposes for which all Governments are instituted."[15] Adams sensed that his own rejoinder offered insufficient insight into an even more important question: Who is to be the judge of this incompetency?

While Adams acknowledged that the people themselves must be the judges of this fact, he also believed a crucial distinction be upheld as to whether "they proceed from passion . . . [or] from principle." If, for example, the social compact is truncated on the belief that a majority opinion claims the right to do whatever it chooses, then the nation may indeed "go through the operation by the plenitude of their irresistible power." The society that is acquainted with no other political standard than the power of its own self-interest may expect to

> meet with ample punishment in their own misery, and the leaders who delude them, in the detestation of their own posterity. It is not by adopting the malignity of a political satyrist . . . that a nation will be justified in resorting to its original strength, to contend against its delegated power. It is not . . . a mechanical horror against the name of a king, or of aristocracy . . . or to the sight of an innocent riband that can authorise a people to lay violent hands upon the Constitution, which protects their rights, and guards their liberties.[16]

The aggrieved majority must feel an actual deprivation of its equal rights, and see an actual impossibility for their restoration in any other manner, before its members can "have a right to lay their hands on their swords" in defense of their liberty. Far from constituting the principles of slavery, these maxims represent "the tenets of the only genuine liberty, which consists in a mean equally distant from the despotism of an individual, as of a million." Jefferson's language in the Declaration appealed to Adams. American patriots, far from thinking they

15. "Publicola No. 3," 76–77.
16. "Publicola No. 4," 78.

inherited a right to do whatever they chose, exposed to the world the various acts of tyranny that had compelled them "to acquiesce in the necessity which denounced the separation," and to appeal "to the Supreme Judge of the world for the rectitude of their intentions." Even though later the Constitution was presented to the people of America in their original character, its endorsement depended upon the assent of nine states. The extreme difficulty that impeded the progress of its ratification provided "the fullest evidence, what a more than Herculean task it is to write the opinions of a free people, upon any system of government whatever."[17]

By a similar authority, Adams asserted that the English had no right to destroy their government, "unless . . . the rights of the people are really oppressed, and unless they have attempted in vain every constitutional mode of obtaining redress." Both theoretic and pragmatic norms of politics colored his defense of the British constitutional order. In one respect, England had less to gain and more to lose than any other European nation in the hazardous event of a revolution. Whatever the people might achieve "must, in all probability, be purchased at the expense of a civil war." In another respect, difficulties abound when the people seek to alter a constitution when "this power is already delegated, with the other powers of legislation." The people, Adams advised, cannot exercise this responsibility except in their original, unrepresented character; therefore, they cannot acquire the right to act in that capacity, at least "until the power which they have . . . conveyed in trust has been abdicated by the extreme abuses of its administration." Those who would champion revolution are obligated to consider the methods by which a people can act in their original character without the total dissolution of civil society. Paine "should have proved what great advantages they would reap as a nation from such a revolution, without disguising the . . . formidable difficulties with which it must be attended."[18]

There are in all European countries, wrote Paine, "a large class of people of that description, which in England are called the *mob*." With the advent of revolution, "those men are rather the followers of the

17. Ibid., 79–80.
18. Ibid., 81.

camp than of the *standard* of liberty, and have yet to be instructed how to reverence it." Adams did not believe that any such multitude, however instrumental in the French Revolution, could be counted upon to accomplish a similar purpose in Britain. While not wanting to "reproach . . . that unhappy class of human beings," Adams refused to treat them as free agents. No friend of humanity should act without caution in mobilizing the tremendous power—competent only to ravage and shatter—belonging to that portion of mankind lacking the inspiration either to create or to preserve. Their frantic enthusiasm and ungovernable fury was apt to be provoked by any provocateur who could inflame their passions or alarm their superstitions.[19] What, Adams asked, has a mob to lose by the incapacitation of civil society?

Without recourse to the formation of rational judgments, "either upon the principles or . . . motives of their own conduct," their rage may be directed at any victim who is pointed out to them. The brutal arm of power is all the assistance they can afford for their revolutionary inspiration. Once this inert mass is set in motion, they "get beyond all restraint and control." Their patron saint is more likely to exhibit the "eccentric vivacity of a madman" than the "sober coolness of phlegmatic reason." The rights of man, in the face of their rage, "oppose but a feeble barrier to them; the beauteous face of nature, and the elegant refinements of art, the hoary head of wisdom, and the enchanting smile of beauty, are all . . . liable to become obnoxious to them."

> In the year 1780, they assembled at London to the number of 60,000, under the direction of Lord George Gordon, and carrying fire and slaughter before them, were upon the point of giving the . . . city of London to one undistinguished devastation and destruction: and this, because the Parliament had mitigated the severity of a . . . tyrannical law of persecution against Roman Catholics. Should these people be taught . . . that the titles of Kings and Nobles, and the wealth of Bishops, are all . . . robberies committed upon them, I believe it would not be difficult . . . to prepare them for every work of ruin.[20]

19. *The Life and Works of Paine*, 51; "Publicola No. 5," 81–82.
20. "Publicola No. 5," 81–82.

The French National Assembly directed "the electric fluid of this popular frenzy" against the ancient fabric of their monarchy; their fatal error, Adams judged, was not being aware of all the consequences that might follow from committing the existence of the kingdom to a popular insurrection, where the object of political power is merely its own enthronement.[21]

Equally dangerous, and even less practical, was Paine's idea of "revolutions by accommodation"—i.e., as applied in England, a convention presumably would be called by act of Parliament to regenerate the constitution. The evils of anarchy and of war are surely lurking when any body of lawmakers, "contrary to nature . . . should venture to perform the most transcendent act of power of which human beings are capable, for the single purpose of divesting themselves of all power whatever." Adams argued that the act itself would prove its own inutility, insofar as no man would willingly endorse such a measure unless the unequivocal wishes of a substantial majority of the people were in favor of altering the government. If public officials are disposed to act in conformity with the representative will of their constituents, then the same power that would enable them to dissolve the government would similarly entitle them to make any corrections that would meet with the wishes of the nation. Recurrence to the people, in their original character, would be unnecessary. The same right that authorizes a member of Parliament "to give his suffrage in the most trifling object of legislation . . . has vested in Parliament, of which he is a member, the whole power of the British nation." The legislator cannot possibly deny their right without denying his own. From this vantage point, the right of the individual depends upon the right of the corporation; the very act of calling a convention would be "assuming the right to dissolve the ties of society, and at the same instant acknowledging that this assumed right was without any sort of foundation."[22]

The normative rationale for any human association—organized for political action—is "in order that the power of the whole may be

---

21. Ibid., 83.
22. Ibid., 85–86.

rendered subservient to the interests of the whole." The very possibility of individual liberty is predicated upon how governmental power is distributed so as to safeguard the public welfare. Political wisdom dictates "the necessity of [nations] delegating their whole power . . . because whatever power is retained by the people, cannot be exercised for their advantage any more than to their injury." Yet Paine offered little instruction on why a nation should not delegate all its powers. Adams distilled from his countryman's reasoning two principal objections: first, that such a government would be arbitrary; and, second, that "there is a paradox in the idea of vitiated bodies reforming themselves." Concerning the first charge, Adams pointed out that the roots of civil society grow out of a body politic, whereby the use of "the whole power (which is not, however, arbitrary power)" ought to be rationally directed toward making men better human beings. This public authority and the character of citizens alike are informed by the principles that make for a free and just society, insofar as they encourage men by the best means and talents at their disposal to put those principles into practice. Adams agreed with Aristotle that happiness—or the life of virtue—accompanies acting well, and that human freedom entails actualizing this potential in a way to promote the common interest. The main concern of politics, as identified by Aristotle in the *Nicomachean Ethics*, is to engender a certain character in the citizens and to make them good and disposed to perform noble actions.

> The reason why man is a being meant for political association, in a higher degree than . . . other gregarious animals can ever associate is evident. . . . The mere making of sounds serves to indicate pleasure and pain, and is thus a faculty that belongs to animals in general. . . . But language serves to declare what is advantageous and what is the reverse, and it therefore serves to declare what is just and what is unjust. It is the peculiarity of man, in comparison with the rest of the animal world, that he alone possesses a perception of good and evil, of the just and unjust, and of other similar qualities; and it is association in [a common perception of] these things which makes a family and a *polis*.[23]

23. *The Life and Works of Paine*, 79; Aristotle, *Nicomachean Ethics*, 23; *The Politics of Aristotle*, 5–6.

Adams could not see a reason why any power claimed in behalf of human freedom should not exist for the benefit of the people. Otherwise, said John Locke, "were it not for the corruption, and vitiousness of degenerate Men, there would be no need" for government. The purpose of living under governments is to preserve all men in their "Lives, Liberties, and Estates," which Locke calls "by the general name, *Property*." To achieve this goal, government must establish "settled, known *Law*," which must be in accord with the law of nature; it must also provide a "*known and indifferent Judge*, with Authority to determine all differences according to the established law." Whenever a constitution is made unalterable by the common legislative authority, "the nation do in reality abdicate all the powers . . . they are said to retain, and declare that very important powers shall . . . be useless . . . from an apprehension that they might possibly be abused to their injury."[24] By failing to delegate the whole power of the nation, the supreme impotence of government might be as prejudicial or fatal as the actual abuse of power.

The true interests of the people required "the distribution of those powers in such a manner as shall . . . guard against the abuses which alone are dangerous to the people." The American Constitution has combined advantages of the French and English examples while "it has avoided the evils of both." For instance, the collective power of alteration—or amending the basic document—was delegated and, thereby, vested in Congress and the state legislatures; at the same time, however, the document provided for alterations by the people themselves in their original character. Adams admonished his countrymen to preserve their commitment to the commonweal and "not be frightened . . . by the words arbitrary power." Manuscript limitations on legislative authority do not always operate as a reliable check upon the actions of a legislature. "Such is the poverty of all human labors," he wrote, "that even a whole nation cannot express themselves upon paper with so much accuracy and precision, as not to admit of much latitude of explanation and construction."[25]

24. Forrest McDonald, *Novus Ordo Seclorum: The Intellectual Origins of the Constitution*, 65; "Publicola No. 7," 91.
25. "Publicola No. 7," 92–93.

Adams's belief in a government of limited powers—expressly set out in the Constitution—did not obviate the need for legislators to "judge . . . the intentions with which the instrument was formed, and to construe . . . the expressions which it contains." As his father wrote in the *Discourses on Davila*, "But it is . . . the function of society so as to organize and arrange the powers of government as best to protect . . . the moral—that is to say, the natural rights of mankind." The younger Adams concurred and advised that both executive and legislative authorities be so constituted that individual rights may never depend upon any one man or body of men. But even the separation of powers doctrine must "depend upon the honest and enlightened spirit of a people for a security which . . . never will obtain, by merely withholding . . . powers, unless that spirit should be constantly kept up." In his "Thoughts On Government," John Adams put the matter succinctly: "Nothing is more certain from the history of nations and the nature of man, than that some forms of government are better fitted for being well administered than others. . . . The foundation of every government is some principle or passion in the minds of the people. The noblest principles and the most generous affections in our nature . . . have the fairest chance to support the noblest and most generous models of government."[26]

Paine's other objection to a nation delegating its powers—the "paradox . . . of vitiated bodies reforming themselves"—was found by Adams to be equally objectionable. The truth of his proposition depends "upon the coincidence of the part vitiated with the part which is to apply the remedy; for unless the defect . . . precludes the possibility of applying the power of reformation, the paradox ceases." There is no more absurdity here than in the example of a physician who relies upon his own prescriptions to heal himself. Adams referred to the act establishing the septennial Parliaments in eighteenth-century England as sufficient proof that the power of altering a constitution itself ought to be delegated, "and even exercised by the Government upon critical occasions." That act occurred at a time when Britain was threatened

26. *The Works of John Adams*, 6:399, 4:193.

with an immediate invasion, when a rebellion had just been quelled, and when the peace and safety of the nation depended upon the use of this power by Parliament. The perils of war may furnish the occasion "when the use even of that [delegated] power may be absolutely necessary" for preservation of the national interest; when, at the same time, "it may be impossible for [a people] to act in [their] original character, with the expedition necessary for [their] salvation."[27]

The reasons given by Adams for a nation to entrust its power are closely tied to the essential principle upon which popular representation in a legislature is to be achieved. The Lockean axiom—that a freeman shall not be bound by any law unless he has consented to it—is impossible except in a very small state. To govern the United States by direct democratic methods—"to pretend to establish . . . a government which according to Rousseau is calculated only for a republic of Gods"—would necessitate "the continual exercise of virtues beyond the reach of human infirmity, even in its best state." In order to supply a mechanism by which every individual should give his voice, the practice of voting by representation was introduced. Yet Burke's argument for the virtual representation of popular sentiment is not without its hazards, for "every representative is actuated by several powerful motives, which could not operate on his constituents." Representative government, Adams believed, is akin to "an *artificial democracy*, which can never perform completely the functions of . . . natural democracy." In addition, the theory of representation embodies the concept of a *personal* trust through which individuals "authorise one man to express their sentiments upon every law which may be enacted for the benefit of the whole people." But, in theory, every representative of the public voice

> ought to be elected by the unanimous vote of his constituents; for how can a man be said to have been consulted in the formation of a law, when the agent authorised to express his opinion was not the man of his choice? Every pecuniary qualification imposed either on the electors or as a condition of eligibility, is an additional restriction upon the natural democracy, and weakens the original purpose of the

27. "Publicola No. 7," 93–94.

institution. Thus far the people of America have submitted to necessity in the constitution of their popular assemblies.[28]

Even the limitations of an artificial democracy, however, "appear to flow
from the natural order of things which a revolution in government
could not reform." The politics of democracy cannot survive in a "society [where] every principle of religion or morality has lost its influence,
and where the only shadow of virtue, public or private . . . among a great
majority of the people is founded upon an imaginary point of honor,
the relict of the exploded age of chivalry."[29] Adams applied this description to the national characters of both England and France.

The final Letters of "Publicola" are directed to Paine's belief in the
superiority of the French constitution upon the subject of making war
and peace. That right, he claims, must be borne by the nation; in
England, however, "the right is said to reside in a *metaphor*, shown at
the Tower for sixpence or a shilling a piece." Adams argued that the
right of committing the energies of the nation to war must be a
delegated power. The French constitution vested this power in the
National Assembly; the English constitution conferred the power of
war on "the supreme executive officer." The representatives of the
people retained the exclusive right of providing for the support of the
war—or withholding the sinews of war—if it should ever be declared
contrary to the sense of the people themselves. Paine expressed reservations about the distinction, and its consequences for democratic
societies: "If the one rashly declares war," he wrote, "as a matter of
right; and the other peremptorily withholds the supplies as a matter of
right, the remedy becomes as bad or worse than the disease." Adams
found Paine's quandary warranted neither by theory nor by the experience of history. The English monarch is the organ of the nation, and he
would "be more than an idiot to declare a war . . . without being
certain of that support." Paine's conclusions, "like the feeble resource
for the satirist," are "drawn by reasoning against the inevitable order of
things, [and] are unworthy of a politician." He built up a straw man

28. "Publicola No. 8," 97–98.
29. Ibid., 95.

197

Philosophy, Politics, and Statecraft

that was easily disassembled without citing examples of this clashing of rights between king and Parliament. Paine, at a later point, seemed to abandon his own objection by saying "that in the manner the English nation is represented, it signifies not where this right resides, whether in the Crown or in the Parliament."[30]

Only the French constitution, Paine declared, united the *right* and the *expense* of waging war in defense of the nation's welfare. Adams, objecting to the impracticability of such a union, asserted that a comparison of the two constitutions pointed to the inherent powers of any government in the domain of foreign policy. At the beginning of his career, Adams raised the constitutional issue that later would mobilize all his political energies, as a congressman, at the time of the Mexican War: "*Whether it is expedient to delegate to the legislature, or whether to the executive authority, the right of declaring war.*"[31]

On the matter of whether a nation has the right to make war upon its neighbors, Adams argued that the people's representatives "must judge, when the provocation is sufficient to dissolve them from all the obligations of morality and humanity, by which nations are bound to preserve the blessings of peace." Adams believed that an integral bond united the defense of the nation with respect for those transcendent principles that give meaning to the everyday operations of democratic government. He was enough of a realist to acknowledge that moral scruples about war are attenuated by "the great law of self-preservation, to which all other laws must give way." Yet he was equally opposed to the amoral workings of "reason of state" in foreign policy—the idea that projecting force is an expedient calculation of necessity about which moral and legal criteria serve only as a convenient rationale. Whether war is justifiable in a particular situation depends upon a determination by elected officials "that the laws . . . enacted in consequence of the primitive contract which united all their power for the benefit of every individual, compel them to appeal for justice to the God of battles." Adams referred at one point to the declaration of war—"the formal act, by which [a people] announce to the world their intention to employ the arm of power in

30. "Publicola No. 10," 103–4.
31. Ibid.

their own defence"—as the proper attribute of executive power. A close reading of the tenth letter suggests that Adams, far from denying the authority of Congress to declare war, was merely differentiating between the justification and prosecution of war as the defense of the nation fell upon coordinate branches of government.

Aware that his distinction might be considered heretical, Adams invoked the reasoning of Rousseau in *The Social Contract*. "The act of declaring war," Rousseau wrote, "and that of making peace, have been considered as acts of sovereignty, which is not the case; for either of those acts is not a law, but only an application of the law; a particular act which determines the operation of the law, as will be . . . perceived when the idea annexed to the word *law* shall be ascertained." This sentiment, Adams claimed, is perfectly agreeable to the spirit of the English constitution. Adams defended executive prerogative in foreign affairs along several lines. First, whenever a dispute between nations culminates in war, it is proper and customary that negotiations be initiated, "in order to use every possible means of settling amicably the dispute." These negotiations—the appointment of agents, and the communication of proposals for accommodation—"are all appropriated to the executive department." Second, the restoration of peace entails the appointment of even more agents, and "proposals of pacification" must again be made. These diplomatic functions, requiring the utmost secrecy and despatch, are "frequently of essential necessity to the welfare of the nation." With reference to the democratic control of foreign policy by the French Assembly, Adams was not sanguine about the prospects for prudence or discretion in the cabinet diplomacy of his day.

> But what secrecy can ever be expected, when every instruction to an ambassador, every article of a proposed treaty, and every circumstance of information from the minister, in the progress of his operations, must be known to twelve-hundred men assembled in the capital. . . . what probability of despatch, when all these things must be debated in this Assembly of 1200 men; where every thing must in the necessary order of events be opposed, by interested individuals and irritated factions, who may protract the discussion for months or years.[32]

32. *Rousseau's Political Writings*, 89–90. "Publicola No. 10," 106.

The Constitution of the United States vested the right to declare war in the legislative power of Congress. But Paine's recommendation of the French example (i.e., placing all responsibility in the democratic-minded nation) is not precisely analogous to the distribution of constitutional authority for decision making in American foreign policy. Adams pointed out that, inasmuch as the legislative power to declare war is concerned, "it is [only] in point of form that it agrees with the Constitution of France." By placing the management of negotiations and treaties, and the appointment of ministers in the executive department, America had adopted the "*principles* of the English Constitution." To emulate the French model would "open a thousand avenues for base intrigue, for furious faction, for foreign bribery, and domestic treason."[33] While defending the conduct of war as an executive function, Adams judged the role of Congress to be central, and indispensable, to the determination of the national interest. The kind of nation worth defending, the amount of domestic resources to be usurped by war, the measure in which the projection of American power can be harmonized with the universal aspiration for human rights—these deliberations would provide the people's representatives with an important brake upon the aggrandizement of executive power in costly military campaigns on distant shores.

II.

Historical scholarship has accepted the central role played by Secretary of State John Quincy Adams in the decisions leading up to the pronouncement of the Monroe Doctrine, both in the diplomatic discussions with Russia and England and in deliberations of the United States Cabinet preceding the formulation of Monroe's celebrated message to Congress in 1823. One important dictum of that address—abstention from European entanglements—was expressed by numerous American leaders from the time of the Revolution until Washington's Farewell Address in 1796 and thereafter, notably by Presidents Jefferson and Madi-

33. "Publicola No. 10," 106–7.

son. Secretary Adams affirmed the policy in a letter of instructions to the American minister to Russia, declining the invitation of Czar Alexander I to join the Holy Alliance. "The political system of the United States," he said, three years before the Monroe Doctrine, "is extra-European. To stand in firm and cautious independence of all entanglement in the European system has been a cardinal point of their policy under every administration of their government from the peace of 1783 to the present day." Less widely noted, however, is that this was—in 1820—not a new thought to John Quincy Adams. His Letters of "Marcellus" and "Columbus" (1793) laid out a course of action that brought him into line with the foreign policy of Washington's Farewell Address, later reiterated in the Monroe Doctrine, and associated with the general concept of the two separate spheres, or systems, of policy.[34] Adams's personal reverence for Washington is an important component in relating his early writings to the volatile debate over America's national interest in a larger world of secret diplomacy and power politics.

George Washington remained John Quincy Adams's hero of history without reproach or reservation. He christened his first child George Washington Adams, born in Berlin in 1801, in memory of the Father of His Country.

> My child was yesterday baptized by the name of George Washington; and may the grace of Almighty God guard his life and enable him . . . to prove himself worthy of it! I was not induced merely by the public character of that great and good man to show his memory this token of respect. Washington was, next to my father, the man upon earth whom I was indebted for the greatest personal obligations. I knew not whether upon philosophical principles it be wise to give a . . . venerable name to such a lottery-ticket as a new-born infant—but my . . . scruples have in this case been overpowered by my instinctive sentiments.[35]

Washington was "one of the greatest names that has ever appeared upon earth for the pride and consolation of the human race. I feel it is an inestimable happiness to have been the contemporary and country-

34. Samuel Flagg Bemis, *American Foreign Policy and the Blessings of Liberty*, 260–61.
35. Bemis, *John Quincy Adams and the Foundations of American Foreign Policy*, 85 n.50.

man of that man." Adams first encountered Washington when visiting his father, the vice president, in New York in 1789. As a young law student, he drafted the address of welcome that the citizens of Newburyport presented to the president on the occasion of his visit. Undoubtedly, Washington knew that it was John Quincy Adams who argued persuasively as "Publicola"; moreover, in 1793, the president took pains to ascertain that it was young Adams who authored the wise counsel of "Columbus" and "Marcellus," widely printed in American newspapers, defending American neutrality against the designs of French diplomacy in the War of the First Coalition.[36]

In 1792, the War of the First Coalition ranged Austria, Prussia, Sardinia, Great Britain, and the United Netherlands against revolutionary France, which was tied to the United States by a treaty of alliance. The French Revolution renewed the contest for principles that Enlightenment philosophers had hoped to replace with the milder contests of interests well understood. "I should desire you particularly to distinguish between the love of our country and that spirit of rivalship and ambition which has been common among nations," Benjamin Franklin's friend, Richard Price, preached in a famous sermon in 1789.

> What has the love of their country hitherto been among mankind? What has it been but a love of domination, a desire of conquest, and a thirst for grandeur and glory, by extending territory and enslaving surrounding countries?
>
> The noblest principle in our nature is the regard to general justice and that good-will which embraces all the world. . . . Though our immediate attention must be employed in promoting our own interest and that of our nearest connexions; yet we must remember, that a narrower interest ought always to give way to a more extensive interest. In pursuing . . . the interest of our country, we ought to carry our views beyond it. We should love it ardently, but not exclusively, We ought to seek its good, by all the means that our different circumstances and abilities will allow; but at the same time we ought to

36. JQA to William Vans Murray, February 11, 1800, 2:453; Bemis, *American Foreign Policy and the Blessings of Liberty*, 261.

consider ourselves citizens of the world, and take care to maintain a just regard to the rights of other countries.[37]

The spirit of what has been described as the "New Diplomacy" of the eighteenth century was strongest in the Girondist phase of worldwide proselytizing, carried to America by Citizen Genêt.[38] Federalists and Republicans alike believed that their country's fate depended on the outcome of events across the Atlantic. There was a direct diplomatic liability to confront. In the French alliance of 1778, the United States guaranteed "forever against all other powers" His Most Christian Majesty's American possessions, just as His Most Christian Majesty had guaranteed the independence and territorial integrity of the United States. Actually these claims at this time consisted of the French islands in the West Indies, plus the two small islands of St. Pierre and Miquelon in the Gulf of St. Lawrence. As the British navy was prepared to attack the West Indian islands, it was difficult to see how America could honorably refuse to defend them, if France demanded it.

Before an historic meeting of the cabinet in April 1793, the secretaries of state and of the treasury debated the moral and legal aspects of American foreign policy commitments. Both Jefferson and Hamilton wished to preserve the neutrality of the United States, but they differed considerably on how best to accomplish this objective. Hamilton argued that the treaties of commerce and alliance should be declared temporarily and provisionally suspended. Moreover, he acknowledged that treaties between nations remained in force regardless of change in the form of government of either signatory; however, in this instance, the rule applied "only in reference to a *change*, which has been finally *established* and secured." It did not apply, he asserted, when, as in this case, such a change was "pending and in contest and which may never be consummated." Writing as "Pacificus" and "Americanus," Hamilton's defense of America's national interest looked less to ambiguous moral and legal axioms and more to the realities

---

37. Richard Price, "Discourse on the Love of Our Country," 1010, 1012.

38. G. J. A. Ducher, an official of the French Foreign Office during the French Revolution, wrote an article in the *Moniteur* of June 9, 1793, entitled "Nouvelle diplomatie." Felix Gilbert, "The 'New Diplomacy' of the Eighteenth Century," 1, 37, n. 110.

of power and the conflicting ambitions that govern the fortune of nations.

> There would be no proportion between the mischief and perils to which the United States would expose themselves, by embarking in the war and the benefit which the nature of their stipulation aims at securing to France; or that which it would be in their power actually to render her by becoming a party. . . . Indeed the rule of morality . . . in this respect is not precisely the same between nations as between individuals. The duty of making its own welfare the guide of its actions, is much stronger upon the former than . . . the latter; in proportion to the greater magnitude and importance of national compared with individual happiness, and to the greater permanency of the effects of national than of individual conduct. . . . The obligation to assist the cause of liberty must be deduced from the merits of that cause and from the interest we have in its support.[39]

Hamilton's case for realism rested on the premise "that the predominant motive of good offices from one nation to another, is the interest or advantage of the nation which performs them."[40]

Jefferson considered the French Revolution "the most sacred cause that ever man was engaged in," but was equally anxious to keep America out of the war. The secretary of state took the position that the Franco-American treaties were compacts between people, not merely between governments. Daniel G. Lang, in his pioneering study on law and diplomacy in the early republic, points out that Jefferson rejected Hamilton's position—abrogation of the treaties—on constitutional, legal, and prudential grounds. He doubted that the executive possessed the authority to suspend the treaties, considered Hamilton's interpretation of the law of nations tendentious, and argued that a price be put on American neutrality. Jefferson's concern was upon what *principles* American neutrality was to be presented to the rest of the world. He explained to Thomas Pinckney, American minister to Great Britain, that the United States would follow the rights and duties of neutrality in its relations with Europe.

39. Alexander Hamilton, "Pacificus No. 4," *The Papers of Alexander Hamilton,* 15:85–86; John C. Miller, "The Federalist Era," 4.
40. Morgenthau, *Defense of the National Interest,* 15–16.

> The general principles of the law of nations must be the rule . . . I
> mean the principles of that law as they have been liberalized in latter
> times by the refinement of manners and morals, and evidenced by the
> Declarations, Stipulations, and Practice of every civilized nation. In
> our treaty with Prussia . . . we have gone ahead of other Nations in
> doing away with restraints on the commerce of peaceful nations, by
> declaring that nothing shall be contraband.[41]

Fearing that Hamiltonian doctrines would steer the government
into a dangerous alliance with monarchism, Jefferson appealed to James
Madison: "For God's sake, my dear Sir, take up your pen, select the
most striking heresies, and cut him to pieces in the face of the public."
Taking the name "Helvidius," Madison sketched out the true "republican" canons of American foreign policy. First, Congress controls foreign policy; the powers of the president in the diplomatic field are
instrumental only. "Can the inference be avoided, that the executive,
instead of a similar right to judge is as much excluded from the right
to judge as from the right to declare?" Second, "war is the nurse of
executive aggrandizement"—and the proclamation of neutrality was a
unilateral interpretation of the Franco-American treaties and enjoined
an impartiality that was irreconcilable with America's legal obligations.
Accordingly, as Lang explains, Madison dismissed Vattel's, Locke's, and
Montesquieu's expositions of executive power because they all wrote
"with their eyes too much on monarchical governments, where all
powers are confounded in the sovereignty of the prince." Yet Madison
accepted Vattel's explanation that neither side possesses the right to
interpret a treaty at its own pleasure: "To decide a question of fact, as
well as of principle, without waiting for such representations and proofs
as the absent and interested party might have to produce, would have
been a proceeding contrary to the ordinary maxims of justice."[42]

With the announcement of Washington's retirement at the end of
his second term in office, intervention of the French ally in domestic
politics again threatened neutrality. In his Farewell Address, embel-
lished by the phraseology of Hamilton, Washington invoked the spirit

---

41. Daniel G. Lang, *Foreign Policy in the Early Republic*, 132–35, 144–45.

42. Lang, *Foreign Policy in the Early Republic*, 136, 138; Miller, "The Federalist Era," 4–6.

of national unity against the divisions of political and sectional factions. America's interest was best served by abstaining from the ordinary vicissitudes of European politics and the ordinary combinations and collisions of her friendships or enmities. In 1796, European politics and power politics were synonymous; there was no other power politics but the one engaged in by the princes of Europe. America's detached and distant position

> enables [her] to pursue a different course. If we remain one people, under an efficient government, the period is not far off, when we may defy material injury from external annoyance; when we may take such an attitude as will cause the neutrality, we may at any time resolve upon, to be scrupulously respected; when belligerent nations, under the impossibility of making acquisitions upon us, will not lightly hazard the giving us provocation; when we may choose peace or war, as our interest, guided by justice, shall counsel.[43]

John Quincy Adams first read Washington's message while serving as American minister to The Hague. "The reception of the President's address to the people might serve as another indicative to France of the temper of our own people," he wrote to Joseph Pitcairn, United States consul in Paris.

> From that let them judge of the success that has attended all their endeavors to tear our benefactor from our hearts; let them see the issue of all their maneuvers and all their libels; of their Baches and Randolphs in America, as well as their Theremins and their Paines in Europe. . . . Can France . . . believe that Mr. Jefferson, or any other man, would dare to start away from that system of administration which Washington has . . . sanctioned, not only by his example, but by his retirement?[44]

American abstention from European power politics was more than a political program. Certain sporadic exceptions notwithstanding, it was an established political fact until the end of the nineteenth century. This fact was the result of deliberate choice as well as the objective conditions of geography. Popular writers often saw in the uniqueness

43. Bemis, *John Quincy Adams and the Foundations of American Foreign Policy*, 62.
44. JQA to Joseph Pitcairn, January 31, 1797, 2:95–96.

of America's geographic position the hand of God, which had un-alterably prescribed the course of American expansion as well as isola-tion. As this period drew to a close, John Bright wrote to Alfred Love: "On your continent we may hope your growing millions may hence-forth know nothing of war. None can assail you; and you are anxious to abstain from mingling with the quarrels of other nations."[45] The general conception the nineteenth century had formed of the nature of foreign affairs combined with specific elements in the American expe-rience to create the belief that involvement in power politics is not inevitable, but only a historic accident, and that nations have a choice between power politics and other kinds of foreign policy not tainted by the desire for power. But more responsible observers, from Washing-ton to John Quincy Adams, were always careful to emphasize the conjunction of geographic conditions and a foreign policy choosing its ends in the light of geography, using geographic conditions to attain those ends.

As partisan attachments crystallized under the impact of the French Revolution, Adams became a Federalist, opposed to Republican or Jeffersonian democracy. As an aspiring Boston attorney, he deplored the heyday of enthusiasm for the French mob and refused to join any of the new democratic societies or to attend one of their civic feasts—the "anarchical dinner[s]"—amid the Jacobin collaborators. He was convinced that the French revolutionary factions had gone wrong in seeking to overthrow other governments by a war of propaganda, particularly in declaring war on England, thus lining up all Europe against France. Many of the ideas, even some of the words, expressed by "Marcellus" and "Columbus" illustrate how closely the position of Adams paralleled Washington's thinking independently of Alexander Hamilton. It is also quite possible, as Bemis suggests, that Vice Presi-dent Adams showed his son's letters to Hamilton. Writing to his father after he perused the text of the Farewell Address, Adams said, "The President . . . has told us, and I am profoundly convinced of the justice and importance of the advice, that we ought not to involve ourselves at

---

45. Merle Curti, *Peace and War: The American Struggle 1636–1936*, 122.

all in the political systems of Europe, but to keep ourselves always distinct and separate from it."[46]

"Marcellus" began by relating political ethics to the foreign policy conduct of *both* the nation and specific individuals. Europe's war made for an interesting question to every American: What course of action "ought to be pursued by the United States . . . and by their citizens as individuals, in relation to the contending parties?" The individual "must follow the dictates of his own discretion"; yet the wisdom of national legislation in this crisis "involves . . . an answer to that [moral issue] which relates to individuals." Washington's proclamation of neutrality was not yet known in Boston when Adams warned his countrymen against privateering under a belligerent flag. He clung to the hope

> that this violation of the laws of nature and nations . . . may not in any instance be carried beyond the airy regions of speculation, and never acquire the consistency of practical execution. If the natural obligations of justice are so feeble among us that avarice cannot be restrained from robbery, but by the provisions of positive law, if the statute book is to be our only rule of morality to regulate . . . our duties towards our fellow creatures, let those whose ideals of equality are so very subservient to their private interests, consult the treaties between the United States and several powers now at war.[47]

Article 6 of the Constitution stipulated that "all Treaties made . . . under the authority of the United States, shall be the supreme Law of the Land." Treaties with France (1778), Holland (1782), and Prussia (1785) required the United States to prevent its citizens from taking out letters of marque or arming privateers with commissions under either of the powers against either of the others. A similar act of hostility against Britain would be a direct violation of the Seventh Article of the Treaty of Peace. Even if the United States was not bound by the treaty stipulations, "the natural obligation of neutrality would operate on us individually, unless the nation should take a decisive part in favor of one of the parties." American citizens would be legally responsible for

---

46. Bemis, *American Foreign Policy and the Blessings of Liberty*, 272.
47. "Marcellus No. 1," 135–36.

property seized with violence under a commission. The commercial interests of the nation dictated that American merchants "should show a peculiar degree of circumspection in their conduct, because the country becomes . . . in some measure responsible for them."[48] Not only did Adams substantiate an ethical link between the actions of individuals and the actions of groups, he also perceived a dire outcome for the national interest if the moral and legal precepts of neutrality were deserted for ill-acquired plunder.

One unmistakable lesson of war through the centuries is that the subjects of belligerent powers are often disposed to violate the rights of neutral nations. Adams laid out a scenario that would become all too familiar for American seamen. "The master and crew of a privateer, fitted out and cruising for the sole purpose of seizing upon defenceless wealth . . . often feel the full force of disappointed rapaciousness, when after a long chase they discover that the ship, under the plunder of whose cargo they had . . . feasted their imaginations, is rescued by the protection of a neutral flag. They are not apt to be nice in their distinctions of morality." In such circumstances, the individuals of the neutral nation have little recourse but to seek through their sovereign a desire for recompensation. The American government could be expected to bring all its force and authority to defend its citizens "in the just and honorable pursuit of their legitimate interest." Yet this obligation could not be incurred without a serious cost to the nation at the precipice of war. Even self-interest should behoove Americans—"as we value our interests, or our reputation"—to deprive adversaries of an opportunity "to retort a complaint that the neutrality was first violated on our part." The United States, Adams said, would never "have an expectation of gaining a compensation for the *injured* individual, unless they can compel the *injuring* individual to make compensation in his turn." A concern for both ethical intentions and political consequences required the American government to "disavow in the most decisive manner, all the acts of iniquity committed by our citizens."[49]

The natural injustice and wickedness of privateering had been roundly

48. Ibid., 136–37.
49. Ibid.

condemned "by the most amiable and virtuous moralists." Further-more, Adams pointed out that Article Twenty-three of the treaty be-tween the United States and Prussia (1785) provided for the following: "All merchant and trading vessels employed in the exchange of prod-ucts of different places . . . shall be allowed to pass free and un-molested; and neither of the contracting parties shall grant . . . any commission to any private armed vessel, empowering them to take or destroy such trading vessels or interrupt such commerce." Adams ren-dered the following verdict: "For if the poet . . . has said, *War is murder*, the plunder of private property, the pillage of all the regular rewards of honest industry and laudable enterprise, upon the mere pretence of a national contest, to the eye of reason and justice, can appear in no other light than that of highway robbery." Beyond "the uncontrollable laws of necessity, or . . . the iniquitous law of war," Americans would certainly have "no possible excuse for those who incur the guilt without being able to plead the palliation." Their will-ingness to violate the rights of nations for indiscriminate, personal rewards would illustrate "that it is only the lash of the executioner that binds them to the observance of their civil and political duties."[50]

III.

John Quincy Adams agreed with Hamilton on the primacy of the national interest for the conduct of American diplomacy; however, he perhaps was closer to Jefferson and Madison in believing that authentic moral choices were at stake in the timing and methods by which the nation defended its security and reputation in foreign affairs. Federal-ists and Republicans alike consented to Locke's doctrine of emergency prerogative beyond the Constitution:

> 'tis fit that the Laws themselves should in some Cases give way to the Executive Power, or rather to this Fundamental Law of Nature and Government, *viz.* That, as much as may be, *all* the Members of the Society are to be *preserved.* For since many accidents may happen,

50. Ibid., 138.

> wherein a strict and rigid observation of the Laws may do harm . . .
> and a Man may come sometimes within the reach of the Law, which
> makes no distinction of Persons, by an action, that may deserve
> reward and pardon; 'tis fit, the Ruler should have a Power, in many
> Cases, to mitigate the severity of the Law, and pardon some Of-
> fenders: For the *end of Government* being the *preservation of all,* as
> much as may be, even the guilty are to be spared, where it can prove
> no prejudice to the innocent.[51]

Indeed, Adams justified a posture of neutrality toward the European
powers as "equally the dictate of justice and policy" to the citizens of
the United States. The second installment of "Marcellus" outlined a
normative framework to guide American statesmen in framing the
obligations and duties of neutrality. Adams turned his attention to "the
line of conduct prescribed to the nation itself . . . by those immutable
laws of justice and equity, which are equally obligatory to sovereigns
and to subjects, to republics and to kings."[52]

Unlike the emphasis of "Pacificus," Adams was not prepared to
make any consideration of general policy—dictated by the national
interest—"a separate subject of inquiry." The reason for his reluctance
was due to one of the most undeniable principles of government—
"that the truest policy of a nation consists in the performance of its
duties." The rights of nations constituted "nothing more than the
extension of the rights of individuals to the great societies, into which
the different portions of mankind have been combined." The precepts
of Christianity *and* modern liberal reason converge upon the principle
of reciprocity in the relations among states. "Whatsoever," says the
author of Christianity, "you would that men should do to you, do ye
even so to them." A parallel assignment is conferred by what the
French Declaration of Rights specifies as the essence of liberty: "Liberty consists in the power of doing whatever is not contrary to the
rights of others." Adams saw a connection between doing nothing
contrary to the rights of others and Americans being able to enjoy and
deserve the blessings of freedom. Each nation "forms a moral person"

---

51. John Locke, *Two Treatises of Government,* 421.
52. "Marcellus No. 2," 139.

and each member of a nation is "personally responsible for his society." Adams rejected the central premise of European *raison d'état*—that the state is subject to no other rule of conduct but its own self-interest. *Salus publica suprema lex.* When the statesman is confronted with a choice between two actions, the one ethical, the other not, of which the latter has a better chance of bringing about the desired result, he must choose the latter. When he acts, however, in a private capacity, he, as any other private individual, must choose the former; "for, while political action is free from ethical limitations, private action is subject to them. The individual as such is moral by nature; political society is amoral, also by nature."[53]

Even the most convinced French protagonists supporting the new republic, Beaumarchais and Vergennes, stuck to the time-honored belief of so many political practitioners that "the national policy which preserves states differs in every respect almost entirely from the civil morality which governs individuals." These are the words of the author of *The Marriage of Figaro.* Count Vergennes was just as unequivocal, informing Louis XVI that "kings are perhaps not subject, when the safety of their people is in question, to the rules of such strict morality as are ordinary individuals in their private actions." The great effort of all idealists—since the time when Machiavelli threw his great challenge into the arena of political discussion—has been directed toward reestablishing some reconciliation between the spheres of politics, emancipated from traditional morality, and morality, loosely but generally identified with the doctrines of Christianity. Benjamin Franklin, after spending eight years as American minister to Paris, gave expression to the ethical impulse behind the New Diplomacy: "Justice is as strictly due between neighbour Nations as between neighbour Citizens. A Highwayman is as much a Robber when he plunders in a Gang, as when single; and a Nation that makes an unjust War, is only a *great Gang.* . . . A War . . . can hardly be just on both sides."[54]

53. Ibid.; Morgenthau, *Scientific Man vs. Power Politics,* 176.
54. E. S. Corwin, *French Policy and the American Alliance of 1778,* 72–77; Benjamin Franklin to Benjamin Vaughan, March 14, 1785, *The Writings of Benjamin Franklin,* 9:296, 299; B. F. Stevens (comp.), *Facsimiles of Manuscripts from European Archives*

Similarly, John Quincy Adams saw no discrepancy between the normative "principles upon which our national conduct is to be grounded" and the "impartial and unequivocal neutrality" that guided America between the contending parties in Europe's war. It was a feature of war, Hobbes believed, that "the notions of right and wrong, justice and injustice have no place." To the contrary, Adams viewed the natural state of nations—with respect to one another—as a state of peace, *demus petimusque vicissim*. It was what America had a right to expect from other nations, and "for the same reason it is our duty to observe it *towards* them." In addition to incurring a natural obligation, the United States was bound by treaties with France, England, Holland, and Prussia; provisions in each accord required America to observe the laws of peace with the subjects of their different governments. This country had no right to interfere in their contentions.

> Whatever may be the current of our sentiments . . . we are not constituted judges of the respective merits of their cause. . . . As men, we must undoubtedly lament the effusion of human blood, and the mass of misery, and distress which is preparing for a great part of the civilized world; but as the citizens of a nation whose happiness consists in real independence, disconnected from all . . . European politics, it is our duty to remain the peaceable and silent, though sorrowful spectators of the sanguinary scene.[55]

Americans might feel gratitude to France and "be disposed to throw a veil over their . . . errors and crimes"; alternatively, as descendants of Englishmen, "we may be willing to lose the memory of all the miseries they inflicted upon us in our first struggle against them."[56] Adams called upon Americans to cast aside momentary political attachments in judging the rectitude of the nation's intentions. In fact, how his countrymen would judge that sanguinary scene depended, in some

---

Relating to America, 1773–1783, 21: No. 1824; Stourzh, *Benjamin Franklin and American Foreign Policy*, 232–33; John Durand, ed. *New Materials for the History of the American Revolution*, 62.

55. Hobbes, *Leviathan*, 101; "Marcellus No. 2," 140.
56. "Marcellus No. 2," 140–41.

measure, upon the degree of self-confidence they were able to draw on to sustain a vision of the national purpose.

In addition to the combined considerations of natural duty and positive stipulation, Adams held that the cause of neutrality could be defended by "a forcible argument . . . derived from our interest." He had in mind the commercial advantages that would be thrown into American hands with the nations of Europe at war. The necessities of the belligerent powers would increase "as their means of supply will diminish, and the profits, which must infallibly flow to us from their wants, can have no other limitation than the extent of our capacity to provide for them." The cost of America becoming a partisan to the conflict would be prohibitive. First, the United States would "be engaged in a quarrel, with the laws of nations against us." Second, any involvement would constitute a "violation of our political duties," thereby signaling "a departure from the principles of natural justice, and an express breach of the positive stipulations of peace and friendship [in America's treaties] with the several . . . powers." Adams conceded that, against the impulses of private avarice and ambition, arguments derived from the "obligations of natural justice, or of written contract will be . . . nugatory." Third, and appealing to those whose "interest is in any degree connected with that of their country," he reasoned that the United States had neither the resources to defend the nation against a substantial external threat nor the ability to make a material difference in the contest of arms. Where, he asked, would American commerce turn when excluded from every market of the earth? Destitute of the defensive apparatus of war, what quarter would "provide us with the arms and ammunition that will be indispensable?" The burden of an accelerating public debt would leave little wherewithal "to support us in the dreadful extremity to which our own madness and iniquity would reduce us."[57] These were hardly imaginary apprehensions or objects of a trivial moment.

The final letter of "Marcellus" was devoted to the eleventh article of the treaty of alliance with France, by which the United States pledged

57. Ibid., 141–42.

to guarantee French possessions in America. Adams evinced four reasons for concluding that the course of events "has either totally absolved us, or . . . suspended the obligation of this clause":

1. The guaranty is *to his most Christian Majesty*; however, after a fifteen-year interval, no clear title to sovereignty could be ascertained. On the one hand, part of the French nation—and the other powers of Europe—will answer "he is the son or the brother of the late Louis the XVIth." On the other hand, the National Convention of the French Republic repudiated any royal claim to authority. The office and all the powers of the monarch had been "extinguished in the blood of the person with whom [the social] contract was made." As to which ruling party is entitled to the claim of performance, this "is not a question to be settled by the . . . civil war, and neither party can call upon us to decide it for them."[58]

2. Even if the revolution in France could be deemed completed, and a republic firmly established, doubts persisted about "whether they have not by their change of government, dissolved this clause of the [1778] treaty." Adams acknowledged that the weight of international law held that treaty obligations survive the internal revolutions of government. This would entitle the republic of France to the benefits of engagements contracted by the former monarch. Yet he also maintained that to this rule there were many exceptions. For example, "the first Constituent Assembly were so fully of this opinion that they thought the nation absolved from all such treaties previously made, as might be injurious to their interests, and the present government have extended the principle much further, when [as] a justification for opening the Scheldt, contrary to the . . . express stipulation of many treaties, they have formally denied the obligation of any compact, which was contrary to *the natural Rights of Men.*" Speculative principles provided little guidance as to whether the French Republic's sovereign control over islands—at a distance of three thousand miles—was consistent with natural rights. Adams knew it was difficult enough to mark the legal distinction that should prohibit every act of jurisdiction exercised by one nation over a river flowing through

58. "Marcellus No. 3," 142–43.

the territories of another. Would not the same difficulty be compounded, he asked, by asserting "supreme authority over colonies placed . . . at so wide a distance from the metropolis?" In this instance, Adams believed that the islands could "no longer be considered as *possessions*, in the same sense in which they were understood when the United States bound themselves to the guaranty."[59]

3. Aside from these extenuating circumstances, Adams next considered what was intended by the guaranty with regard to America's duty to intervene in the domestic affairs of other nations. Clearly, the guaranty carried certain limits—moral and political—for America's obligations even *before* the decimation of the French monarchy. Even if the authority of the sovereign had "been guided by the maxims of speculative freedom or of practical tyranny; had he provoked a rebellion in the islands, by oppressing the planters or by liberating their slaves; the guaranty in the treaty would not have bound us to assist him . . . in enforcing an absurd and unnatural Government against the perpetual resistances which it would . . . provoke." Armed with quotations from international jurists, he laid down as a "universal principle, that no stipulation contained in a treaty, can ever oblige one nation to . . . support the folly or injustice of another." Since the 1789 revolution in France, the island inhabitants had been in a constant state of civil war and rebellion; masters and slaves were divided against each other as "the torch of the furies has been applied to the composition." The state of desperation led a delegation of the colonists to solicit the protection of the British government, with the king of England agreeing to hold them in trust for the French crown. The power of America's guaranty to France was mediated by the fact that the time had not yet come for a successful drive toward independence by the island patriots. The justice of their cause "would avail them . . . little against the powerful injustice of their oppressors." In addition, American intervention would defy "all moral and political consistency" by supporting the French in their oppressive administration over the colonies, especially "as a reward for rescuing them from the oppression of Great Britain."[60]

59. Ibid., 143–44.
60. Ibid., 145.

4. Finally, Adams judged the guaranty to be unsupportable since France had declared war against the naval powers of Europe. Taking part with the French Republic would unite the rest of Europe against the United States. Upon every rational calculation of probability, this would lead the nation to almost certain ruin. Adams again returned to the confluence of power and moral principle in explaining why America's legal obligation had "been rendered impracticable." The United States was obliged to adhere to "that uncontrollable law of nature, which is paramount to all human legislation, or compact, to remain at peace." Objective limits on the nation's resources in war and diplomacy, however, did not diminish America's wish "that laureled Victory may sit upon the sword of justice, and that . . . success may always be strewed before the feet of virtuous Freedom."[61]

IV.

Before turning to Adams's commentary on the diplomatic mission of Citizen Genêt, it will be instructive to compare briefly the words of "Marcellus" and "Columbus" with the essential foreign policy objectives of the Washington Administration. Conspicuous among the admonitions outlined in the Farewell Address are 1) to exalt patriotically the national words, *America, American, Americans*; 2) to beware of foreign intrigue; and 3) to have no political connections with the foreign nations of Europe with their different set of primary interests. As Bemis noted, "All three of these features of the . . . document can be discerned [in] the thought of John Quincy Adams."[62]

Americanism

JQA: Is this a condition tolerable of the imagination of American freemen? . . . Was it worthy of the generous and heroic self-devotion, which offered the slaughtered thousands of our friends

---

61. Ibid., 146.
62. Bemis, *American Foreign Policy and the Blessings of Liberty*, 272.

and brethren, as a willing sacrifice at the holy altar of American Independence, to be made the miserable babbles of foreign speculation, to be blown like feathers to and fro as the varying breath of foreign influence should be directed: to be bandied about, from one nation to another, subservient to the purposes of their mutual resentments, and played with as the passive instruments of their interests and passions? Perish the Americans whose soul is capable of submitting to such . . . servitude![63]

GW: The name of AMERICAN, which belongs to you in your national capacity, must always exalt the just pride of Patriotism, more than any appellation derived from local discriminations. With slight shades of difference, you have the same Religion, Manners, Habits and political Principles. You have in a common cause fought and triumphed together. The independence and liberty you possess are the work of joint councils, and joint efforts, of common dangers, sufferings and successes.[64]

Foreign Intrigue

JQA: Among the nations of antiquity, the *Athenians* were equally distinguished for the freedom of their government, the mildness of their laws, the sagaciousness of their understanding. . . . Their Constitution was purely democratic, and their penal laws were few; but the bare appearance of a stranger in the assemblies of the people, they made punishable with death, from a . . . well-grounded conviction that of all the dangers which encompass the liberties of a republican State, the intrusion of a foreign influence into the administration of their affairs, is the most alarming, and requires the opposition of the severest caution. . . . [65]

GW: Against the insidious wiles of foreign influence (I conjure you to believe me fellow-citizens), the jealousy of a free people ought to be *constantly* awake; since history and experience prove that for-

---

63. "Columbus No. 2," 159.
64. Paltsits, *Washington's Farewell Address*, 169.
65. "Columbus No. 2," 157–59.

eign influence is one of the most baneful foes of Republican Government. . . . [66]

Political Connections with Foreign Nations

JQA: . . . as the citizens of a nation at a vast distance from the continent of Europe; of a nation whose happiness consists in a real independence, disconnected from all European interests and European politics.[67]

GW: The Great rule of conduct for us, in regard to foreign Nations is in extending our commercial relations to have with them as little *political* connection as possible. So far as we have already formed engagements let them be fulfilled, with perfect good faith. Here let us stop.[68]

Washington's policy of neutrality was subjected to a severe test by the extravagant conduct of the young and vainglorious first minister from the French Republic, Citizen Edmond Genêt. Regarded with undisguised hostility by the Federalists even before reaching the nation's capital in 1793, he was welcomed by a lone cabinet member, Jefferson. Genêt's visit, Republicans claimed, "would furnish occasion for the *people* to testify their affections without respect to the cold caution of their government." His roaring reception, upon arriving in Charleston, South Carolina, persuaded this revolutionary hotspur that American opinion overwhelmingly favored intervention on the side of France; he was not convinced that Washington's proclamation accurately represented the popular will. The Francophile editors along the eastern seaboard agreed with the excitable Frenchman, one of them exulting: "Thanks to our God, that *sovereignty* still resides with THE PEOPLE, and that neither proclamations, nor *royal demeanor and state* can prevent them from exercising it. Of this the independent freemen

---

66. Paltsits, *Washington's Farewell Address,* 169.
67. "Marcellus No. 1," 140.
68. Paltsits, *Washington's Farewell Address,* 155.

of this metropolis [Philadelphia] gave a striking example in their reception of Mr. Genêt."[69]

In his study of Washington's presidency, Forrest McDonald notes that Genêt was armed with commissions for raising an *Armé du Mississippie* and an *Armée des Florides*—which, if successful in liberating Louisiana and Florida, would yield untold wealth. Similarly, Genêt issued licenses for plundering by sea: commissions for American vessels to act as privateers and attack unarmed British merchant vessels, haul them into American ports to be sold as prizes of war, and share the proceeds with the government of France, two-thirds going to the privateer. In later years, John Adams, vice president in 1793, reminisced to Jefferson: "You certainly never felt the terrorism excited by Genêt, in 1793, when ten thousand people in the streets of Philadelphia, day after day, threatened to drag Washington out of his house, and effect a revolution in the government, or compel it to declare war in favor of the French Revolution and against England." From the time of his arrival in Philadelphia until his departure, Genêt fitted out fourteen privateers, which brought back over eighty prizes, some of them taken within American waters. John F. Watson later recorded his childhood memories:

> I remember with what joy we ran to the wharves at the report of cannon, to see the arrivals of the Frenchman's prizes,—we were so pleased to see the British union down! Although most of us understood no French, we had caught many national airs . . . such as these: "Allons, enfans de la patrie, le jour de gloire est arrivé. . . ." It was a time, when . . . boys usurped the attributes of manhood; and the men, who should have chastened us, had themselves become very puerile![70]

The privateering exploits of Genêt were flagrant violations of the neutrality of the United States. "Never in my opinion, was as calamitous an appointment made, as that of the present minister of France

---

69. *National Gazette* (Philadelphia), May 22, 1793, 2:4; Bailey, *A Diplomatic History of the American People*, 74–76.

70. McDonald, *The Presidency of George Washington*, 124; *Works of John Adams*, 10:47; John F. Watson, *Annals of Philadelphia* (Philadelphia, 1881), 1:180.

here," Jefferson admitted after a few weeks of trying to deal with this incorrigible. He thought it would be "true wisdom in the Republican party to approve unequivocally of a state of neutrality" and "to abandon Genêt entirely, with expressions of strong friendship & adherence to his nation and confidence that he has acted against their sense." One device, which has long been a standard tool of psychological warfare when nations are at war, is to appeal to "the people" over the head of the chief executive of the nation. Genêt's exhortation of Americans to oppose their president elicited a swift response from Washington. "Is the minister of the French Republic to set the acts of this government at defiance *with impunity*? And then threaten the executive with an appeal to the people? What would the world think of such conduct, and of the government of the United States in submitting to it?"[71] In August 1793, the cabinet unanimously voted to request his recall. Robespierre gladly consented and, in return, asked for the recall of Gouverneur Morris, whose intrigues at Paris had been about as suspect as Genêt's in Philadelphia.

Writing as "Columbus," John Quincy Adams insisted on treating Genêt as a diplomat who was bound to conform to treaty arrangements and customary diplomatic usage. He held "it to be a moral and religious duty," not only to discountenance the defamation of Washington by this *opéra bouffe* bungler, but to defend "the integrity . . . and public respectability . . . of the diplomatic art." In view of the many years of foreign service that Adams later would undertake for his nation, the spirited commentary of "Columbus" is a useful example of why he refused to separate ethical impulses from political aims in the methods of diplomatic negotiation. Albert Sorel, writing about the character of traditional diplomacy throughout the seventeenth and eighteenth centuries, observed that negotiations of the *ancien regime* were "governed only by self-interest." The "reason of state reigned" as the "Old Europe had no scruples and no pride in false delicacy." While mindful of the sacrifices states sometimes endure for their national interests, Adams argued that recognizable norms of international be-

---

71. Samuel Eliot Morison, Henry Steele Commager, and William E. Leuchtenburg, *Growth of the American Republic,* 1:301; *Writings of George Washington,* 12:302.

havior were at stake whenever diplomats, like Genêt, resort to "the science of typographical negotiation." Beyond probing the interrelation of methods and purposes in diplomacy, Adams himself was not immune to the stirrings of political opportunity in taking up the defense of the Administration. The proud words of his father are self-explanatory.

> Washington was . . . under obligations to him [J. Q. A.] for turning the tide of sentiment against Genêt, and he was . . . grateful for it. The enthusiasm for Genêt and . . . the French Revolution was, at this time, almost universal throughout the United States. . . . J. Q. Adams' writings first turned this tide. . . . Not all Washington's ministers, Hamilton and Pickering included, could have written these papers, which were so fatal to Genêt. Washington saw it . . . and took great pains to find out the author. The first notice I had of his decision to appoint my son to a mission abroad was from his Secretary of State Randolph, who told me he had been ordered to enquire of the members of Congress, and others, concerning the life and character of J. Q. Adams, and, he was, that day to report in favor of his appointment.[72]

Genêt's conduct raised the question of the appropriate actions to be taken against an ambassador who conspires against a ruler to whom he is accredited. The ambassador, according to French diplomatist Jean Jusserand, is to be more exacting for himself as he is much more in the public eye, and since others may have a strong motive in taking advantage of his faults and foibles. He will become acquainted with all sorts of people "but be careful to keep absolutely aloof from internal politics and avoid taking sides with one party or another, especially . . . in republican states." Callières warned against a similar failure in the representative character of the diplomat: "This care to seek out everybody, this kind of popularity, must not be accompanied by anything that might lead people to suppose that the envoy is endeavouring to enter into the detail of domestic affairs, which he should not, or to profit of the multiplicity of the members composing the sovereignty, to sow division among them." Furthermore, he would at once become sus-

---

72. "Columbus No. 1," 149–50; Albert Sorel, *Europe under the Old Regime*, 60; *Writings of John Quincy Adams*, 1:148 n.1.

pected. "The republican . . . spirit of liberty, which liberty, to be solid, must rest on internal union, ever leads all the other affections to this rallying point." The envoy who neglects these truths "becomes useless to his government in the country where he is and in all others."[73]

International lawyers such as Gentiles, Grotius, Zouche, and Bynkershoeck, discussed this question and formulated general principles concerning diplomatic immunities and privileges. Yet, as Stephen Kertesz points out, most problems connected with precedence—particularly the rules for permanent embassies—were not settled until after the Congress of Vienna in 1815. Although it may have been "a novelty in the diplomatic world, to see the [French] envoy of a foreign nation assuming a character like this," Adams balanced a concern for diplomatic immunity with the workings of a democratic society. Genuine freedom in republican government makes it "unquestionably the right of every . . . citizen, to express without control his sentiments upon . . . the conduct of public men." Representatives of the electorate, "being only the dispositaries of their power," are accountable to the voters for the execution of their trust. Yet this principle, Adams contended, ought not—in common cases—to be extended to the conduct of foreign ministers. So long as the agent of a friendly nation confined himself "within the circle of his own rights," the demands of his country—however offensive those pretensions might be—"ought not be a subject of personal animadversion upon him."[74]

The conduct of Genêt precipitated a debate involving both diplomatic protocol and executive authority in the "right of political communication with foreign powers [accredited] to the government of the union." As a foreign agent, Genêt's official powers were circumscribed within the limits of his commission; his right to negotiate, then, was only commensurate with his credentials. These did not permit the French envoy to arm himself with "all the weapons of a wordy war" and negotiate with the American populace through any other medium

73. Jean J. Jusserand, *The School for Ambassadors and Other Essays*, 52–53; Francois de Callières, *On the Manner of Negotiating with Princes*, 16, 20, 25, 51, 120ff.

74. Stephen D. Kertesz, *The Quest for Peace through Diplomacy*, 4–5; "Columbus No. 1," 149.

than that of their government. In his letters home, Genêt gloated over his own matchless deeds.

> The whole of America has risen to acknowledge in me the minister of the French Republic. . . . I live in the midst of perpetual feasts. I receive addresses from all parts of the continent. I see . . . that my way of negotiating pleases our American brothers, and I am founded to believe . . . that my mission will be a fortunate one from every point of view! I include here with American gazettes in which I have marked the articles concerning myself. . . . I am in the meantime provisioning the West Indies; I excite Canadians to break the British yoke, I arm the Kentukois, and I prepare a naval expedition which will facilitate their descent on New Orleans.[75]

Washington so underestimated Genêt's impact that he left for a vacation in Mount Vernon just before the emissary arrived. "The people," says Junius, "are seldom mistaken in their *opinions,* in their *sentiments* they are never wrong." Adams understood that, in a state of civil and political liberty, "parties are to the public body, what the passions are to the individual." He realized, but not without a certain degree of apprehension, that "the animated and vivifying spirit of party seems to be . . . essential to the existence of genuine freedom."[76]

Yet even the French foreign minister in Paris was persuaded that Genêt had violated his letter of diplomatic instructions.

> You invoke your instructions from the "Conseil exécutif" of the Republic; but your instructions enjoin you quite the reverse: they order you to treat with the *government,* not with a *portion* of the people. . . . You say that Washington *does not pardon you your success,* and that he hampers your moves in a thousand ways. You are ordered to treat with the American Government; there only can you attain real successes; all the others are illusory and contrary to the interests of your country.[77]

Adams thought it his moral duty to censure the French ambassador, in part because any foreign conspiracy "of arming one part of *America*

---

75. "Columbus No. 2," 152–53; *Correspondence of the French Ministers to the United States,* 214–17.
76. "Columbus No. 2," 158.
77. Jean J. Jusserand, *With Americans of Past and Present Days,* 251–52.

against the other" generated domestic "excesses destructive to . . . the enjoyment of our most valuable rights." He appreciated that minority rights, anchored in higher law and venerable traditions, are soon cut adrift by the frenzy that delivers popular causes beyond "the exertion of restraint and regulation." The ambassador's example illustrated how "the candidates of popular favor" conceal their private views "by standing forth as advocates . . . of the public interest." With Madison, Adams agreed that the general welfare "is perhaps promoted, by placing the jealousy of one patriot as a guard over the ambition of another." Beyond this step, however, the interference of foreign agents in domestic affairs "must be inevitably fatal to the liberties of the State, as the admission of strangers to arbitrate . . . the domestic differences of man and wife is destructive to the happiness of a private family." The national interest is endangered if

> the partizans of any . . . faction cease to rely upon their own talents and services to support their influence among their country men, and link themselves in union with an external power. . . . [Then] the principles of self-defence, the instinct for self-preservation . . . will suggest a similar connection to their opponents; whichever of the party nominally prevails, the whole country is really enslaved; alternately the sport of every caprice, that directs the two foreign sovereigns . . . may disguise under the mask of friendship and benevolence.[78]

By pointing to the link between internal faction and external power, Adams took with him a powerful reminder of the resentments engendered by foreign intervention in the domestic divisions of rival nations.

In addition, Genêt's application to Congress to pass judgment upon his conduct raised important constitutional issues. The framers of the Constitution delegated to Congress the power to regulate commercial intercourse with foreign nations (Article 1, sec. 8); however, the president was assigned the responsibility of negotiating with ministers of other nations (Article 2, sec. 3), and with the concurrence of the Senate, to makes treaties with them. The president was also directed to "take care that the laws be faithfully executed"; and, "if . . . a difference of

78. "Columbus, No. 2," 159.

opinion on the meaning of a national compact should arise between him and the agent, they [the people] had not reserved to themselves the right of judging between them." Nor did the framers imagine that they had imparted to the chief magistrate "a power in the smallest degree arbitrary." In all cases affecting ambassadors, for example, the Supreme Court has original jurisdiction (Article 3, sec. 2). Furthermore, if the president "proceeded upon a wilful and treacherous misinterpretation" of his constitutional duties, the rules of impeachment (Article 1, sec. 2) provide for his removal from office. Inasmuch as no appellate jurisdiction was assigned to the elected representatives of the people, the intention of the French minister "was no less hostile to the Constitution, than insulting to the government of the Union."[79]

Moreover, presidential authority in foreign policy conduct was called into question by Genêt's letter to the secretary of state, challenging the revocation of an exequatur awarded to a French vice consul (Antoine Charbonet Duplaine). In June 1793, Citizen Duplaine received from President Washington an exequatur recognizing him as vice consul for the Republic of France, within the states of New Hampshire, Massachusetts, and Rhode Island. On October 10 of that year, the president revoked the exequatur. Washington's reasoning was that "the said Duplaine having under the colors of his . . . office committed sundry encroachments and infractions on the laws of the land, and . . . having caused a vessel to be rescued with an armed force out of the custody of an officer of justice, who had arrested the same by process from his court, it was . . . no longer . . . consistent with the obedience due to laws, that . . . Duplaine should be permitted to continue in the said functions, powers, and privileges." In his letter, Genêt argued that the Constitution "has not given the President the right of exercising this authority [i.e., revocation]; and that it can be exerted *only by the sovereign* of the agent, or by the one to which he is sent." Accordingly, Genêt demanded that the president refer Duplaine's conduct to the legislature of Massachusetts. This led Adams to inquire, "whether by the *Laws of Nations,* there is in every sovereign state, a power compe-

79. Ibid., 151–52.

tent to dismiss the agent of a foreign power for encroachment upon . . . the laws of the land, under colour of executing the duties of his office."[80] Adams's affirmative defense of presidential authority was closely tied to his understanding of international law.

The same warning against extremes that characterized Adams's moral reasoning about the national interest applies to his reflections on the legal basis of state relations. A core of legal norms, laying down the rights and duties of states in relation to each other, developed in the sixteenth and seventeenth centuries. These rules were securely established in 1648, when the Treaty of Westphalia brought the religious wars of Europe to an end and made the territorial nation state the cornerstone of the modern state system. On numerous issues—frontiers, the rights of diplomats and foreign nationals, the laws of war and amicable settlement, treaty violations and the enforcement of sanctions—legal rules determine the mutual rights and obligations of states if anarchy and violence are not to be the order of the day. Hugo Grotius's *On The Law of War and Peace*, published in 1628, is the classic codification of that early system of international law. It is also worth mentioning that, during the four hundred years of its existence, the bulk of international law has, in most instances, been scrupulously observed. Adams believed that the existence and application of international law derived from objective social forces (i.e., identical or complementary interests of states and the distribution of power among them). One of the foremost modern scholars of international law summarized the reality that makes the ideal of lawful international society a practical possibility in an otherwise anarchic arena:

> The first and principal moral is that a Law of Nations can exist only if there be an equilibrium, a balance of power, between the members of the Family of Nations. If the Powers cannot keep one another in check, no rules of law will have any force, since an overpowerful State will naturally try to act according to discretion and disobey the law. As there is not and never can be a central political authority above Sovereign States that could enforce the rules of the Law of Nations, a

80. "Columbus No. 3," 162.

balance of power must prevent any member of the Family of Nations
from becoming omnipotent.[81]

Adams contended that there lies, at the foundation of any legal
system, a body of principles that incorporates the guiding ideas of
justice and order to be expounded by the rules of law. International law
embraces "principles of reciprocal justice and equity, which common
sense and natural reason dictate as having the greatest tendency to
promote the mutual advantage and happiness of all nations." Legal
rules always refer to ethics and mores for the determination of their
meaning. The obligations of states inhere in "that fundamental maxim
of nature and religion, to do unto others as we would that they should
do unto us." This universal rule of right enables the ethicist to judge
"every political question that can arise among nations as well as individuals." The opposition between man and society, individual and
political action, is a mere figure of speech insofar as the individual
political actor is confronted with a collectivity which is supposed
likewise to act. Once the opposition between man and society is reduced to the opposition between different kinds of individual actions,
it becomes obvious that the difference in moral character between the
two kinds of actions is, at best, a relative one. The action of society, of
the nation, or any other collectivity, political or otherwise, as such has
no empirical existence. At the same time, Adams knew that international law involves political agreements among states, thereby incor-
porating certain interests and rights subject to change and the most
contradictory interpretations. Applying a universal code to the political transactions of different societies would "occasion perpetual alter-
cation among them, unless some less comprehensive principles were
admitted as deducible from it." For the statesman, subordinate axioms
of conduct must be relied upon to support any national act that does
not "militate against the stronger obligations of natural justice." Similarly, those writings that constitute the science of national jurisprudence are acknowledged by the common consent of nations "as evidence of the conclusions, which in particular cases are to be drawn

81. L. Oppenheim, *International Law*, 1:80.

from the general principle." These secondary sources of law and obligation are not "infallible guides, but to be recurred to as experienced conductors, and consulted as impartial advisors."[82]

Adams claimed that the revocation of Duplaine's exequatur could be defended by the recourse of international law to the principles of natural reason and national custom. Principles of "public justice" required that some power in government should be available to remove the servant of another sovereign, "who makes the duties of his office a cloak for the most violent infraction of the laws of the land." If such a power did not exist, the liberty and property of citizens would be perpetually at the mercy of a stranger. In addition, the expedient proposed by Genêt—complaining to the sovereign of the culprit for the purpose of his recall—was a very inadequate remedy when that sovereign is at a distance of three thousand miles. Genêt's remedy had little applicability beyond minor offenses that do not require a speedy reparation, and where the removal of the official is "considered as a penalty for the past, rather than a precaution against future guilt." Adams opposed "this mendicancy of justice" for it left no reasonable alternative between a degrading dependence of America upon France for reparation and the furies of war. What, for example, would be the government's response if the demand for removal or recall was met with indifference or disagreement? The right of doing justice, Adams insisted, is itself very distinct from that of requesting that justice be done: both, however, "are equally necessary, inherent and unalienable by a nation as much as the right of personal liberty in the individual."[83]

Both intentions and consequences mattered in the removal of Duplaine's privilege. By depriving Duplaine of the power of repeating the crime, the revocation "affords a security against his evil intentions to the nation which has already been prejudiced by them." The ethical mark of administration policy was that it violated "none of the natural or civil rights of the man himself" and deserved the praise of lenity. It was equally important that care be taken so that "the rights and interests of his constituents suffer no detriment, in consequence of his

82. Morgenthau, *Scientific Man vs. Power Politics,* 187–88; "Columbus No. 3," 164–65.
83. "Columbus No. 3," 167.

dismission." The principles of reciprocal benefit and utility require that the removal of a foreign agent "not be permitted to interfere with the rights, and as little as possible with the transient interests of the other nation." In so doing, the justice of the other party can never consider it as an act of aggression. Common sense, if not a common humanity, teaches that the interests of all nations "ought to multiply as far as possible the means of avoiding war."[84]

In the diplomatic intercourse between sovereign states, moral methods counted as much as those broad conceptions of national purpose shaping foreign policy goals. Considering the Duplaine affair on the footing of national custom, Adams quoted leading authorities of international jurisprudence. Regarding the immunities of diplomats, Grotius distinguishes between what may be done by nations in the way of self-defense and what may be done in the way of punishment. Although the law of nations does not allow an ambassador's life to be taken away as punishment for a crime, this law does not oblige the state "to suffer him to use violence without endeavoring to resist it." In the words of Vattel,

> But shall an ambassador with impunity cabal against the state where he resides, plot its ruin, stir up subjects to revolt, and . . . foment the most dangerous conspiracies, under assurance of being supported by his master, if he behaves as an enemy, shall it not be allowable to treat him as such? The case is unquestionable with regard to an ambassador who takes up arms and uses violence; for then whom he attacks may repel him, self-defense being part of the law of nature.[85]

The inviolability attached to the public character of a foreign minister may be relaxed only before the paramount right of self-preservation and necessity. Both Martens and Vattel acknowledge that a minister, whenever and however his mission is terminated, still remains entitled to all the privileges of his public character until his return to his own country. This regard for his position is "so necessary for the correspondence of nations, and to the dignity of the prince represented, that the

84. "Publicola No. 10," 107–8.
85. Vattel, *The Law of Nations*, 536–37.

conduct of his minister should be complained of to him, and reparation demanded; and if nothing can be obtained, and the importance of his faults . . . requires that a stop be put to them, not to carry resentment beyond an abrupt dismission."[86] The revocation of Duplaine's exequatur was an act of this description. Adams contended that Washington's decision embodied two basic obligations: 1) an obligation to the nation by depriving the minister of the power of repeating the crime; and 2) an obligation to remain impartial before the interests of another sovereign by not trespassing "upon the natural or civil rights" of an accredited agent.

86. Ibid. 536.

SIX

The Ethics of Power
in American Diplomacy

The Statecraft of John Quincy Adams

The political vision and diplomatic legacy of John Quincy Adams testifies to the significance of moral reasoning in the statesman's effort to uphold the national interest in a world where nations live together in a state of nature, acknowledging no superior on earth. Recourse to principles of political ethics afforded Adams a vantage point from which to evaluate the volatile problem of intervention— viewed in terms of the moral responsibilities and limits of American power—at a crucial turning point in the diplomatic history of the young republic. Important in this connection is how Adams attempted to reconcile the blessings of liberty with the methods and purposes of American diplomacy within and beyond the Western Hemisphere. Attention now turns to the sources and meaning of statesmanship for Adams who—as perhaps the nation's most experienced diplomat and accomplished secretary of state—judged the obligations and opportunities of American power from a perspective that considered moral precepts and international law as compatible with the prudent pursuit of American national interest in world affairs.

To understand Adams properly one must move away from the view that realism and idealism in foreign policy are mutually exclusive cate-

231

gories. In fact, Adams's conception of political ethics was closely related to the Jeffersonian heritage in American politics and diplomacy. Both Jefferson and Adams had a vision of statecraft whereby power and principle dialectically interact in the working out of an American public philosophy. The question of intervention in world politics repeatedly precipitates national debate about the moral auspices of American power in foreign policy. How did Adams's ethical impulses inform his reactions to European intervention in the Western Hemisphere? American incursions into Spanish Florida? Declarations of independence in Latin America and Europe? The war with Mexico? What is striking about the diplomatic heritage of the Founders' era and a generation thereafter—the balance of power, moral considerations in foreign policy, and democratic control in foreign policy—is the marked identity between their political and intellectual interests and ours. The question of intervention is an old—and persistent—one. Adams spoke across the generations with the message that America's duty to champion freedom around the world takes its inspiration from the internal purposes of republican government.

Believing themselves to be the beneficiaries of the *novus ordo seclorum*, early American statesmen understood the nation's identity as a testament to the triumph of universal rights and an ordered scheme of "liberty under law." "America," Morgenthau once observed, "has conceived itself not as a link in a historic chain that began in the distant past and in distant places and may never end, but as the creator of a new world, *ex nihilo*, owing to its virtue and providential design."[1] The constitutional debate between Federalists and Anti-Federalists touched directly upon the diplomatic mission of the new republic. In choosing the new constitution the country implicitly recognized the possibility of national self-extension and continental empire, but Anti-Federalist fears about the consequences of such a vision remained a latent topic

---

1. The founding as an epochal moment in our own and in world history was the guiding theme of several essays collected under the "The New Face of the American Founding" in the *Social Science Quarterly* 68 (December 1987): 653–744; Hans J. Morgenthau, "The Founding Fathers and Foreign Policy: Some Implications for the Late Twentieth Century," 15.

of partisan controversy. These reservations surfaced a decade later in the reaction of Jeffersonians to the actions of Federalist Presidents Washington and John Adams. Jeffersonian and Hamiltonian factions vigorously debated the limits and requirements of American security. For all its rancor, however, the partisanship reflected, as it were, a family quarrel, a point Jefferson himself sought to make when he asserted in his first inaugural address that in spite of differences of opinion, "we are all republicans, we are all federalists."

Adams's political career symbolized in significant ways the values and principles inherent in Jefferson's bipartisan appeal to those who would defend a union dedicated to perpetuate the blessings of liberty. Aristocratic by education and temperament, he proclaimed himself a republican; initially identified as a Federalist, he came to support Jefferson's party; though a New Englander, he made the Union his passion. This act of nonpartisan independence, he noted late in his career, "marked the principle by which my whole public life has been governed from that day to this." His moral and political compass was the standard his father had laid down many years before: "The magistrate is the servant not of his desires, not even of the people, but of his God." George Frisbie Hoar acknowledged that Adams's New England demeanor was: "fit for exact ethical discussion, clear in seeing general truths, active, unresting, fond of inquiry and debate, but penetrated and restrained by shrewd common sense. . . . He had a tenacity of purpose, a lofty and inflexible courage, an unbending will, which never qualified or flinched before human antagonist, or before exile, torture or death."[2]

I.

"From the time of the Declaration of our Independence," according to Henry Kissinger, "Americans have believed that this country has a moral significance for the world." The United States was created in a conscious act by a people dedicated to a set of political and ethical

2. John F. Kennedy, *Profiles in Courage*, 33.

principles they held to be of universal meaning. A new generation of American statesmen, looking beyond Cold War rivalry, are called upon to affirm certain truths to be virtually self-evident: that the United States is a great power with a unique national identity; that what we do will affect not only our own survival but the fate of Western civilization as well; that men fighting for freedom are moved by great ideals; and that, for these reasons, it is urgent that we see ourselves and that others see us as acting in accord with ideals that are sharable and worthy of respect. Today, Jefferson's common human faith in the rights of man will certainly find acceptance in a wider immediate circle than he ever dreamed of.

> Convinced that the republican is the only form of government which is not eternally at open or secret war with the rights of mankind, my prayers and efforts shall be cordially distributed to the support of that we have so happily established. It is . . . an animating thought, that while we are securing the rights of ourselves and our posterity, we are pointing out the way to struggling nations, who wish like us to emerge from their tyrannies also. Heaven help their struggles, and lead them, as it has done us, triumphantly through them.[3]

The two great religious-moral traditions that infused early American thinking—New England Calvinism and Virginian Jeffersonianism—arrive at similar conclusions about the meaning of American national character and destiny. In *Wonder Working Providence of Zion's Saviour* (1650), Edward Johnson spoke of New England as the place "where the Lord would create a new heaven and a new earth, new churches and a new commonwealth altogether." A century later, Ezra Stiles of Yale preached a sermon on "the United States elevated to glory and honor" in which he defined the nation as "God's American Israel." Jefferson and John Adams called the amalgam "the dictates of reason and pure Americanism." The self-interpretive symbols of American nationhood look in two directions: "towards the truth of man's existence personally, socially, and historically, on the one hand; and toward the persuasive and evocative articulation of that truth in the founda-

---

3. Henry A. Kissinger, "Morality and Power," 59; Adrienne Koch, *Power, Morals, and the Founding Fathers*, 151.

tion myth of the new community, on the other hand." The vision at the center of American politics, then, is structured by insights into human reality "taken to be universally valid for all mankind, even as they are adapted to the concrete conditions of time and place at the moment of the articulation of the new nation as an entity politically organized for action in history."[4]

Jefferson's conception of the innocency and virtue of the new nation was not informed by the biblical symbolism of the New England tracts. His religious faith was a form of Christianity that had passed through the rationalism of the French Enlightenment. His moral transcendence was expressed through the belief in the power of "nature's God" over the vicissitudes of history. Jefferson was moved to acknowledge that nature's God had a very special purpose in founding this new community. America had a political mission to fulfill, for itself and before the eyes of the world: to prove that reason, order, and law are the genuine fruits of an educated people governing themselves. "The eyes of the virtuous all over the earth are turned with anxiety on us, as the only depositories of the sacred fire of liberty, and that our falling into anarchy would decide forever the destinies of mankind, and seal the political heresy that man is incapable of self-government." Every nation has its own form of spiritual pride. These examples of American self-appreciation could be matched by corresponding sentiments in other nations. To know that nations are subject to the moral law is one thing, while to pretend to know with certainty what is good and evil in the relations among nations is quite another.[5] The tragic conception of politics and diplomacy, however, need not recommend cynicism or complacency with respect to fundamental moral choices. Indeed, it will make a difference whether the particular culture in which the policies of nations—the actions of statesmen—are formed is only as

4. Thomas Jefferson to Edward Rutledge, June 24, 1797, *Writings*, 9:409; John Adams to Benjamin Rush, July 7, 1805, in John A. Schutz and Douglass Adair, ed. *Spur of Fame: Dialogues of John Adams and Benjamin Rush, 1805–1813*, 30; Sandoz, *A Government of Laws*, 35, 35–36, 38, 83–84, 105, 114–15, and 123; Eric Voegelin, *New Science of Politics*, chaps. 1–3.

5. Thomas Jefferson to John Hollis, Esq., May 5, 1811, *Writings*, 13:58; Morgenthau, *Politics among Nations*, 11.

deep and as high as the nation's highest ideals; or whether there is a dimension in the culture from which the element of vanity in all human achievements is discerned. Jefferson's inaugural appeal to Federalists and Republicans was less important as a conciliatory overture than as a subtle intimation of the moral resources in American politics and statecraft.

That the national unity of all Americans carried a distinctive message for mankind can be seen by noting the relationship between power and morals in Jefferson's philosophy. Of particular importance is how the natural and inalienable rights of man are derived from, or connected with, natural law. For example, Jefferson affirmed the rights of man on a preponderantly moral basis of preference and appropriateness to human nature. Jefferson's convictions were concisely stated in the following terms: "We believed, with them, that man was a rational animal, endowed by nature with rights, and with an innate sense of justice; and that he could be restrained from wrong and protected in right, by moderate powers, confided to persons of his own choice, and held to their duties by dependence on his own will." Self-realization, always in the interpersonal context of other selves, may be the natural moral goal. Natural law constitutes the system of governing norms, rules, and duties that bind man—the correlative, in short of the natural rights that he claims. Natural law in its widest legal sense (what Jefferson referred to as "the law of nature and nations") includes this meaning plus the usages and customs of nations dealing with other nations in the interest of peace and under the controlling ideal of more humane and civilized practice.[6]

Enduring moral principles (e.g., the worth of every human being, equality of consideration to which all are entitled in society, justice, and fraternity) are in no way limited to a given time or society but invoke the vision of a brotherhood of man. The important point is that one hereby asserts a moral limit on power politics; one condemns force and violence as an extensive, wholesale instrument of national or international policy. Jefferson urged justice upon nations if they would have

---

6. Thomas Jefferson to Judge William Johnson, June 12, 1823, *Writings*, 15:441; Koch, *Power, Morals, and the Founding Fathers*, 44–45.

the firm friendship of other countries. Of Great Britain, unable to win allies in the great battle with Napoleonic France, Jefferson wrote that she was a living example "that no nation however powerful, any more than any individual, can be unjust with impunity. Sooner or later public opinion, an instrument merely moral in the beginning, will find occasion physically to inflict its sentence upon the unjust." The lesson, he believed, was as useful to the weak as well as to the strong. The law of nature and nations, then, becomes another illustration of Jefferson's theory of natural rights. Each nation "forms a moral person" and each member of a nation is "personally responsible for his society."[7]

The only exception to the laws of nature and nations is the transcendent right to resist self-destruction. As there are circumstances that sometimes excuse the non-performance of contracts between man and man, so nations may annul their obligations "if performance becomes self-destructive to the party." Only "the law of self-preservation overrules the laws of obligations in others." In addition, Jefferson was enough of a realist to see clearly that no nation can fully transcend its own interests. "All know the influence of interest on the mind of man, and how unconsciously his judgment is warped by that influence." In 1812, when Napoleon was at the pinnacle of his power, Jefferson was unprepared to contemplate moral principles apart from the political exigencies of American national security. His was the hope that "the powers of Europe may be so poised and counterpoised among themselves, that their own security may require the presence of all their forces at home, leaving the other quarters of the world in undisturbed tranquility."[8]

This was also a realism that made room for political ideals and declarations of rights. The Thomas Jefferson who wrote in 1809 that "I am persuaded no constitution was ever before so well calculated as ours for extensive empire and self-government" could also write in 1817 that America's role in the world was to "consecrate a sanctuary

7. Thomas Jefferson to James Madison, April 23, 1804, *Writings*, 8:300.
8. Thomas Jefferson, "Opinion on the Question Whether the United States Has a Right to Intervene to Renounce Their Treaties with France," *Writings*, 3:228; "Autobiography," *Writings*, 1:120; Morgenthau, *Defense of the National Interest*, 20–21.

for those whom the misrule of Europe may compel to seek happiness in other climes." America's influence was not to be military but moral in nature: "This refuge once known," he declared, "will produce happiness even of those who remain there, by warning their taskmasters that . . . another Canaan is open where there subjects will be received as brothers." The struggle for political power is inseparable from the pursuit of justice. Consider in this connection Jefferson's admonition that "it is true, that nations are to be judges for themselves; since no nation has the right to sit in judgment over another, but the tribunal of our consciences remains, and that also of the opinion of the world."[9]

Modern perspectives of realism or idealism in American diplomacy often sharpen the power/morality dichotomy in such a fashion as to ignore the manner in which a statesman's political responsibility is part and parcel of his role as a moral witness to the actions of his nation. The importance of America as a democratic example to others—the need to nourish the tree of liberty—is possible only by pursuing a foreign policy that seeks reform and liberation from the inside out rather than by crusades and protracted engagements abroad. For the diplomatist, the Jeffersonian legacy is not a doctrine or mere ideological credo; rather, his contribution (although not alone here among the Founding Fathers) underscores the centrality of political ethics for relating the national interest to structures of community and justice beyond the parochial nation state. The issue is one that points to the need for a meeting ground upon which the philosopher and statesman can momentarily converge.

II.

Arthur Schlesinger, Jr., refers to John Quincy Adams, and several of his contemporaries, as honest Jeffersonians. Admittedly, the categoriza-

9. Robert N. Bellah, *The Broken Covenant*, 89; Dante Germino, unpublished paper delivered at the Claremont Institute Conference on the American Bicentennial, Claremont, California, February 23–25, 1984; Jefferson, "Opinion on the Question Whether the United States Has a Right to Intervene to Renounce Their Treaties with France," *Writings*, 3:228.

tion is arguable in light of several profound differences in political and philosophical orientation; however, Schlesinger's paradox is not entirely lost with reference to a common intellectual inclination on the part of both leaders to affirm, however precariously, the moral basis of American power and expansion. Moreover, they arrived at this conclusion by divergent paths, even while disagreeing on the origins and merits of republican and democratic politics. "We are . . . as Mr. Jefferson forty years ago said, all federalists—all republicans, but not all *Democrats*, no more than we are all Aristocrats or Monarchists." Yet Adams, the only Federalist in the United States Senate to support Jefferson's purchase of the Louisiana territory, acknowledged in this transaction that "fortune claims to herself the lion's share. To seize and to turn to profit the precise instant of the turning tide, is itself among the eminent properties of a Statesman, and if requiring less elevated virtue than the firmness and prudence that withstand adversity, or the moderation which adorns and dignifies prosperity, it is not less essential to the character of an accomplished ruler of men." Adams, with Jefferson, knew too well that "the selfish and the social passions are intermingled in the conduct of every man acting in a public capacity." Moreover, the good that an individual can do for his fellow citizens "is seldom proportioned to his dispositions and the inclination to do good itself, unless enlightened by a clear perception, guided by a discriminating judgment, and animated by . . . active resolution, evaporates in the dreams of imagination."[10]

No American was better qualified to shape and direct American foreign policy during the 1814–1828 era than John Quincy Adams. In support of President Adams's promotion of his son to minister plenipotentiary to Prussia in 1797, George Washington wrote, "Mr. Adams is the most valuable public character we have abroad, and . . . there remains no doubt in my mind that he will prove himself to be the ablest, of all our diplomatic corps." Thomas Jefferson spoke of Secretary of State Adams's momentous state paper defending General Jackson's actions in Florida as "among the ablest compositions [he had]

10. Arthur M. Schlesinger, Jr., *The Age of Jackson*, 313; John Quincy Adams, *The Social Compact*, 30; Adams, *Lives*, 83–84; *Memoirs*, 2:13, 5:13.

ever seen, both as to logic and style" and recommended that it be thoroughly circulated in Europe as an illustration of the level of American statecraft. European diplomacy at this time was peculiarly a personal diplomacy. Adams alone knew the leading statesmen of Europe—particularly Tsar Alexander, Talleyrand, Nesselrode, Capodistrias, and Castlereagh—and understood the political and social values essential to cabinet diplomacy at the time of the Congress of Vienna following the defeat of Napoleon. It would be hard to quarrel with Brooks Adams's profile of his grandfather as "the most interesting and suggestive personage of the early nineteenth century."[11]

Upon being appointed secretary of state in 1817, Adams acknowledged the partisan controversy in the wake of his appointment with the pointed judgment that President Monroe would "neither require nor expect from me any sacrifice of principles inconsistent with my own sense of right."[12] Although several classic works chronicle Adams's diplomacy and political career, few have attended to his unfailing preoccupation with the normative foundations of the national interest in an uncertain and threatening world arena. His *Memoirs* and *Writings* provide invaluable commentary on why American diplomacy ought not be insulated from concepts of virtue and right in the political lives of men and nations. Adams's statecraft, then, offers an important historical backdrop against which future generations will be called upon to rethink the relationship of the original objects of American society to the methods and purposes of foreign policy. Precisely how ethical and political principles of universal significance were to guide the destiny of the nation was the challenge Adams confronted in trying to balance the requirement of the nation's security with emanations of the European balance of power in the New World.

Adams rejected the ethical dualism underlying the European diplomatic heritage of *raison d'état* by considering the "American Union as a

11. George Washington to John Adams, February 20, 1797, in *Works of John Adams*, 8:529; Thomas Jefferson to President Monroe, January 18, 1819, *Writings of Thomas Jefferson*, 10:122; Brooks Adams, "Introduction," in Adams, *Degradation of Democratic Dogma*, 13.

12. JQA to Abigail Adams, April 23, 1817, 6:182.

moral Person in the family of Nations." His religious faith held that men owe their existence to, and act in the light of, the presence of a Divine Will that created and nurtures an immutable moral order. In his "Marcellus" letters, defending Washington's Proclamation of Neutrality in 1793, Adams applied the golden rule to the affairs of state. Precepts of national conduct were closely related to those of personal morality; the rights of nations "are nothing more than an extension of the rights of individuals."[13]

Against the Machiavellian view of the state as originating in "ineluctable necessity" and through which power becomes the state's "first law of motion," Adams viewed the statesman as a moral witness to the values and actions of the nation. In particular, Adams declined to ask "of heaven success, even for my country, in a cause where she would be in the wrong." *Fiat justitia, pareat coelum.* He judged harshly "all patriotism incompatible with the principles of eternal justice." Adams held it to be one of the most undeniable principles of government, "that the truest policy of a nation consists in the performance of its duties." Primary among these, "binding in chains more adamantine than all the rest the conscience of the Chief Magistrate of this Union," is "to maintain *peace* amidst the convulsions of foreign wars, and to enter the list as parties to no cause, other than our own."[14] The existential predicament of human legislators, therefore, is to seek that always precarious balance between ubiquitous self-interest and those eternal and immutable principles that help define man's moral nature.

The most explicit manifestation of the order of nature governing the intercourse of nations was the existing body of international law. Describing the United States as an "Independent Christian Nation, recognizing the general principles of the European law of nations," Adams wrote,

> The laws of social intercourse between sovereign communities constitute the law of nations, all derived from three sources:—the laws of

13. JQA to Charles W. Upham, February 2, 1837, in Edward Tatum, "Ten Unpublished Letters of John Quincy Adams," 383; East, *John Quincy Adams, The Critical Years, 1785–1794,* 179.

14. John Adams to JQA, August 1, 1816, 6:61–62; Adams, *Lives,* 87; JQA to Hugh Nelson, April 28, 1823, 7:371.

nature . . . or the dictates of justice; usages, sanctioned by custom; and treaties or national covenants. Super-added to these, the *Christian* nations, between themselves, admit, with various latitudes of interpretation, and little consistency of practice, the laws of humanity and mutual benevolence taught in the gospel of Christ.[15]

"The general history of mankind," he claimed, "for the last three thousand years, demonstrates beyond all contradiction the progressive improvement of the condition of man, by means of the establishment of International Law, tending to social benevolence and humanity."[16] Conversant with the teachings of Grotius, Vattel, and Martens, Adams usually found ample support in the public law of Europe to vindicate major American diplomatic objectives.

He frequently relied upon the law of nature and nations in his efforts to achieve liberal principles of commercial exchange, in particular resulting in the opening up of South American ports to the commerce of the world and in the relaxing of the whole system of British imperial commercial restrictions. As part of the American delegation to negotiate the Peace of Ghent following the War of 1812, Adams was the only commissioner who knew where to turn in Martens's *Receuil des traités* for opening negotiations with the enemy. Aggressions of British sea power against the rights of neutrals were considered attacks on the fundamental rights of nations. Later, as secretary of state, Adams claimed that "the principles of justice, humanity, and Christianity demanded, in particular, that free or neutral ships should make free goods and the neutral goods should be safe in enemy ships."[17]

A sovereign nation assumed external rights and obligations that, Adams declared, remained unchanged by any internal revolution of government. He cited chapter and verse of Martens and Vattel against the arguments of Spanish authorities who questioned the obligation of their government to ratify the 1819 treaty. At issue was whether Spain

15. Adams, *Newburyport Oration*, 17.
16. Ibid., 17–18.
17. Bradford Perkins, *Castlereagh and Adams, England and the United States, 1812–1823*, 40–41; JQA to Levett Harris, November 15, 1814, 5:187; JQA to Abigail Adams, November 23, 1814, 5:208; Lipsky, *John Quincy Adams, His Theory and Ideas*, 22–24.

could be relieved of a responsibility to ratify a treaty that had been signed by a plenipotentiary, even though he had acted on unqualified instructions of a sovereign whose authority was subsequently limited by a legislative body asserting a new constitutional power to pass on treaties. Adams argued that "by the universal assent of civilized nations, nothing can release the *honor* of a sovereign from the obligation of a promise thus unqualified." The words of Vattel are "but to refuse with honor to ratify that which has been concluded in virtue of a full power, the sovereign must have strong and solid reasons for it; and particularly, he must show that his minister transcended his instructions." According to Martens,

> Every thing that has been stipulated by an agent in conformity with his full powers, ought to become obligatory on the state from the moment of the signing, without ever waiting for the ratification. However, not to expose a state to the errors of a single person, it is now become a general maxim that public conventions do not become obligatory until ratified. The motive of this custom clearly proves that the ratification can never be refused with justice, except when he who is charged with the negotiation, keeping within the extent of his public full powers, has gone beyond his secret instructions, and . . . rendered himself liable to punishment, or when the other party refuses to ratify.[18]

Contested interpretations of these two passages entered into the letters exchanged between the American minister to Madrid, John Forsyth, and the Duke of San Fernando. The latter suggested that the very authorities cited by Forsyth (upon instructions from Adams) "literally declare that the sovereign, for strong and solid reasons, *or* if his minister has exceeded his instructions, may refuse verification (Vattel, book 2, chap. 12)"; and that "public treaties are not obligatory until ratified (Martens, book 2, chap. 3)." Studying the Spanish response and its reference to Vattel, Adams countered that the duke "substituted for the connective *and* . . . the disjunctive term *or*, which presents it

18. National Archives, Records of the Department of State, *Diplomatic Instructions, All Countries*, 9:8; JQA to Don Francisco Dionisio Vivés, May 8, 1820, 7:18; Vattel, *The Law of Nations*, 256–57.

[proof of instructions transcended in order to withhold ratification] as an alternative, and unnecessary on the contingency of other existing . . . reasons." The citation from Martens presented a similar problem. The duke's contention—"that public treaties are not obligatory until ratified"—disregards the preceding sentence, "by which Martens asserts that a treaty signed in conformity to full powers is in rigor obligatory from the moment of signature." He also omits the following sentence, which asserts that this usage can never be resorted to in justification of a refusal to ratify, unless the minister has exceeded his secret instructions. In stripping the obligation of all qualifying context, the Spanish rejoinder disregards the "immoveable foundation of eternal justice in the law of nature." Adams's position appealed both to the national interest and moral sensibilities of sovereign states,

> There would be no more security, no longer any commerce between mankind, did they not believe themselves obliged to preserve their faith and keep their word. This obligation . . . is as necessary as it is natural . . . between nations that live together in a state of nature, and acknowledge no superior on earth, to maintain order and peace in their society. Nations and their conductors ought . . . to keep their promises and their treaties inviolable. This great truth, *though too often neglected in practice*, is generally acknowledged by all nations.[19]

The obligation of states to keep their promises and adhere to their treaties was morally right and essential for the maintenance of international order. The strictures of law proved to be a valuable political ally for one who advised that the diplomat must acquire his expertise, and pursue rigorous studies, in the "history, internal interest, and external *relations* of his own nation, as well as of other nations."[20]

Adams was acutely conscious of the significance and implication of diplomatic maneuver, and his first contacts with the British government provided him with early experience in the art. Sir Charles Bagot was the most successful British minister he had known. This fact impressed him because success was based perhaps on the minister's mediocre talents, and this possibility staggered Adams's "belief in the

19. JQA to Don Francisco Dionisio Vivés, May 8, 1820, 19–20.
20. JQA to Christopher Hughes, December 25, 1816, 6:129.

universality of the maxim that men of the greatest talents ought to be sought out for diplomatic missions." In a revealing profile, Adams noted,

> The principal feature of his character is discretion, one of the most indispensable qualities of the good negotiator. . . . His temper is serious, but cheerful. He has no depth of dissimulation, though enough to suppress his feelings when it is for his interest to conceal them. . . . To neutralize fretful passions and soothe prejudices, a man of good breeding, inoffensive manners, and courteous deportment is nearer to the true diplomatic standard than one with the genius of Shakespeare, the learning of Bentley, the philosophical penetration of Berkeley, or the wit of Swift.[21]

Adams understood the delicacy and danger in bestowing diplomatic confidences; "but, crafty and fraudulent as the trade has the reputation of being, I give it as the result of my experience that confidence judiciously . . . bestowed is one of the most powerful and efficacious instruments of negotiation." Adams also knew that improper methods, or morally questionable means, may exact a high price. What is here done with good intentions but unwisely, and hence with disastrous results, is morally defective; for it violates the ethics of responsibility to which action affecting others, and political action par excellence, is subject.[22]

Moral principles, as expressed in the law of nations, counseled a disposition in states to pursue peace and practice nonintervention. To seek peace is not, unfortunately, to ensure it; peace depends on the conduct of other states. "The peace of every nation," Adams wrote, "must depend not alone upon its own will, but upon that concurrently with the will of all others." Adams's devotion to commands of law and morality in the affairs of nations was tempered by the realization that a government cannot morally transcend what the nation regards as essential to its survival. The nation may be a moral person; however, self-preservation is also the first law of nature. Nations acknowledge no judge between them on earth. Adams advised that "there is a point

---

21. *Memoirs*, 4:339.
22. Ibid., May 28, 1819, 339; Morgenthau, *Scientific Man vs. Power Politics*, 186.

beyond which every sacrifice to preserve Peace, only serves to defeat its own purpose; and that perfidy or dishonour are too high a price to pay even for the first of national blessings." America had "committed many great errors" in confounding the principles of internal government with those of external relations. Adams never extended normative sanction to the presence of self-interest in political life. But there "must be force for the government of mankind, and whoever in this world does not choose to fight for his freedom, must turn Quaker or look out for a master." The "doctrine and the creed of Washington . . . from the first organization of the government," no less than "the most profitable lesson" of the 1812 war, pointed to "the primary duty of the nation to place itself in a state of permanent preparation for self-defence."[23] The greater good of mankind is no less real for having to recognize the moral and political accountability of the statesman to his nation's survival and material well-being; for Adams the claims of the society of states and the society of Americans tended to complement one another.

The imperfect relationship between law and morality was exemplified by the victims of impressment who seek indemnity for captured cargoes and vessels. Adams acknowledged that the argument of abstract right is strong; however, "the justice obtainable from foreign nations is at all times . . . very imperfect, and . . . the only alternative in cases of denial of justice is abandonment of the claim or war." The government, after exhausting every pacific expedient for obtaining justice, "neither partakes of the injustice done nor makes itself responsible to the sufferer." Statesmen are confronted with the demanding task of determining what is right amidst the complexity of competing—sometimes conflicting, and sometimes compatible—moral ends. Immediate consequences must be weighed against ultimate consequences. The destruction of life, for example, results in the immediate destruction of moral values. War, even if it eventually obtains justice for that sufferer, "secures it by the sufferings of thousands of others

23. Adams, *Lives,* 88–89; Morgenthau, *Defense of the National Interest,* 14–15; JQA to Elbridge Gerry, February 20, 1798, in Tatum, "Ten Unpublished Letters of John Quincy Adams," 373; JQA to William Vans Murray, July 22, 1798, 2:344.

equally unmerited, and which must ultimately remain unindemnified." A nation, however much it may desire justice or equity, "cannot incur the obligation which it is unable to enforce."[24]

Nevertheless, Adams was mindful that the irrational and the self-serving components of the human will can become magnified in the conduct of nations. He sometimes complained that "moral considerations seldom appear to have much weight in the minds of our statesmen, unless connected with popular feelings." War posed particular difficulties: for Adams "*fraud* is never justifiable where *force* would not be equally justifiable to affect the same object." Fraud is a "weapon . . . belonging to the relations of war and to be used sparingly even when justifiable" since it may "impair the confidence of mankind in the sincerity and integrity of him who uses it." That the statesman qua man is part of an existential reality bounded by the polarities of grace and power is affirmed by Adams with an eloquence all too rare in modern political discourse.

> If it is not [in] the uniform course of human events that virtue should be crowned with success, it is at least the uniform will of Heaven that virtue should be the duty of man. There is one event to the righteous and to the wicked. Time and chance happeneth to them all. So says Divine Revelation, and so proves constant experience. The path of virtue is . . . not always clear, and in the complication of human affairs, artifice and simulation itself must occasionally be practiced. The sternist moralists allow it in time of war.[25]

Adams's devotion to the precepts of natural law is not invalidated by pointing out that, on occasion, he departed from his principles, although the departure itself was explained in terms of moral and legal obligation. Concerning the acquisition of Louisiana, for example, Adams believed that the consent of the inhabitants should have been solicited. He conceded, however, that circumstances made it impracticable to obtain their acquiescence prior to the treaty and that "theoretic principles of government" had to be modified to meet the "situations of human events and human concerns." The treaty-making power had

24. Adams, *Memoirs*, 11:382–83.
25. *Memoirs*, 5:47–48.

been used constitutionally in acquiring the territory; a plebiscite might have denied the results of the treaty. Yet the United States could not be relieved of an obligation to procure the consent of the inhabitants after ratification of the treaty. As Adams explained, "And as nothing but necessity can justify even a momentary departure from those principles which we hold as the most sacred laws of nature and of nations, so nothing can justify extending the departure beyond the bounds of necessity. From the instant when that [necessity] ceases the principle returns in all its force, and every further violation of it is error and crime." The law of nature, then, determines the extent of deviation that necessity may occasion from its guidance. A certain relativistic ethos pervades these lines, even if general principles are operative as a self-activating brake on national pretense. Adams once wrote in his *Memoirs* that principles should be "adhered to strongly only to the degree of their importance and of the importance of results deriving from their application." Adams would not accept our dichotomy of realism and idealism; he would, as one political thinker explains, emphasize the complementary relationship of principle and prudence. "Principles are not self-applying: They do not tell you what to do. They require prudence and judgment for their application. Prudence is not self-sufficient either; it requires principles for guidance."[26]

Neither morality nor interest were entirely reliable as indicators of foreign policy; subversive of both ran strong countercurrents of emotion. Taking exception to Jeffersonian optimism about human rationality, Adams warned that a reliance upon "the operation of measures, from their effect on the *interests,* however clear and unequivocal of nations, cannot be safe against a counter current of their passions." Jefferson's economic measures against the British did not work because they naively assumed a reasonable British attachment to their interests—commerce—would prevail over the lust for war:

> nations, like individuals, sacrifice their peace to their pride, to their hatred, to their envy, to their jealousy, and even to the craft, which

26. Adams, "Notes on Speech on Motion," *Writings,* 3:28–29; *Memoirs,* 9:58; Nathan Tarcov, "Principle and Prudence in Foreign Policy: The Founders' Perspective," 48.

the cunning of hackneyed politicians not infrequently mistakes for policy. . . . That national madness is infectious, and that a paroxysm of it in one people, especially when generated by the Furies that preside over war, produces a counter paroxysm in their adverse party. Such is the melancholy condition as yet of associated man.[27]

Moral pretension in the behavior of nations is but a reflection of a general inclination in human nature, that men as the agents of history are apt to forget that they are also creatures in the very historical process in which they must take responsible action. In this realist portrait of human nature, Adams remained a Federalist, yet he allowed himself more optimism about human progress than most Federalists, perhaps because he had seen how easily monarchies fell under the Furies' spell.

The French Revolution taught Adams about the deadly ends often associated with the universalistic aims of modern nationalism. The national madness inspired by mass ideologies and the exclusive claim to justice and virtue for one's country are infectious. The very sensitive honor of nations can always be appeased by the blood of their citizens, and no national ambition seems too base or petty to claim and to receive the support of a majority of their citizens. It is a characteristic aspect of all politics, domestic as well as international, that frequently its basic manifestations do not appear as what they actually are— manifestations of a struggle for power. The true nature of policy is concealed by ideological justifications and rationalizations. "It is not for want of admirable doctrine," exclaims Shelley in the *Defense of Poetry,* "that men hate and despise and censor and deceive, and subjugate one another." The deeper the individual is involved in the power struggle, the less likely he is to see the power struggle for what it is. The words that Hamlet addressed to his mother might be addressed with equal lack of success to all hungry for power:

> . . . Mother, for love of grace,
> Lay not that flattering unction to your soul,
> That not your trespass, but my madness speaks.[28]

27. Adams, *Lives,* 88.

28. Morgenthau, *Scientific Man vs. Power Politics,* 156; Morgenthau, *Politics among Nations,* 88; Reinhold Niebuhr, *Moral Man and Immoral Society,* 93.

III.

Adams brought his conception of political ethics—an arena within which power and principle curiously intermingle and work out their uncertain compromises—to bear upon national and international events that would shape the destiny of future generations. His approach to intervention may gain in depth by considering his outlook on: 1) the nature of American Continentalism; 2) the European balance of power and its significance for American foreign policy in the Western Hemisphere; and 3) the problem of preserving domestic liberties and supporting human rights in the nation's external conduct. Adams took the lead in helping to formulate foreign policy goals at a time when the United States encountered such new challenges as a proposal for Anglo-American cooperation; rumored European intervention in Latin America; Russian extension of colonial establishments in the northwest; and the tsar's denunciation of republican principles upon which every independent state in America was now based.

Of particular importance, especially in judging Adams's clarion call for a reinvigorated militia and navy, was the expansionist views he harbored toward the North American continent. This was, however, an expansionism that looked to geography and not to war. His support for Jefferson's acquisition of the Louisiana territory, and for Madison's embargo, signaled a course of commercial and continental expansion that he would help consolidate as diplomat, secretary of state, and president. To the projection of American power was added a powerful strain of idealism. American success would erode European colonial claims elsewhere and perhaps even affect European practice at home. Mutual respect would replace overbearing imperialism as the basis of the relations between the Old and New Worlds. Unlike Jefferson, Adams saw the United States as a player in the game of nations; unlike Hamilton, Adams thought that the United States could pursue an active neutrality.

As the principal architect of the noninterference clause of the Monroe Doctrine, Adams had begun to think of the American continent as a special preserve of the United States long before the president's message to Congress in 1823. "The whole continent of North America appears to be destined by Divine Providence to be peopled by one nation," he wrote to John Adams in 1811, "speaking one language, professing one general system of religious and political principles." The world, he later declared at a cabinet meeting in 1819, "must be familiarized with the idea of considering our proper dominion to be the continent of North America." He concluded, "From the time we became an independent people it was as much a law of nature that this should become our pretension as that the Mississippi should flow to the sea. Spain had possessions upon our southern and Great Britain upon our northern border. It was impossible that centuries should elapse without finding them annexed to the United States."[29]

In a heated exchange in 1821 with British Minister Stratford Canning regarding the English claim to Oregon in the convention of 1818, Adams informed his adversary that "there would be neither policy nor profit in cavilling with us about territory on this North American continent." A similar theme prevailed in Adams's exchange with Baron Tuyll, minister of Russia, over the ukase of 1821 establishing Russian territorial claims to the Pacific northwest. He informed Tuyll that the United States "would contest the right of Russia to any territorial establishment on this continent, and that we should assume . . . the principle that the United States are no longer subjects for any new European colonial establishments." When Secretary Adams drew up in November 1823 the customary sketch of foreign policy topics that might interest the president in connection with his forthcoming message, he included in the paragraph on the Russian negotiations a reference to the new dogma. That paragraph was taken over almost without verbal change by Monroe and thus it appeared in his communication to Congress.[30]

In addition, Adams drew upon commercial, geopolitical, and legal arguments to justify the American cause. Noncolonization would, in the first instance, militate against bringing the intrigues and conflicting territorial ambitions of Europe across the seas into the New World. The letters of instruction dispatched by the secretary of state to Minis-

29. JQA to John Adams, August 31, 1811, 4:209; *Memoirs*, 4:438f.
30. *Memoirs*, 5:252f, 6:157; Dexter Perkins, *The Monroe Doctrine, 1823–1826*, 13–14.

ters Rush (London) and Middleton (St. Petersburg) indicate that Adams's general objective was to prevent the establishment on this continent of new colonial dependencies of European powers. These were objectionable by reason of the restrictions and exclusions on commerce and navigation that, at that time, formed part of the European colonial systems. Adams insisted that the "principle of mutual treatment upon a footing of equality with the most favored nation" was "the great foundation of our foreign policy." After declaring that the American continents will henceforth no longer be open for colonization, he went on to say, "Occupied by civilized independent nations, they will be accessible to Europeans and to each other on that footing alone, and the Pacific Ocean in every part of it will remain open to the navigation of all nations, in like manner with the Atlantic. . . . The application of colonial principles of exclusion, therefore, cannot be admitted by the United States as lawful upon any part of the northwest coast of America, or as belonging to any European nation." Apart from its legal justification, however, Adams's principle represented an adroit diplomatic maneuver. It committed the United States to no specific policy of any kind; it left open for debate the courses of action necessary to defend the new doctrine; it left open the possibility of a diplomatic retreat while giving the impression of great definiteness. Finally, the noncolonization principle drew its moral inspiration from Adams's belief that "from the moral and physical nature of man . . . colonial establishments cannot fulfill the great objects of government in the just purpose of society."[31]

It is doubtful that the United States alone had the wherewithal to oppose European power committed to testing the Monroe Doctrine, although the American position had improved considerably over the previous decade. For Adams, however, geography and the operation of the European balance could be included as assets in the United States'

31. JQA to Henry Middleton, July 5, 1820, 7:46–51; Adams to Richard Rush, February 6, 1821, 7:92–94; Adams to Caesar Augustus Rodney, May 17, 1823, 7:437ff; Adams to Richard C. Anderson, May 27, 1823, 7:457–61; Perkins, *The Monroe Doctrine*, 20–26; Henry Wheaton, *Elements of International Law*, 82n; Dangerfield, *The Era of Good Feelings*, 268–69.

ledger. Writing in the last year of his father's presidency, but in language equally significant for his brother's worldview at the close of the Napoleonic Wars, Thomas Boylston Adams observed, "It must always happen so long as America is an independent Republic . . . that the balance of power in Europe will continue to be of the utmost importance for her welfare." Adams joined his brother in praising the Founding Fathers for maintaining America's national interest in view of the shifting military and political fortunes of European nations. On noncolonization, Adams recognized the convergence of American and British interests. As Norman Graebner observed, "Together Adams and Monroe had wedded American policies to the *status quo* in the Atlantic, a *status quo* which, if threatened, would have the defense of the British navy itself."[32] Prudence dictated keeping a vigilant eye on European affairs, on which American security might depend.

In a letter of instruction to Henry Middleton, American minister to Russia, he analyzed the political system of Europe growing out of the treaties concluded in Vienna, Paris, and Aix-la-Chappelle. The core of that system is "that of a compact between the five principal powers . . . for the preservation of universal peace"; the primary goal, in eliminating the influence of the French Revolution, was "the substitution of a system which would preserve them from that evil; the preponderancy of one power by the subjugation, virtual if not nominal, of the rest." Whether European nations "perceived [the system] in its full extent, considered in its true colors, or provided by judicious arrangements for the revolutionary temper of the weapons by which they had so long been assailed, and from which they had so severely suffered, is a question now in a course of solution. Their great anxiety appears to have been to guard themselves each against the other." Declining the tsar's overture to the United States to become a formal partner in the Holy Alliance, Adams argued that "for the repose of America as well as Europe, the European and American political systems should be kept as separate and distinct from each other as possible." Yet, on the eve of the French invasion of Spain in 1823, Adams realized that a pledge of

---

32. Bemis, *John Quincy Adams and the Foundations of American Foreign Policy*, 86; Graebner, "John Quincy Adams and the Federalist Tradition," 123.

neutrality did not alleviate the threat from Europe. The fact of American diplomatic history had illustrated that this policy, "however earnestly and perseveringly it was maintained, yielded ultimately to a course of events by which the violence and injustice of European powers involved the immediate interests and . . . essential rights of our own country." With the Holy Alliance in mind, he alluded to "a number of projects, hitherto abortive, of interposing in the revolutionary struggle between Spain and her South American colonies."[33]

While Adams forthrightly rejected European intervention in the Western Hemisphere, his attitude toward American intervention was more complex and more equivocal. His interest in continental expansion was balanced by his concern for maintaining the nation's moral integrity and reputation; earlier indifference gave way to acute concern over the impact of expansion on the strength of slavery. Thus Andrew Jackson's champion against the Spanish in Florida in 1818 became James Polk's adversary over the war with Mexico in 1847. Intervention consistent with the nation's character might be defended; intervention that violated the national commitment to natural rights could not.

Of all the major events in foreign affairs during Adams's tenure at the State Department, none was more challenging in the complexity of negotiations than the long-standing controversy with Spain over the western boundary of Louisiana and the possession of the Floridas. While Secretary Adams negotiated with Luis de Onís for the acquisition of Florida, a dramatic and unexpected development threatened to disrupt completely all diplomatic relations between Spain and the United States. Spain had weakened her authority in East Florida by withdrawing troops in order to subdue South American insurgents. Amelia Island, once a Spanish outpost near the Georgia border, was transformed into an intolerable nest for buccaneers and unscrupulous speculators. A military expedition, authorized by the United States government, seized the island in 1817. Far more threatening, however, were the Seminole Indians of Florida, who, joined by runaway slaves and white renegades, crossed the border into Georgia on raiding parties.

33. JQA to Henry Middleton, July 5, 1820, 7:47, 7:47–51; JQA to Hugh Nelson, April 28, 1823, 7:370.

Confrontations between them and frontiersmen culminated on November 30, 1817, when the Seminoles jumped an American ship sliding along the slow-moving Apalachicola River, and killed thirty-four soldiers, seven women, and four children.[34] Although the Seminoles had long-standing grievances against the United States, the willingness of Spanish officials to grant refuge to these marauders violated the "good neighbor pledge" contained in the Pinckney Treaty of 1795. Tensions escalated on both sides as Spain was virtually powerless to control or restrain these outlaws or stop their incursions.

In 1817, Andrew Jackson was commissioned by the Monroe administration to confront the Seminoles. His instructions were as broad as they were vague; and he was authorized to pursue the Indians across the Spanish boundary, if necessary. At the same time, his instructions obligated him to respect all posts under the Bourbon flag. Years later, Jackson maintained that Monroe sent him further instructions, through Congressman John Rhea, authorizing a seizure of the Spanish towns. Although Monroe denied the point, there is little doubt that Jackson apparently believed that he was proceeding with the support of the administration. Jackson, with no deficit of ill-will for either Spaniards or Indians, occupied the military post of St. Marks in April 1818. Two British citizens—Alexander Arbuthnot and Robert Armbrister—were summarily court-martialed and executed. Jackson reported these events to the secretary of war, John C. Calhoun: "I hope the execution of these two unprincipled villains will prove an awful example to the world, and convince the Government of Great Britain, as well as her subjects, that certain, though slow retribution awaits those unchristian wretches who, by false promises, delude and excite an Indian tribe to all the horrid deeds of savage war." Within a few short weeks, Adams had reprimanded the Indians, stormed Pensacola and St. Augustine, confiscated the royal archives, ousted the Spanish governor and named an American in his place, and declared in force "the revenue laws of the United States."[35]

---

34. Shepherd, *The Adams Chronicles*, 259.

35. R. R. Stenberg, "Jackson's 'Rhea Letter' Hoax," *Journal of Southern History* II (1936):480–96; Bailey, *A Diplomatic History of the American People*, 169.

The news that the "ruffian" Jackson had murdered two British subjects led to an explosion of indignation in England. "We can hardly believe," one London journal remarked, "that anything so offensive to public decorum could be admitted, *even in America!*"[36] The popular clamor in Britain was for disavowal, apology, and reparation. The words of America's minister to England, Richard Rush, provide a graphic footnote to the affair.

> Out-of-doors, excitement seemed to rise higher and higher. Stocks experienced a slight fall. The newspapers kept up their fire . . . [giving] vent to angry declamation. They fiercely denounced the Government of the United States. Tyrant, ruffian, murderer, were among the epithets applied to their commanding general. He was exhibited in placards through the streets. The journals, without distinction of party, united in these attacks.[37]

Americans grew concerned that the British government might demand redress—even at the risk of war. Lord Castlereagh helped to defuse the crisis, however, declaring that Armbrister and Arbuthnot were engaged in "practices of such a description as to have deprived them of any claim on their own government for interference." Castlereagh later informed Rush that war might have broken out "if the ministry had but held up a finger." An examination of the British press suggests Castlereagh claimed too much. That England was angry is beyond question; that her citizens really wanted a confrontation with the United States is much less certain.[38]

Secretary of State Adams stood virtually alone in the cabinet in his defense of Jackson's actions. These were circumstances that Adams readily conceded were "embarrassing and complicated, not only as involving that of actual war with Spain, but that of Executive power to authorize hostilities without a declaration of war by Congress." In cabinet sessions, and against the strong objections of John C. Calhoun and William Wirt, Adams "produced as authority Martens" in defend-

36. Bailey, *Diplomatic History.*
37. Ibid.; Richard Rush, *A Residence at the Court of London,* 412.
38. Perkins, *Castlereagh and Adams: England and the United States, 1812–1823,* 288–90.

ing the proposition that the general's action had been "defensive, neither an act of war nor in violation of the constitution." His reasoning was "that Jackson took Pensacola only because the Governor threatened to drive him out of the province by force if he did not withdraw"; therefore, Jackson was "only executing his orders when he received the threat . . . and could not withdraw his troops from the province consistently with his orders." His "only alternative was to prevent the execution of the threat." Adams reminded Onís, that "by the ordinary laws and usages of nations, the right of pursuing an enemy, who takes refuge from actual conflict within a neutral territory is uncontestable." Peace between the United States and Spain "required that henceforth the stipulations by Spain to restore by force her Indians from all hostilities against the United States should be faithfully and effectually fulfilled."[39]

Adams conceded that Jackson's conduct fell within the realm of "political necessity," that it "was necessary to carry the reasoning upon my principles to the utmost extent it would bear to come to this conclusion." Yet even considering "the question was dubious, it was better to err on the side of vigor than of weakness, on the side of our own officer, who had rendered . . . eminent services to the nation, than on the side of our bitterest enemies." Desirous of avoiding a posture of "truckling to Spain," Adams saw a larger moral and political challenge to American statecraft. "But the mischief of this determination lies deeper: 1. It is weakness, and a confession of weakness. 2. The disclaimer of power in the Executive is of dangerous example and of evil consequences. 3. There is injustice to the officer in disavowing him, when in principle he is strictly justifiable." America, he believed, could never expect to hold a position of dignity and honor in world affairs while she pursued a pusillanimous policy in her relations with other nations. In the very first test of his ability to handle a delicate international situation, Adams insisted on taking a clear stand for the right of the United States to be treated with respect by other nations and sounded a bold tone for the future course of American diplomacy.[40]

Adams's defense of Jackson, as noted by one historian, "was a virtu-

39. *Memoirs*, 4:107–15; JQA to George W. Erving, November 28, 1818, 6:174.
40. *Memoirs*, 4:115; Tatum, *The United States and Europe, 1815–1823*, 230–32.

oso performance that added luster and reach to the theme of merciless savages and outside agitators." Although struggling to evince a moral justification for acts of political necessity, Adams pushed the dialectic of power and principle to its breaking point. Even Adams could never fully insulate his fierce nationalism from the ideological rationalization of power. Instructive in this connection was a principle his father had laid down some years before. "Power always thinks it has a great soul and vast views beyond the comprehension of the weak and that it is doing God's service when it is violating all His laws. Our passions, ambitions, avarice, love and resentment . . . possess some much metaphysical subtlety and so much overpowering eloquence that they insinuate themselves into the understanding and the conscience and convert both to their party."[41] Furthermore, John Quincy Adams's concern for disturbing signs of national weakness left serious questions unanswered regarding the moral or legal restraints that would be applicable to his conviction that defensive acts of hostility might by authorized by the executive.

Another volatile question was whether or not America had an obligation to recognize and intervene in behalf of Latin American independence. While this issue is examined in greater detail in a subsequent chapter, it touches upon the role of human rights in American foreign policy conduct. Henry Clay's moralism—"the glorious spectacle of eighteen millions of people struggling to burst their chains and be free"—was a popular response to the position, circulated by French publicist Abbé de Pradt, that European powers might act to establish the region's independence on terms that would keep the new nations aligned with the Continent. Adams took a conservative view by emphasizing the moral and practical limits of American power in the domestic affairs of these nations. He also doubted their readiness for self-government. Adams answered Clay along the following lines:

> That it was our true policy and duty to take no part in the contest, . . . was equally clear. The principle of neutrality to *all* foreign wars was,

---

41. Richard Drinnon, *Facing West: The Metaphysics of Indian-Hating and Empire-Building*, 108–11; Morgenthau, *Politics among Nations*, 90–91.

in my opinion, fundamental to the continuance of our liberties and of our Union. So far as they were contending for independence, I wished well to their cause; but I . . . see not prospect that they would establish free or liberal institutions of government. . . . Arbitrary power, military and ecclesiastical, was stamped upon their habits, and upon all their institutions. . . . I had little expectation of any beneficial result to this country from any future connection with them, political or commercial.[42]

Latin American independence was desired in Washington as an additional bulwark for American isolation, but it was not supported with sufficient ardor to risk a European war. So long as Europe did not actively intervene, Monroe and Adams were content to stand aside and let Spain fight it out with her colonies, but they would certainly oppose any attempt by the Holy Alliance to interpose.[43]

Following the reconquest of Spain by France in 1823, Adams's attention turned toward the possible reconquest of the Spanish Empire under the aegis of the Holy Alliance. His enunciation of the "no transfer principle," opposing the transfer of any remaining colony of Spain in the New World, was a direct response to the prospect of collusion among European powers to undermine the national interest of the United States. The war in Europe opened the possibility that Great Britain, in return for assisting Spain against France, might be compensated by a transfer of Cuba to her possession. At a cabinet meeting on March 17, President Monroe proposed to offer Great Britain a mutual promise not to take Cuba. Adams, joined by Calhoun, counseled against such a move since the United States could be plunged "into the whirlpool of European politics." In a letter of instruction to Hugh Nelson, American minister at Madrid, Adams considered Cuba to be of "transcendent importance to the political and commercial interests of our union." Any change in the condition of Cuba would seriously affect "the good understanding between us and Spain" and justify the United States in supporting subsequent movements of national liberation.[44]

42. *Memoirs*, 5:324–25.
43. Morrison and Commager, *The Growth of the American Republic*, 1:454.
44. *Memoirs*, 6:138; JQA to Hugh Nelson, April 28, 1823, 7:372, 381.

Adams drew on related arguments in an attempt in 1822 and 1823 to persuade President Monroe to moderate his open endorsement of the revolutionary cause in Spain and Greece. In the first draft of his historic message to Congress, Monroe proposed to reprove the French invasion of Spain, to acknowledge the independence of Greece, and to ask Congress for a diplomatic mission to Athens. This position, Adams said, would be akin to "a summon to arms . . . against all of Europe, and for objects of policy exclusively European—Greece and Spain." It would "throw down the gauntlet . . . to all of Europe" and perhaps even prompt a decision by Spain, France, and Russia to break off diplomatic intercourse with the United States. Even if the Holy Alliance were determined to take issue with the United States, Adams warned that "it should be our policy to meet, and not to make it." He advised, "We should retreat to the wall before taking up arms, and be sure at every step to put them as much as possible in the wrong. . . . The ground that I wish to take is that of earnest remonstrance against the interference of European powers by force with South America, but to disclaim all interference on our part with Europe; to make an American cause, and adhere inflexibly to that."[45]

On August 16, 1823, British Foreign Secretary George Canning put to Richard Rush, American minister at London, a request that both nations issue a joint declaration opposing any attempt by France or other European nations to take possession of Spain's colonies. Canning's offer confronted the Monroe administration with a fundamental dilemma: Did the nation's hemispheric interests require the projection of American influence into European politics, or could the United States entrust the independence of the Western Hemisphere to protections afforded by the Atlantic, British naval power, and Latin American resistance? As Canning's request was being transmitted to Washington, Baron de Tuyll advised Adams that, unless the United States remained neutral, Russia might countenance European action within the Spanish empire. While other administration officials considered this development as of sufficient warrant to accept Canning's offer,

45. *Memoirs*, 6:193–98.

Adams considered any military threat from the Holy Alliance dubious and realized that Britain had the will and power to prevent it in any case. Canning's motive was less in soliciting a superfluous American pledge than preventing, through a self-denying agreement, future American expansion into Texas and the Caribbean. Such a pledge, of course, would later prove inconvenient if Cuba voted herself into the United States. Adams argued that the time was propitious to take a stand against the Holy Alliance while declining the overture from Britain. "It would be more candid, as well as more dignified, to avow our principles explicitly to Russia and France, than to come in as a cock-boat in the wake of the British man-of-war."[46]

Accusations that Adams's foreign policy ethics amounted to little more than a shield for American empire building are belied by his repeated concern that the nation avoid the "prospects and temptations to aggrandizement." Nowhere were these convictions more vividly expressed than in Congressman Adams's indefatigable opposition to the annexation of Texas and to the nation's "most unrighteous war" against Mexico in 1847–1848. Adams, in 1843, tried unsuccessfully to block the annexation of Texas by proposing to the Committee of Foreign Affairs of the House that they bring forward his propositions of 1838: 1) a denial of the power of Congress or any department of Government to annex any foreign *state* or *people*; and 2) a declaration that any attempt by an act of Congress or by treaty to annex Texas would be a violation of the Constitution, null and void, to which free states of the Union and their people *ought not* to submit. As debate on the annexation resolution unfolded in 1845, Adams hesitated whether "to sit and witness in silence the perpetration of a wrong which I too clearly saw was unavoidable." Yet Adams could hardly remain passive on an issue that he deemed contrary to the fundamental purpose of the nation: "to secure the blessings of liberty to ourselves and our posterity." Annexation would be "identical with dissolution of the Union."[47]

46. Graebner, *Foundations of American Foreign Policy, A Realist Appraisal from Franklin to McKinley*, 169; *Memoirs*, 6:177, 180–81; Varg, *United States Foreign Relations, 1820–1860*, 52–56.

47. Adams, *The New England Confederacy of 1643*, 6; *Memoirs*, 12:6; Lipsky, *John Quincy Adams, His Theory and Ideas*, 324; *Memoirs*, 11:330, 12:150–51.

Certainly not lost upon Adams were the diplomatic and political implications of contiguous Mexican territory for the course of American continental expansion. Secretary of State Calhoun spoke for the Tyler administration in presenting the Texas annexation treaty to the Senate as an instrument necessary to prevent the interference of Britain with slavery in the nation rather than as a necessary step in national expansion. The British foreign secretary had frankly acknowledged diplomatic intervention to bring about Mexican recognition of Texas independence—valuable to Great Britain only in a commercial way— and implied that the abolition of slavery there would be an acceptable equivalent. In a letter of instruction to the new British minister in Washington, dated December 23, 1843, Lord Aberdeen wrote, "It must be and is well known both to the United States and to the whole world, that Great Britain desires, and is constantly exerting herself to procure, the general abolition of slavery throughout the world."[48]

Adams dissented and argued that Britain was interested more in preserving the independence of Texas as a counterweight to the power of North America than in the abolition of slavery there. "The policy of the British Government is to cherish, sustain, and protect the institution of slavery in our Southern States and Texas, and their task is to do it by humbugging the abolitionists in England into the belief that they intend directly the reverse. . . . I perceive nothing, as yet, to relieve the deep distrust, which I would fain discard if I could, of the British ministerial policy with regard to slavery in Texas and in our Southern states."[49] Yet Adams conceded that the stronger part of the Southern argument for annexation was the spectacle of an independent Texas becoming the Uruguay of North America, a creature of the British balance of power in the New World. Adams warned his countrymen that the methods devised to safeguard American security—the very justification of necessity—had an intrinsic bearing upon the vitality of national purpose before the eyes of the world.

In what can be considered an important qualification of his nationalism, Adams dismissed claims that Texas was to be delivered to the

---

48. Bemis, *John Quincy Adams and the Union*, 470–71.
49. *Memoirs*, 11:406–7.

Union by any principle of natural right or provisions of the Louisiana Purchase. Adams acknowledged that he himself, as secretary of state, had tried to include Texas during the negotiations with Spain, and as president to purchase it from Mexico. In fact, he was prepared to "vote for annexation tomorrow" provided that "slavery were totally abolished in Texas, and the voluntary consent of Mexico could be obtained." Upon learning in July 1845 that the congress of Texas accepted the terms of annexation to the United States—"the heaviest calamity that ever befell myself and my country"—Adams saw the tragic judgment of history at work. "If the voice of the people is the voice of God, this measure has now the sanction of Almighty God. I have opposed it for ten long years, firmly believing it tainted with two deadly crimes: 1, the leprous contamination of slavery; and 2, robbery of Mexico. *Victrix causa Deo placuit.*" In a letter to Richard Rush, former American minister to England from 1817 to 1825, Adams wrote that "our country . . . is no longer the same" and spoke of the disintegration of American moral fibre.

> The polar Star of our Foreign Relations at that time was Justice it is not Conquest. Their vital Spirit was then Liberty it is not Slavery. As our Dominion swells she becomes dropsical and by the time when our Empire shall extend over the whole Continent . . . we shall be ready for a race of Caesars to subdue the South or to fall at the feet of Pompey's Statue. Liberty has yet her greatest warfare to wage in this Hemisphere. May your posterity and mine be armed in Celestial Panoply for the conflict.[50]

President Polk's war message signaled the "apoplexy of the Constitution" and the climax of a vile conspiracy against Mexico for the perpetuation of slavery throughout the Union. Objecting to the movement of Gen. Zachary Taylor's troops to the east bank of the Rio Grande and never believing that "we had a shadow of right beyond the Sabine," Adams charged "there is no aspect of right and wrong of which we can claim the benefit in this controversy." The Mexican War, he wrote in 1847, "has never to this day been declared by the Congress

50. Bemis, *John Quincy Adams and the Foundations of American Foreign Policy*, 120–21; *Memoirs*, 12:152–53, 173, 202; Bemis, *John Quincy Adams and the Union*, 479.

of the United States. . . . It has been recognized as existing by the Act of Mexico, in direct and notorious violation of the truth." Adams, as Arthur Schlesinger points out, tried to distinguish the congressional *recognition* of a state of war from the Constitution's provision for a congressional *declaration* of war. The Polk administration's use of the former illustrated how presidential control of troop deployment might make for gaping holes in the congressional war-making power. In the words of Adams, "It is now established as an irreversible precedent that the President of the United States has but to declare that War exists, with any Nation upon Earth, by the act of that Nation's Government, and the War is essentially declared." Adams's earlier invocation of executive prerogative in the defense of Jackson did not deter him, when he was nearing his eightieth year, from the belief that in *this* case the assertion of presidential power could prove fatal to liberty and to all that the Union meant, physically and morally.

> Texas and slavery are interwoven in every banner floating on the Democratic breeze. "Freedom or death" should be inscribed on ours. A war for slavery! Can you enlist under such a standard? May the Ruler of the universe preserve you from such degradation! "Freedom! Peace! Union!" be this the watchword of your camp; and if Ate, hot from hell, will come and cry "Havoc!" fight—fight and conquer, under the banner of universal freedom.[51]

"I live in the faith and hope of the progressive advancement of Christian liberty, and expect to abide by the same in death."[52]

---

51. *Memoirs*, 4:32, 107–15; Arthur Schlesinger, Jr., *The Imperial Presidency*, 26–27, 41–42; Bemis, *John Quincy Adams and the Union*, 499–500; Quincy, *Memoir of the Life of John Quincy Adams*, 282–83, 422.
52. Ibid.

Conclusion

I N MEETING THE CHALLENGE of the post–Cold War era, American leaders embark upon a mission no less formidable than the one that confronted Federalist leaders two centuries ago. Part of that challenge is relating America's national interest to new configurations and imbalances of power. Yet the nature of America's foreign policy obligations, as well as the resources committed to them, will also reflect the self-image of a nation, its national morale and quality of government. The task is no longer founding a political order but building the confidence and leadership through which the national interest may be harmonized with the public philosophy of a free people. A government that is truly representative—not only in the sense of parliamentary majorities, but above all in the sense of being able to translate the inarticulate convictions and aspirations of its people into international objectives—has the best chance to marshal national morale in support of those policies. The creative imagination of the statesman must grasp the indispensable link between external patterns of power and those fundamental intellectual and moral traits that give each nation its unmistakable distinctiveness.

The phrase *the idea of America* is open to grave misunderstandings. There is no single correct idea that can sum up the multiple, and sometimes contradictory, aspects of American history. American virtues rarely come pure, and there may be plausible reasons for the nation's impaired popularity in the world at large. For Adams, America's national purpose in politics and diplomacy achieved coherence within a public realm based upon objective standards of universal validity. The assumption of a substantive, transcendent, and objective order was conceived in both religious and secular terms.[1] The goals of American nationhood were modified also by the objective conditions that confronted the builders. This is the nature of an experiment, where ideas guide activity to test certain conclusions and reach intended outcomes.

Adams's view of the national purpose was shared by Madison, who defined the role of America in a little-known letter to a friend. He wrote,

> The free system of government we have established is so congenial with reason, with common sense, and with a universal feeling, that it must produce approbation and desire of imitation . . . Our country, if it does justice to itself, will be the *officina Libertatis* [workshop of liberty], to the Civilized World, and do more than any other for the uncivilized.[2]

The idea of America convinced Madison and Adams that work and liberty are intimately connected. America must *work* to achieve a free society. Liberty, which does not come cheap, must be established by men who cherish it, and maintained by a society that concedes its value. American liberalism holds certain truths to be self-evident, which no majority has the right to abrogate and from which the legitimacy of majority rule derives. These truths can be subsumed under the proposition that the individual—his integrity, happiness, and self-development—is the ultimate point of reference for the political order, and that his nature owes nothing to any secular order or human institution. It is on this transcendent foundation that the philosophy of genuine democracy rests. Neither Madison nor Adams endorsed the sort of relativism that makes truth a function of political power in the mar-

1. Morgenthau, *The Purpose of American Politics*, 17–18.
2. Koch, "The Idea of America," 228–30.

ketplace of ideas. Higher law principles of right and justice are entitled to prevail of their own intrinsic excellence, regardless of the attitude of those who wield the physical resources of the community.

The "workshop" is also a symbol of technology for a society that guards the intellectual freedom of its thinkers and scientists. In one respect, the realization of representative democracy was grounded in a social-scientific critique of monarchies, aristocracies, dictatorships, and in hypotheses about the functioning of a democratic state. In another, Adams was interested less in "machine worship" than in the control of machines for liberty, for bettering man's estate. Liberty of conscience as a great desideratum arises in this experimental setting. The spirit of controlled experimentation, even in the laboratory of human relations, did not preclude Madison's "universal feeling" for America as both presupposition and fruition of the *novus ordo seclorum*. It must be emphasized that we are not dealing here with doctrines or creeds but with philosophical issues embracing the intellectual, spiritual, and in-stitutional roots of American experience. While full treatment of these issues is beyond the pale of this inquiry, Ellis Sandoz has summarized the motivational synthesis of reason and science that marked the Founders' work.

> This kind of . . . recognition of the layered structure of reality and the need for pluralistic approaches to a pluralistic reality is rooted in mutually-reinforcing foundations of Western thought: the Creation story in Genesis, with its layering of the cosmos and man, created between brute and angelic beings . . . given dominion over all the earth; and the hierarchical structure of being of the Hellenic philoso-phers, for whom reality ranges from the material to the divine, man's composite nature being such as to participate in all layers and thus be their epitome.[3]

What distinguishes the workshop of liberty from the society of the concentration camp is the absence of monocausal and reductionist fallacies that obliterate the hierarchical structure of being in favor of ideological dreamworlds. The pursuit of happiness in the workshop

---

3. Sandoz, *A Government of Laws*, 155–56.

can best be understood in the Aristotelian sense, implying the happiness appropriate to the human condition, *substantial* happiness that is realized by the mature development of man's fullest potentialities.

The legacy of modernity, however, illustrates that material progress can be bought at the price of moral retrogression and that technology can come to replace wisdom or knowledge respecting the ends of human existence. What theologian Reinhold Niebuhr described as the irony of power in American history—the tendency of virtues to turn into vices when too complacently relied upon—may be applied to the transforming power of technology and cognitive power of science. The "indeterminacy of history" was Niebuhr's symbol for a baffled creature who no longer experiences his freedom as controlling and who has become the hapless object of technological developments. Increasing control over the natural and social worlds has also brought new forms of totalitarianism, the threat of nuclear extinction, and increasing divorce, suicide, and crime rates. The task that lies ahead for democratic civilization will be to conserve the quantitative, technological advances of modernity while correcting trends toward the squandering and misuse of these advances through spiritual or qualitative deterioration. In other words, the increase in man's power over the phenomenal world must bring heightened awareness of the need for *moral restraint* in the use of power.[4]

The workshop of liberty may also be interpreted in a more literal way to include America's original role as a beacon to the oppressed of all countries who seek work in freedom. Yet an obligation to defend the rights of man takes its inspiration from a clear domestic example of the broad purposes for which freedom may harness individual talents to a public philosophy. What one political thinker has characterized as "theocentric humanism" points to the importance of infusing modern, secular liberalism—the belief in the dignity of man—with an appreciation for the transcendent sources of human authority. In the popular mind, nothing precedes and transcends society; whatever exists in the social sphere has been created by society itself. Man-

4. Dante Germino, *Beyond Ideology*, 222–23.

in-the-mass, the majority of men in a given society at a given time, becomes the measure of all things. The theocentric foundation for liberalism's advancement from the negative to the positive concept of freedom—freedom understood above all as spiritual development and growth—was identified by T. H. Green in his essay "Liberal Legislation and Freedom of Contract":

> We shall all agree that freedom . . . is the true end of all our effort as citizens. But when we . . . speak of freedom, we should consider carefully what we mean by it. We do not mean . . . freedom from restraint or compulsion. We do not mean . . . freedom to do as we like irrespectively of what it is that we like. We do not mean a freedom that can be enjoyed by one man . . . at the cost of a loss of freedom for others. When we speak of freedom as something to be highly prized, we mean a positive power . . . of enjoying something worth doing or enjoying.[5]

The "ideal of freedom," Green wrote, is "the maximum of power for all members of human society alike to make the best of themselves." Therefore, the freedom to do what one will is not separate from "the liberation of . . . powers of all men equally for contribution to the common good."[6]

In the end, the freedom of the individual is not the result of one specific constitutional device or institutional arrangement. Freedom, as Adams insisted, reposes on the social order as a whole, on the distribution of concrete values to which a society is committed. The freedom of both the wolves and lambs in society will depend upon the values that society attributes—not in the abstract, but in carving out concrete spheres of action—to the freedom of the wolves and the lambs. Society will inevitably have to intervene, deciding the values it wishes to put upon their respective capabilities and interests, and assigning to each a sphere and mode of action. Reinvigoration of America as a workshop of liberty will require the liberalism of the future to involve itself far more

5. J. R. Rodman, ed. *The Political Theory of T. H. Green,* 43–73; Germino, *Beyond Ideology,* 223–26.

6. Rodman, ed., *Political Theory of T. H. Green,* 1–40.

immediately than ever before with providing richer cultural opportunities to increasing numbers of people.

The statesmanship of John Quincy Adams—distinguishing between methods and purposes in national conduct—has lost no significance for the foreign policy debate of the 1990s. Adams would be among the first to advise that the ethics of diplomacy contain an inevitable ambiguity because the factors of interest and power, which are regarded as an irrelevance in pure morality, must be tentatively admitted to the realm of social morality. The risks and dangers of power, however, must be channeled for two constructive purposes: to assure a proper counterweight against power in the interest of justice; and to provide for the coercion that is necessary for the order and stability of any community. Adams looked upon moral reasoning in diplomacy as a practical art by which the statesman seeks to reconcile competing moral claims flowing from divergent interpretations of a nation's interest in a particular situation and at a particular time.

Regarding America's moral mission to the world, Adams believed that the purpose of our foreign policy is not to bring enlightenment or happiness to the rest of the world but to ensure the life, liberty, and happiness of the American people. Yet foreign policy, like all human activities, partakes of the judgment made by both the actor and the witnesses to the act when they perceive the act. Adams believed that there are certain basic moral principles applicable to all human beings, that there exists a moral order in the universe that God directs, the contents of which we can only imperfectly understand. Fundamental principles concerning the dignity and sacredness of human life are not a product of history, but are something objective that are to be discovered.

Ethical debate about America's national purpose reveals a vast and perhaps unbridgeable gap between those who would affirm the final ends of society and let it go at that and those who strive to relate means and ends. Adams spoke for the latter alternative. Affirming a nation's ultimate ends may bring a flush of moral self-satisfaction, but it is hardly a substitute for giving content to purposes in a changing historical context. Adams believed that acting in good faith and with justice toward all nations entails the ethical responsibility of self-judgment. A moral approach to foreign policy begins with the acceptance of one's limitations, of the need to bring national commitments and undertakings into a reasonable relationship with the real possibilities for acting upon the international environment. The connection between power and responsibility—between the sowing and the reaping—is integral.[7] The American Revolution, to quote Paine, "was not made for America alone, but for mankind." In the sphere of foreign affairs, however, those universal principles proclaimed by the Founders were not to be exported by fire and sword if necessary, but they were to be presented to the rest of the world through the successful example of the United States.

Second, the promotion of human rights in foreign policy involves a judgment about ourselves as much as about the actions of others. Adams raised the question of whether any democratic nation can separate the national interest from the larger purposes of civil society. Additionally, do foundations of liberal-democratic political culture in the early nineteenth century provide any useful instructions for an American society consumed by crass materialism and lacking in objective standards of excellence from which to distinguish an honorable national commitment to public virtue? Registering his opposition to American involvement in the Vietnam War before the Senate Foreign Relations Committee, George F. Kennan testified that

> as John Quincy Adams says, there are limits to what our duties and our responsibilities are, and our first duty is to ourselves, and if we get lost in the attempt to rescue or even to establish in many instances the liberties of others, and particularly of people who have never known them as we know them in this country, who don't even know what the words mean that we use, we can lose our own substance and . . . we can have very little to show for it when it is all over.[8]

Kennan, no less than Adams, argued that a prudently and modestly conceived national interest prescribes its own morality. Any rigorous defender of the idea must accept that other nations have their legitimate interests too. The recognition of equal claims sets bounds on

---

7. George F. Kennan, "Morality and Foreign Policy," 212, 215.

8. Statement of the Honorable George F. Kennan before the Senate Foreign Relations Committee of the United States, February 10, 1966.

intervention or aggression. Unless transformed by an injection of moral righteousness, the idea of national interest cannot produce ideological crusades for unlimited objectives.[9]

Adams's legacy testifies to important procedural aspects, often neglected, in defining the concept of the national interest. The national interest, he claimed, is not a detached interest in the international environment *for its own sake,* independent of a nation's aspirations and problems. A nation's values, history, resource needs, and international relationships are components of the national interest. Moreover, the national interest does not consist in the pursuit of abstractions such as peace or just war or other legal definitions. Adams also insisted that the national interest is not simply a question of purpose or objective; it is also a question of method. On this last point, Kennan explained,

> A study of the great decisions of national policy in the past leaves the historian impressed with the difficulty of analyzing the future clearly enough to make reliable calculations of the consequences of national action. It also reveals that too often the motives of national action are ones dictated for government by developments outside of its control. Its freedom of action, in these cases, lies only in the choice of method— in the *how* rather than the *what.*[10]

Third, Adams's diplomatic record suggests that a commitment to human rights does not in itself resolve the question of intervention or nonintervention. This turns in part on what is meant by human rights. When human rights are understood as the universal enjoyment of individual rights to life, liberty, and happiness, they seem to point to intervention against all tyrannical governments and to the replacement of the modern state system by international organization. When the promotion of human rights in foreign policy is understood as moral precepts that are rooted in the principle of consent and filtered through circumstances of time and place, they seem to point in the direction of nonintervention and a disposition to work within the state system. The difficulty of the latter view is that it implicitly permits the conservation

9. Arthur Schlesinger, Jr., "National Interests and Moral Absolutes," 23–24.
10. George F. Kennan, "The National Interest of the United States," 730, 736, 738.

of tyrannical regimes: "foreign officials must act *as if* [tyrannical regimes] were legitimate"; the difficulty of the former view is the invitation to empire in the name of human rights.[11]

Fourth, Adams recognized basic logical and pragmatic hindrances to a consistent policy of defending freedom fighters and revolutionary movements abroad. On the one hand, it is not the prime business of a state among other states to defend human rights; on the other, the defense of human rights can and must come into conflict with *other* interests that may be more important in a particular instance.[12] To conclude from the omnipresence of the moral element in foreign policy that a country has a mission to apply its own moral principles to the rest of humanity is something else. For there exists an enormous gap between the judgment we apply to ourselves, our own actions, and the universal application of our own standards of action to others. As important as America's obligation to confront ruthless aggressors around the world is the courage with which it confronts the limitations of its own moral example. For Adams, the security of the United States (as a regime that protected rights) had priority over the extension of human rights in other states. In choosing not to aid the Hungarians in 1956 or the Czechs in 1968, American policymakers, in effect, gave peace priority. Human rights goals in foreign policy must be filtered through the intermediary of changing historic and social circumstances, thereby leading to uneven results in different times and under different circumstances.

Fifth, Adams knew that a workable foreign policy consists in bringing into balance, with a comfortable surplus of power in reserve, the nation's commitments and the nation's power. His hesitations about involving the United States in Latin American and European politics in defense of liberty grew partly out of a sense of the material and political limits of American power and of the difficulties in attempting to transfer democratic institutions to other cultures. "The issue is not the value of free-

11. Michael Walzer, "The Moral Standing of States: A Response to Four Critics," 216; Tarcov, "Principle and Prudence in Foreign Policy," 56–58.
12. Hans J. Morgenthau, *Human Rights and Foreign Policy*, 1–5.

dom. Instead, it is what power can accomplish in spreading freedom."[13] The United States in the twentieth century possesses considerably more resources than the nation Adams knew and, accordingly, has more power to project; even so, those resources are not unlimited and must be husbanded as carefully as Adams sought to do 170 years ago. Recognition that men and nations proclaim goals transcending national defense or sovereignty is a first step, but not a solution to, the moral problem in international politics. It is both moral and political wisdom to choose the most moral alternative through which expedience and ethics are served.

Finally, Adams's role as both moral thinker and diplomatist suggests a limited, but important, point of convergence between the callings of the statesman and the philosopher. Diplomacy, like politics, is preeminently a realm of ways and means. It is the avenue along which ideals and objectives are realized. At some point the philosopher, however amateur in matters affecting the organization of the state, must venture across the line that separates thought and action. The notion is often advanced that the intellectual stops being an intellectual by being practical. In becoming a practitioner, he ceases to be the conscience of society, becoming instead its ideologue. Yet a conscience that has never known the deep pathos of social action and the tragic choices of statesmen inevitably views the political scene from the false security of moral and intellectual superiority. Much of the present-day social and political criticism in the United States rings with a note of "holier than thou." When the organic connection is destroyed between the philosopher's world and the world of shadows and imperfections, the philosopher loses a zest for discrimination in practical affairs and declares a plague on every man's house. If there is a germ of truth in the diagnosis of the unhealthy state of American intellectual life, then one is certainly justified in approaching rather in the spirit of a dialogue the continuing interplay between philosophy, diplomacy, and politics.[14]

13. Robert W. Tucker, "Ideology and Foreign Policy," 14.
14. Kenneth W. Thompson, *American Diplomacy and Emergent Patterns*, xvii-xviii.

Bibliography

Adair, Douglass. "'That Politics May Be Reduced to a Science': David Hume, James Madison, and the Tenth *Federalist*." *Huntington Library Quarterly* 20 (August 1957): 343–60.

Adams, Abigail. *Letters of Mrs. John Adams, the Wife of John Adams.* Boston: Wilkins, Carter & Company, 1848.

Adams, Charles Francis, ed. *Memoirs of John Quincy Adams.* 12 vols. Philadephia: J. B. Lippincott, 1874–1877.

————. *Works of John Adams.* 10 vols. Boston: Little, Brown, 1850–1856.

Adams, Henry. *The Degradation of the Democratic Dogma.* New York: Macmillan, 1920.

Adams, James Truslow. *The Adams Family.* Boston: Little, Brown, 1930.

Adams, John. *A Defence of the Constitutions of Government of the United States of America.* 3 vols. New York: DeCapo Press, 1971.

Adams, John Quincy. *An Address Delivered at the Request of a Committee of the Citizens of Washington; on the Occasion of Reading the Declaration of Independence, on the Fourth of July, 1821.* Washington, D.C.: Davis & Force, 1821.

————. *Argument by John Quincy Adams before the Supreme Court of the United States, in the Case of the United States, Appellants vs. Cinque, and Others, Africans, February 24, and March 1, 1841.* New York: Negro University Press, 1969.

———. *A Discourse on Education.* Boston: Perkins & Marvin, 1840.

———. *Eulogy on Lafayette.* New York: Craighead & Allen, 1835.

———. *The Jubilee of the Constitution. A Discourse Delivered at the Request of the New York Historical Society, in the City of New York, on Tuesday, the 30th of April 1839; Being the Fiftieth Anniversary of the Inauguration of George Washington As President of the United States, on Thursday, the 30th of April, 1789.* New York: Berford & Company, 1848.

———. *Lectures on Rhetoric and Oratory.* 2 vols. New York: Russell & Russell, 1962.

———. *Letters of John Quincy Adams, to His Son, on the Bible and Its Teachings.* Auburn, N.Y.: James Alden, 1850.

———. *Life in a New England Town: 1787, 1788; Diary of John Quincy Adams.* Boston: Little, Brown, 1903.

———. *Lives of Celebrated Statesmen.* New York: William H. Graham, 1846.

———. *The Lives of James Madison and James Monroe.* Buffalo: George Derby & Company, 1850.

———. "The Nature of Federal Government," In *Speeches of the American Presidents,* edited by Janet Podell and Steven Anzouin. New York: H. W. Wilson, 1988.

———. *The New England Confederacy of 1643, a discourse delivered before the Massachusetts Historical Society at Boston on the 29th of May, 1843.* Boston: C. C. Little & J. Brown, 1843.

———. *An Oration Addressed to the Citizens of the Town of Quincy on the Fourth of July, 1831.* Boston: Richardson, Lord & Holbrook, 1831.

———. *An Oration Delivered at Plymouth, December 22, 1802, at the Anniversary Commemoration of the First Landing of Our Ancestors at That Place.* Boston: Russell & Cutler, 1802.

———. *An Oration, Delivered before the Cincinnati Astronomical Society on the Occasion of Laying the Corner Stone of an Astronomical Observatory.* Cincinnati: Shepard & Company, 1843.

———. *An Oration Delivered before the Inhabitants of the Town of Newburyport at their request, on the Sixty-first Anniversary of the Declaration of Independence, July 4, 1837.* Newburyport: Charles Whipple, 1837.

———. *An Oration Pronounced July 4, 1793 at the Request of the Inhabitants of the Town of Boston.* Boston: Benjamin Edes & Son, 1793.

———. "An Oration upon the Importance and Necessity of Public Faith, to the Well Being of a Community," July 17, 1787, Adams Manuscripts.

———. *Parties in the United States.* New York: Greenberg, 1941.

———. *Poems of Religion and Society.* Auburn, N.Y.: Miller, Orton & Mulligan, 1848.

———. *The Social Compact, Exemplified in the Constitution of the Commonwealth of Massachusetts; with Remarks on the Theories of Divine Right of Hobbes and of Filmer, and the Counter-theories of Sidney, Locke, Montesquieu, and Rousseau, Concerning the Origin and Nature of Government.* Providence: Knowles & Vose, 1842.

Adams, John Quincy, and Charles Francis Adams. *The Life of John Adams.* Philadelphia: J. B. Lippincott, 1871.

Adams, John Quincy, and John Adams. "Letters of John Adams and John Quincy Adams," *Bulletin of the New York Public Library* 10 (April 1906): 244–50.

Adams, John Quincy, and James H. Hackett. *The Character of Hamlet.* New York: J. Mowatt, 1844.

Allen, J. H. *Christian History in Its Three Great Periods: Third Period, Modern Phases.* Roberts Brothers, 1891.

Arendt, Hannah. *On Revolution.* New York: Penguin Books, 1990.

Aristotle, *Nicomachean Ethics.* Translated by Martin Ostwald. New York: Bobbs-Merrill, 1962.

Bailey, Thomas. *A Diplomatic History of the American People.* New York: F. S. Crofts, 1946.

Bailyn, Bernard. *The Ideological Origins of the American Revolution.* Cambridge: Harvard University Press, 1967.

Barker, Ernest, ed. *The Politics of Aristotle.* New York: Oxford University Press, 1977.

———. *Traditions of Civility.* Cambridge: Cambridge University Press, 1948.

Barrow, Isaac. *Theological Works.* 8 vols. Oxford: Oxford University Press, 1830.

Bellah, Robert. *The Broken Covenant.* New York: Seabury Press, 1975.

Bemis, Samuel Flagg. *John Quincy Adams and the Foundations of American Foreign Policy.* New York: Alfred A. Knopf, 1949.

———. *John Quincy Adams and the Union.* New York: Alfred A. Knopf, 1956.

Blackstone, Sir William. *Commentaries on the Laws of England.* 4 vols. New York: Garland, 1978.

Bondanella, Peter, and Mark Musa, eds. *The Portable Machiavelli.* New York: Penguin, 1987.

Bowring, John, ed. *The Works of Jeremy Bentham.* 22 vols. New York: Russell & Russell, 1962.

Bull, Hedley. "Hobbes and the International Anarchy," *Social Research* 48 (Winter 1981): 717–38.

Burke, Edmund. *Selected Speeches and Writings.* Edited by Peter J. Stanlis. Chicago: Regnery-Gateway, 1963.

———. *The Works of the Rt. Honourable Edmund Burke.* 12 vols. Boston: Little, Brown, 1889.

Bush, Douglas, ed. *The Portable Milton.* New York: Viking Press, 1949.

Butterfield, Lyman H., ed. *Adams Family Correspondence.* 4 vols. Cambridge: Harvard University Press, 1963–1973.

Callières, Francois de. *On the Manner of Negotiating with Princes.* Translated by A. F. Whyte. Boston: Houghton Mifflin, 1919.

Cicero, Marcus Tullius. *Disputations 2 and 5.* Translated by A. E. Douglas. Westminster, England: Aris and Phillips, 1990.

———. *On the Nature of the Gods.* Translated by Hubert Poteat. Chicago: University of Chicago Press, 1950.

Clark, Bennett Champ. *John Quincy Adams.* Boston: Little, Brown, 1932.

Clark, William, and William Aldis Wright, eds. *The Complete Works of William Shakespeare.* New York: Grossett and Dunlap, 1911.

Clinton, W. David. *The Two Faces of National Interest.* Baton Rouge: Louisiana State University Press, 1994.

Corwin, Edward S. *French Policy and the American Alliance.* Princeton: Princeton University Press, 1916.

———. *The "Higher Law" Background of American Constitutional Law.* Ithaca: Cornell University Press, 1979.

Current, Richard. *Daniel Webster and the Rise of National Conservatism.* Boston: Little, Brown, 1955.

Curti, Merle. *Peace and War: The American Struggle 1636–1936*. New York: W. W. Norton, 1936.

Dangerfield, George. *The Era of Good Feelings*. New York: Harcourt, Brace & World, 1963.

Davis, William T., ed. *Bradford's History of Plymouth Plantation, 1606–1646*. New York: Charles Scribner's Sons, 1908.

Drinnon, Richard. *Facing West: The Metaphysics of Indian-Hating and Empire-Building*. Minneapolis: University of Minnesota Press, 1980.

Durand, John, ed. *New Materials for the History of the American Revolution*. New York: Henry Holt, 1889.

East, Robert. *John Quincy Adams, The Critical Years: 1785–1794*. New York: Bookman Associates, 1962.

Elliot, Jonathan, ed. *The Debates in the Several State Conventions on the Adoption of the Federal Constitution*. 5 vols. Philadelphia: J. B. Lippincott, 1901.

Everett, Edward. *A Eulogy on the Life and Character of John Quincy Adams*. Boston: Dutton & Wentworth, 1848.

Farrand, Max, ed. *The Records of the Federal Convention of 1787*. 4 vols. New Haven: Yale University Press, 1937.

Fitzpatrick, John C., ed. *The Writings of George Washington, 1745–1799*. 39 vols. Washington, D.C.: U.S. Government Printing Office, 1931–1944.

Ford, Paul Leicester, ed. *Essays on the Constitution of the United States*. Brooklyn: Historical Printing Club, 1888.

———, ed. *Pamphlets on the Constitution of the United States*. New York: Ben Franklin, 1971.

———, ed. *The Works of Thomas Jefferson*. 12 vols. New York: G. P. Putnam's Sons, 1904–1905.

———, ed. *The Writings of Thomas Jefferson*. 10 vols. New York: G. P. Putnam's Sons, 1892–1899.

Ford, Worthington C., ed. *The Writings of John Quincy Adams*. 7 vols. New York: Macmillan, 1913.

Gebhardt, Jürgen. *Americanism, Revolutionary Order and Societal Self-Interpretation in the American Republic*. Baton Rouge: Louisiana State University Press, 1993.

Gellman, Barton. *Contending with Kennan: Toward a Philosophy of American Power*. New York: Praeger, 1984.

Gentz, Friedrich von. *The Origin and Principles of the American Revolution, Compared with the Origin and Principles of the French Revolution.* Translated by John Quincy Adams. Delmar, New York: Scholars' Facsimiles & Reprints, 1977.

Germino, Dante. *Beyond Ideology.* New York: Harper & Row, 1967.

————. *Machiavelli to Marx.* Chicago: University of Chicago Press, 1972.

————. Paper delivered at the Claremont Institute Conference on the American Bicentennial, Claremont, California, February 23–25, 1984.

Gilbert, Felix. "The New Diplomacy of the Eighteenth Century," *World Politics* 4 (October 1951): 1–38.

Graebner, Norman A. *Foundations of American Foreign Policy, A Realist Appraisal from Franklin to McKinley.* Wilmington: Scholarly Resources, 1985.

————, ed. *Traditions and Values: American Diplomacy, 1790–1865.* Lanham: University Press of America, 1985.

Grayson, David Allen, et al. eds. *Diary of John Quincy Adams.* 2 vols. Cambridge: Belknap Press, 1981.

Hadas, Moses, ed. *The Basic Works of Cicero.* New York: Modern Library, 1951.

Hamilton, Alexander, James Madison, and John Jay. *The Federalist Papers.* New York: New American Library, 1961.

Hanscom, E. D. *The Heart of the Puritan.* New York: Macmillan, 1917.

Haraszti, Zoltan. *John Adams and the Prophets of Progress.* Cambridge: Harvard University Press, 1952.

Hargreaves, Mary W. M. *The Presidency of John Quincy Adams.* Lawrence: University of Kansas Press, 1985.

Hartz, Louis. *The Liberal Tradition in America.* New York: Harcourt Brace, 1955.

Hendel, Charles, ed. *David Hume's Political Essays.* New York: Liberal Arts Press, 1953.

Hobbes, Thomas. *Leviathan.* Edited by Michael Oakeshott. Oxford: Oxford University Press, 1947.

Houston, Alan Craig. *Algernon Sidney and the Republican Heritage in England and America.* Princeton: Princeton University Press, 1991.

Israel, Fred H., ed. *The State of the Union Messages of the Presidents, 1790–1966.* New York: Chelsea House, 1966.

Jusserand, Jean J. *The School for Ambassadors and Other Essays.* New York: G. P. Putnam's Sons, 1925.

———. *With Americans of Past and Present Days.* New York: Charles Scribner's Sons, 1916.

Kelley, Alfred, and Winfred Harbison. *The American Constitution,* 5th ed. New York: W. W. Norton, 1976.

Kennan, George F. "Lectures on Foreign Policy," *Illinois Law Review* 45 (January-February 1951): 718–42.

———. *Memoirs, 1925–1950.* Boston: Little, Brown, 1967.

———. "Morality and Foreign Policy," *Foreign Affairs* 64 (Winter 1985–1986): 205–18.

———. "Statement of the Honorable George F. Kennan before the Senate Foreign Relations Committee of the United States," 10 February 1966.

Kennedy, John F. *Profiles in Courage.* New York: Harper, 1956.

Kertesz, Stephen. *The Quest for Peace through Diplomacy.* Englewood Cliffs: Prentice-Hall, 1967.

Kissinger, Henry A. *A World Restored: Europe After Napoleon.* Gloucester: Peter Smith, 1973.

———. *Diplomacy.* New York: Simon & Schuster, 1994.

———. "Morality and Power," In *Morality and Foreign Policy,* edited by Ernest W. Lefever. Washington, D.C.: Ethics and Public Policy Center of Georgetown University, 1977.

Koch, Adrienne. "The Idea of America," *Yale Review* 41 (December 1951): 223–33.

———. *Power, Morals, and the Founding Fathers.* Ithaca: Cornell University Press, 1961.

———, and William Peden, eds. *The Selected Writings of John and John Quincy Adams.* Westport: Greenwood Press, 1981.

LaFeber, Walter, ed. *John Quincy Adams and the American Continental Empire.* Chicago: Quadrangle, 1965.

Lang, Daniel G. *Foreign Policy in the Early Republic.* Baton Rouge: Louisiana State University, 1985.

Laslett, Peter, ed. *Patriarcha and Other Political Works of Sir Robert Filmer.* Oxford: Blackwell, 1949.

Levin, Phyllis Lee. *Abigail Adams, A Biography.* New York: Ballantine Books, 1987.

Locke, John. *An Essay Concerning Human Understanding.* Edited by John Yolton. London: J. M. Dent, 1961.

―――. *Two Treatises of Government.* Edited by Peter Laslett. New York: Mentor, 1965.

Lodge, Henry Cabot. *The Works of Alexander Hamilton.* 12 vols. New York: Federal Edition, 1904.

Longinus, Dionysius. *On the Sublime.* London: C. Whittingham, 1800.

Lovejoy, A. O. *The Great Chain of Being.* Cambridge: Oxford University Press, 1936.

Lippmann, Walter. *The Public Philosophy.* New York: New American Library, 1955.

Lipscomb, Andrew A., and Albert Bergh, eds. *The Writings of Thomas Jefferson.* 20 vols. Washington, D.C.: Jefferson Memorial Association, 1904–1905.

MacDonald, Lee Cameron. *Western Political Theory.* 3 vols. New York: Harcourt, Brace, Jovanovich, 1984.

Machiavelli, Niccolò. *The Prince and the Discourses.* New York: Modern Library, 1950.

McAdam, E. L., ed. *The Yale Edition of the Works of Samuel Johnson.* 16 vols. New Haven: Yale University Press, 1977.

McDonald, Forrest. *Novus Ordo Seclorum: The Intellectual Origins of the Constitution.* Lawrence: University of Kansas Press, 1985.

―――. *The Presidency of George Washington.* Lawrence: University of Kansas Press, 1974.

McWilliams, Wilson Carey. "On Equality as the Moral Foundation for Community." In *The Moral Foundations of the American Republic,* edited by Robert Horwitz. Charlottesville: University Press of Virginia, 1986.

Miller, John C. "The Federalist Era." In *The Critical Years of American Foreign Policy, 1793–1823,* edited by Patrick C. White. New York: John Wiley, 1970.

Milton, John. *Paradise Lost and Other Poems.* Edited by Maurice Kelley. New York: Walter Black, 1943.

Montesquieu. *The Spirit of the Laws.* 2 vols. Translated by T. Nugent. New York: Colonial Press, 1899.

Morgenthau, Hans J. *In Defense of the National Interest.* New York: Alfred A. Knopf, 1951.

———. *Dilemmas of Politics.* Chicago: University of Chicago Press, 1958.

———. "The Founding Fathers and Foreign Policy: Some Implications for the Late Twentieth Century," *Orbis* 20 (Spring 1976): 15–25.

———. *Human Rights and Foreign Policy.* New York: Council on Religion and International Affairs, 1979.

———. *A New Foreign Policy for the United States.* New York: Praeger, 1969.

———. *Politics among Nations,* 5th ed. New York: Alfred A. Knopf, 1973.

———. *The Purpose of American Politics.* New York: Alfred A. Knopf, 1960.

———. *Scientific Man vs. Power Politics.* Chicago: University of Chicago Press, 1946.

Morison, Samuel Eliot, Henry Steele Commager, and William E. Leuctenburg. *The Growth of the American Republic.* 2 vols. New York: Oxford University Press, 1969.

Morse, J. T. *John Quincy Adams.* New York: Houghton Mifflin, 1882.

Mulgan, R. G. *Aristotle's Political Theory.* Oxford: Oxford University Press, 1977.

National Archives. Records of the Department of State. *Diplomatic Instructions,* All Countries, Vols. 8–10.

Nettleship, H., ed. *The Satires of A. Persius Flaccus.* Hildesheim: Georg Olms Verlagsbuchhandlung, 1967.

Nevins, Allan, ed. *The Diary of John Quincy Adams, 1794–1845.* New York: Longmans Green, 1928.

Niebuhr, Reinhold. *Moral Man and Immoral Society.* New York: Charles Scribner's Sons, 1932.

———. *The Nature and Destiny of Man: A Christian Interpretation.* 2 vols. New York: Charles Scribner's Sons, 1941–1943.

Oppenheim, L. *International Law,* 2nd ed., 2 vols. London: Longmans and Green, 1912.

Ovid (Publius Ovidius Naso). *Metamorphoses.* Translated by Rolfe Humphries. Bloomington: Indiana University Press, 1955.

Paley, William. *A View of the Evidences of Christianity.* 2 vols. London: F. Faulder, 1796.

Paltsits, Victor H. *Washington's Farewell Address, in Facsimile, with Translations of All the Drafts of Washington, Madison, and Hamilton, Together with Their Correspondence and Other Supporting Documents, Edited with a History of Its Origin, Its Reception by the Nation, Rise of the Controversy Respecting Its Authorship, and a Bibliography.* New York: New York Public Library, 1935.

Parton, James. *Life and Times of Benjamin Franklin.* Boston: Houghton Mifflin, 1987.

Perkins, Bradford. *Castlereagh and Adams, England and the United States, 1812–1823.* Berkeley and Los Angeles: University of California Press, 1964.

Perkins, Dexter. "John Quincy Adams," In *The American Secretaries of State and Their Diplomacy,* edited by Samuel Flagg Bemis. New York: Cooper Square Publishers, 1963.

———. *The Monroe Doctrine, 1823–1826.* Cambridge: Harvard University Press, 1927.

Poetical Works of Johnson, Parnell, Gray and Smollett. With explanatory notes by the Rev. George Gilfillan. Edinburgh: James Nicol, 1855.

Pope, Alexander. *Collected Poems.* London: J. M. Dent, 1983.

Price, Richard. "A Discourse on the Love of Our Country, Delivered on November 4, 1789, at the Meeting-House in the Old Jewry, to the Society for Commemorating the Revolution in Great Britain," In *Political Sermons of the American Founding Era, 1730–1805,* edited by Ellis Sandoz. Indianapolis: Liberty Fund Press, 1991.

Quincy, Josiah. *Memoir of the Life of John Quincy Adams.* Boston: Phillips, Sampson & Company, 1859.

Remini, Robert. *Henry Clay: Statesman for the Union.* New York: W. W. Norton, 1991.

Richards, Leonard L. *The Life and Times of Congressman John Quincy Adams.* New York: Oxford University Press, 1986.

Richardson, J. D., ed. *Messages and Papers of the Presidents, 1789–1897.* 10 vols. Washington, D.C.: U.S. Government Printing Office, 1987.

Ritter, Allan, and Julia Conaway Bondanella, eds. *Rousseau's Political Writings.* New York: W. W. Norton, 1988.

Rodman, J. R., ed. *The Political Theory of T. H. Green.* New York: Appleton-Century-Crofts, 1964.

Rousseau, Jean-Jacques. *The Social Contract.* Translated by Charles M. Sherover. New York: New American Library, 1974.

Rousseau, Lousene G. "The Rhetorical Principles of Cicero and Adams," *The Quarterly Journal of Public Speaking* 2 (October 1916): 397–409.

Rush, Richard. *A Residence at the Court of London.* Philadelphia: Lea and Blanchard, 1845.

Sandoz, Ellis. *A Government of Laws: Political Theory, Religion, and the American Founding.* Baton Rouge: Louisiana State University Press, 1990.

———. *Political Apocalypse, A Study of Dostoyevsky's Grand Inquisitor.* Baton Rouge: Louisiana State University Press, 1971.

Schlesinger, Arthur M. *The Age of Jackson.* Boston: Little, Brown, 1945.

———. *The Imperial Presidency.* Boston: Houghton Mifflin, 1973.

———. "National Interests and Moral Absolutes," In *International Ethics in the Nuclear Age,* edited by Robert J. Myers. Lanham: University Press of America, 1987.

Schutz, John A., and Douglass Adair, eds. *Spur of Fame: Dialogues of John Adams and Benjamin Rush, 1805–1813.* San Marino, California: Huntington Library, 1980.

Schwartz, Bernard. *The Great Rights of Mankind.* New York: Oxford University Press, 1977.

Seward, William. *Life and Public Services of John Quincy Adams.* Auburn, N.Y.: Derby, Miller & Company, 1851.

Shakespeare, William. *Measure for Measure.* Edited by James Coles and Rex Gibson. Cambridge: Cambridge University Press, 1991.

Shepherd, Jack. *The Adams Chronicles, Four Generations of Greatness.* Boston: Little, Brown, 1975.

Sidney, Algernon. *Discourses on Government.* London: London and Westminster, 1698.

Smith, Adam. *An Inquiry into the Nature and Causes of the Wealth of Nations.* New York: Modern Library, 1937.

Smyth, Albert Henry, ed. *The Writings of Benjamin Franklin.* 10 vols. New York: Macmillan, 1905–1907.

Sorel, Albert. *Europe under the Old Regime.* Translated by Francis H. Herrick. Los Angeles: Ward Ritchie Press, 1947.

Stenberg, R. R. "Jackson's 'Rhea Letter' Hoax," *Journal of Southern History* 2 (1936): 480–96.

Stevens, B. F., comp. *Facsimiles of Manuscripts from European Archives Relating to America, 1773–1783.* 24 vols. London: Malby & Sons, 1889–1895.

Stourzh, Gerald. *Benjamin Franklin and American Foreign Policy.* Chicago: University of Chicago Press, 1954.

———. *Alexander Hamilton and the Idea of Republican Government.* Palo Alto: Stanford University Press, 1970.

Strauss, Leo. *The Political Philosophy of Hobbes.* Chicago: University of Chicago Press, 1952.

Syrett, Harold C., and Jacob Cooke, eds. *The Papers of Alexander Hamilton.* 26 vols. New York: Columbia University Press, 1961–1979.

Tarcov, Nathan. "Principle and Prudence in Foreign Policy: The Founders' Perspective," *Public Interest* 76 (Summer 1984): 45–60.

Tatum, Edward H., ed. "Ten Unpublished Letters of John Quincy Adams, 1796–1837," *Huntington Library Quarterly* 4 (April 1941): 369–85.

———. *The United States and Europe, 1815–1823.* Berkeley and Los Angeles: University of California Press, 1936.

Thomas, W. Moy, ed. *The Poetical Works of William Collins.* London: George Bell & Sons, 1901.

Thompson, Kenneth W. *American Diplomacy and Emergent Patterns.* New York: New York University Press, 1962.

———. *Political Realism and the Crisis of World Politics.* New York: Columbia University Press, 1960.

Thucydides, *The Peloponnesian War.* Translated by Rex Warner. New York: Penguin, 1980.

Tucker, Robert. "Ideology and Foreign Policy," In *World Politics 87/88,* edited by Suzanne Ogden. Guilford: Dushkin, 1988.

Turner, F. J., ed. "Correspondence of the French Ministers to the United States," In *Annual Report of the American Historical Association for the Year 1903.* 2 vols. Washington, D.C., 1904.

U.S. Congress, *Congressional Globe,* 23rd Congress, 1st Session to 30th Congress, 1st Session.

————. *Register of Debates*, 22nd Congress, 1st Session to 24th Congress, 2nd Session.

Varg, Paul. *United States Foreign Relations, 1820–1860*. East Lansing: Michigan State University Press, 1979.

Vattel, Emmerich de. *The Law of Nations; or, Principles of the Law of Nature, Applied to the Conduct and Affairs of Nations and Sovereigns*. Washington, D.C.: Carnegie Institute, 1916.

Virgil: The Aeneid. Translated by John Dryden. New York: Heritage Press, 1944.

Voegelin, Eric. *New Science of Politics*. Chicago: Henry Regnery, 1952.

Walzer, Michael. "The Moral Standing of States: A Response to Four Critics," *Philosophy & Public Affairs* 9 (Spring 1980): 209–229.

Watson, John F. *Annals of Philadelphia*. 2 vols. Philadelphia: P. H. Nicklin, 1829.

Watts, Isaac. *The Improvement of the Human Mind*. New Brunswick: L. Deare, 1813.

Weyde, William van der, ed. *The Life and Works of Thomas Paine*. 10 vols. New Rochelle: Thomas Paine National Historical Association, 1925.

Wheaton, Henry. *Elements of International Law*, 8th ed., London: Milford, 1936.

Whitaker, Arthur. *United States and Latin American Independence, 1800–1830*. Baltimore: Johns Hopkins University Press, 1941.

Wills, Garry. *Explaining America: The Federalist*. Harmondsworth: Penguin, 1981.

Index

Aberdeen, Lord, 262
Adams, Abigail, 10–12, 14, 32
Adams, Brooks, 4, 240
Adams, Charles Francis, 10, 23, 55, 57
Adams, George Washington, 85
Adams, Henry, 4
Adams, John, 11, 15, 17, 38, 78, 180, 206, 219; *A Defence of the Constitutions of Government of the United States of America*, 25; on Thomas Paine's *Rights of Man*, 26–27; on Citizen Genêt, 27; recalls JQA from post in Berlin, 31; science of politics, 123; commercial policy, 127–28; virtue of emulation, 166–67; *Discourses on Davila*, 194; "Thoughts on Government," 194; on power, 258
Adams, John Quincy: realism and idealism, 2–3, 5–6, 131, 141, 173, 197, 231–32, 248, 250; July 4, 1821 oration, 3, 138–41; appeal to natural law, 4–5, 146–47; skeptical view of science, 5; influence of Alexander Pope on JQA, 6; Letters of "Publicola," 6, 26, 179–99 *passim*; Letters of "Marcellus," 7, 27, 58, 201, 207–16 *passim*, 241; Letters of "Columbus," 7, 27, 201, 220–30 *passim*; tragic sense of politics, 8, 235, 274; early life and education, 10–15; travel to Europe, 15–18; attends Harvard, 18–23; 1787 commencement address, 23–24; study and practice of law, 24–26; political creed of JQA, 27; minister to The Hague, 28; marries Louisa Catherine Johnson, 28; on the French Revolution, 29–30; travel through Silesia, 30–31; removed by Jefferson as commissioner of bankruptcy, 32; election to Massachusetts State Senate, 33;

election to U.S. Senate, 33; on the Louisiana Purchase, 34–35, 247–48; as Harvard Professor of Literature and Rhetoric, 38–39; minister to Russia, 39–42; commissioner to negotiate peace at Ghent, 42–43; minister to the Court of St. James, 43–44; as secretary of state, 44–50 *passim*; conduct as a diplomat, 45–46; on the acquisition of Florida, 46–47, 254–55; exchange with Stratford Canning, 47–48, 251; support for independence movements, 48–49, 131–34, 135–37, 158–60; and Monroe Doctrine, 50; political ambitions of JQA, 51; presidential election of 1824, 51–52; presidency of JQA, 52–55; on internal improvements, 53–54, 112–13; literary and scientific interests, 55–56; retirement to Quincy, 57; election to U.S. House of Representatives, 57–65 *passim*; economic philosophy of JQA, 58–59; on the Missouri Compromise, 59; supports right to petition in Congress, 60–61; opposes nullification and secession, 61, 155–57; defense of *Amistad* slaves, 62; opposes annexation of Texas and Mexican War, 63, 197, 261–64; creation of the Smithsonian Institution, 64; death of JQA, 64–65; analysis of Hamlet's tragedy, 68–70; on human nature, 70–75, 79–80, 86, 91–92, 96–97, 167–68, 171, 175, 241, 249; and puritanism, 77–78; belief in God, 78–79; religious faith of JQA, 81–83; on death and immortality, 83–85, 87; the Bible and Christianity, 85–95 *passim*, 110–11, 235; Ralph Waldo Emerson and transcendentalism, 94; political philosophy of

JQA, 95–105 *passim*; social contract, 99–103, 146, 147, 164, 165–66; opposes Rousseau's concept of democracy, 101–2; cites Aristotle's classification of governments, 102–4; exchange with Jeremy Bentham, 105–8; promotion of science, 108–10; preference for practical ethics, 110–11; purposes of government, 111–13, 173–74, 266–67; on the national interest, 134, 226, 271–72; role of intervention in U.S. foreign policy, 140–41, 212–13; on the Declaration of Independence, 145–48, 158; struggle for English and American liberties, 149–54; opposes Articles of Confederation, 154–58; on the U.S. Constitution, 158–60; support for the balance principle, 159; favors a Bill of Rights, 159–60; republican virtue of statesmen, 160–61; view of democracy, 161–62; on the idea of posterity, 162–63, 176; heritage of the Puritans, 164–66, 171; communalism of the Pilgrims, 168–69; glory of the Founders, 172–73; JQA's party preference, 177–78; on higher law tradition in America, 183–84; influence of Burke on JQA, 186–87; nature of representation, 195–96; comparison of French and English constitutions, 196–99; admiration of George Washington, 200–201; on French Alliance of 1778, 202–204; condemns privateering, 208–209; view of nations as "moral persons," 210–11; foreign policy views compared to those of George Washington, 216–18; moral methods of diplomacy, 229–30; rejects reason of state, 240–41; on international law, 241–44; qualities of the successful diplomat, 244–45; relation of morality to power in foreign policy, 245–50; on American continental expansion, 250–52; on the European balance of power, 252–54; defense of Jackson's invasion of Florida, 255–58, 264; declines Canning's offer of a joint declaration of nonintervention, 260–61; JQA's foreign policy legacy for the 1990s, 270–74 *passim*

Adams, John Quincy, II, 10
Adams, Louisa Catherine, 28
Adams, Thomas Boylston, 30, 253
Addison, Joseph, 15
Alcibiades, 120
Alexander I, 39–40, 42, 46, 200, 240; ukase of 1821, 50
Americanism, 234–35
American Revolution, 30
Ames, Fisher, 22, 33, 58
Antony, Mark, 13
Aquinas, Thomas, 4, 143
Arbuthnot, Alexander, 255
Arendt, Hannah, 175–76
aristocracy, 19, 21, 103–4, 105, 106, 177
Aristotle, 6, 56, 68, 80, 102–4, 117, 125; on self-love, 75–76; happiness and virtue, 192, 268
Armbrister, Robert, 255
Articles of Confederation, 7, 154–58 *passim*
Astor, John Jacob, 47
Augustine, Saint, 22, 75

Bacon, Ezekiel, 39
Bacon, Francis, 7, 83, 117, 156
balance of power, 45, 50, 232, 240, 252–54
Barker, Sir Ernest, 143
Barrow, Isaac, 95
Bathurst, Lord, 44
Bayard, James A., 42
Beaumarchais, Pierre Augustin Caron de, 17, 211
Beckley, John, 180, 181
Belknap, Jeremy, 23
Bemis, Samuel Flagg, 6, 206
Bentham, Jeremy, 43, 105–8
bios theoretikos, 117
Blackstone, William, 105, 151–52, 157, 186
Boleyn, Anne, 170
Bossuet, Jacques Bénigne, 56
Boston Massacre, 10
Boston Tea Party, 10
Bowdoin, James, 178
Bradford, William, 154, 165
Brahe, Tycho, 64
Brewster, William, 164
Bright, John, 206

Brock, Sir Isaac, 40
Brownson, Orestes, 94
Bryant, William Cullen, 135
Bulwer-Lytton, Edward Robert, 55
Burke, Edmund, 7, 17, 141, 180, 182; defense of virtual representation, 104, 195
Burns, Robert, 154
Butler, Samuel, 56
Bynkershoeck, Cornelius van, 222

Cabot, George, 32
Cabot, Henry, 57
Caesar, Julius, 37
Calhoun, John C., 49, 58, 63, 136, 255, 256, 259, 262
Callières, Francois de: qualities of the diplomat, 134, 221–22
Calvin, John, 170
Canning, George, 44, 49, 260
Canning, Stratford, 48
Carver, John, 154
Castlereagh, Robert Stewart, Viscount, 44, 240, 256
Catherine of Aragon, 170
Catherine the Great, 16
Catiline, 13
Cato, 68
Charles I, 98, 149, 170
Charles II, 105
Christ, 21, 22, 80, 81, 83, 86, 92–93, 98, 107, 161, 170
Christianity, 6, 21, 24, 41, 75, 110–11, 210, 211, 267
Chryssipus, 80
Cicero, Marcus Tullius, 6, 13, 38, 55, 56, 57; detestation of war, 10; just war doctrine, 22; on immortality, 83, 88; subjugation of the passions, 90–91; and higher law, 143, 185
citizenship, 6
Clay, Henry, 42, 43, 48, 53, 65, 131, 136, 258
Coercive Acts, 151
Coke, Sir Edward, 143
Collins, William, 100
Columbus, Christopher, 164
Congress of Vienna, 45, 222, 240
Constant, Benjamin, 42
Constantine, 21
constitutionalism, 6, 185–89, 209–10

Constitution of the United States, 7, 25, 158–60, 162, 193–94; statehood for Louisiana, 35–36; and Missouri Compromise, 59–60; Mexican War, 63; idea of counterpoise, 73; Tenth Amendment, 157; declaration of war, 199, 264; treaties as supreme law, 207; issues raised by Citizen Genêt, 224–25
Convention of 1818, 47
Cook, Orchard, 39
Corwin, Edward S., 142
Cranmer, Thomas, 170
Crawford, William, 46, 52

Dana, Francis, 16
Declaration of Independence, 7, 145–48, 152, 155, 158, 233
democracy, 19, 21, 36, 53, 54, 61, 76–77, 101–2, 103–4, 105, 107–8, 142, 144, 177, 195–96, 267
Demosthenes, 38, 56
de Staël, Madame, 41–42
Dickinson, John, 117
diffidence, 13
diplomacy, 4, 29, 45–46, 49, 134, 198, 220–21, 244–45, 274
Dryden, John, 71
Duplaine, Antoine Charbonet, 225, 228–30

education, 12, 18, 111
Emerson, Ralph Waldo, 94
Endicott, Charles Moses, 154
equality, 19, 20, 61, 77, 129
Essex Junto, 32
Euclid, 34
Everett, Edward, 11, 138

faith, 81, 100, 169
Falstaff, Sir John, 98, 99
Federalist party, 32, 33, 36, 37, 57, 58
Filmer, Sir Robert: *Patriarcha* and defense of monarchy, 98–99
foreign policy: and American Founders, 115–17; in classical political thought, 117–21; in modern political thought, 121–31; legalistic approach, 122–23; ethics of, 133–34, 197–98, 203, 216, 245–50, 270–71, 274
Forsyth, John, 243

Fox, Charles James, 17, 27
Franklin, Benjamin, 13, 17, 71, 201; on
  new diplomacy, 211
Frederick I, 148
Frederick the Great, 17
freedom, 26, 75, 83, 108, 133, 161, 269
French Revolution, 7, 26, 27, 29, 107–8,
  123, 168, 179, 190, 201, 203, 215, 219,
  253

Gallatin, Albert, 42, 47, 135, 136
Garrison, William Lloyd, 94
Garth, Samuel, 15
Gebhardt, Jürgen, 176–77
Genêt, Edmond Charles, 27, 218–30
  passim
Gentiles, Albericus, 222
Gentz, Friedrich von, 30
George III, 146, 150, 151
Giles, William B., 57
Graebner, Norman, 253
Granger, Gideon, 40
Great Chain of Being, 6
Green, Thomas Hill, 269
Grotius, Hugo, 22, 165, 222, 226, 242
Guthrie, William, 15, 38

Hadrian, 84
Hamilton, Alexander, 5, 32, 58, 204,
  206, 209, 221, 250; defense of power
  politics, 116; equality and the law of
  nations, 122; on sea and commercial
  power, 126–28; on virtue and inequal-
  ity, 129; critique of perpetual peace,
  130, 158; "Pacificus" and "Ameri-
  canus" essays, 202–3
Hamlet, 68–70, 249
Hampden, John, 150
happiness, 89, 123, 266
Harrington, James, 7, 117, 123
Hartz, Louis, 115
Harvard University, 18, 57, 172
Henry VIII, 170, 171
Henry, Patrick, 116, 125
Hoar, George Frisbie, 233
Hobbes, Thomas, 62–63, 75, 98, 99,
  122, 128, 212; on power, 97
Holland, Lord, 43
Holy Alliance, 45, 46, 49–50, 137, 200,
  253, 254, 259, 260, 261

Horace, 93
Houston, Sam, 63
Hull, William, 40
human nature, 2, 21, 24, 25, 64, 66–67,
  70, 71–72, 73, 74, 79, 81, 82, 108–9,
  123, 129, 134, 140, 181
human rights, 36, 131, 135, 271, 272–73
Hume, David, 7, 16, 75, 109, 127; on
  "modern policy," 128–29; on the
  Puritans, 153
Hundred Years' War, 149
Huss, John, 169
Hyde de Neuville, Baron Guillaume-
  Jean, 159

idealism, 2, 5, 115
internal improvements, 4, 53–54, 61
international law, 28, 42–43, 106, 122,
  148–49, 203–4, 207, 213, 214, 222,
  225, 226–28, 241–44
intervention, 3, 131–32, 204–5, 231,
  232, 254
Isocrates, 56

Jackson, Andrew, 44, 47, 51–52, 54, 58,
  59, 254, 255–58
James I, 170
James II, 150
Jay, John, 28, 58, 181
Jay Treaty, 28
Jefferson, Thomas, 2, 17, 31, 32, 40, 47,
  58, 74, 146, 158, 181, 203, 209, 218,
  233, 250; commends JQA to George
  Washington, 28; on the Louisiana
  Purchase, 35; on Paine's Rights of
  Man, 180; on Citizen Genêt, 220; and
  republican government, 234; relation
  of natural law to natural rights, 236;
  morality and statecraft, 236–38; on
  human nature, 239; praises JQA's state
  paper defending Jackson's actions in
  Florida, 239–40
Johnson, Edward, 234
Johnson, Joshua, 28
Johnson, Samuel: on sovereignty, 151
Jusserand, Jean, 220–21
justice, 14, 63, 81, 88, 175, 185, 204,
  227, 228, 238
Juvenal, 30, 79

Kennan, George F.: duties to self and duties to others, 270–71; procedural aspects of the national interest, 272

Kepler, Johannes, 64

Kertesz, Stephen, 222

Kissinger, Henry A., 233

Knox, John 170

Lafayette, Marquis de, 17

LaFontaine, Jean de, 17

Lang, Daniel G., 203–4

Laplace, Pierre Simon, 17

Lee, Arthur, 15

Leland, John, 38

Leo X, 170

LeSage, Alain René, 17

liberalism, 8, 94–95, 131, 161, 210, 268–69

liberty, 7, 13, 18, 62–63, 76, 77, 83, 93–94, 104–5, 111, 130, 132, 138–39, 153, 159, 169, 182, 188, 192, 228, 235, 263, 267

Lincoln, Abraham, 60–61

Lippmann, Walter: on American public philosophy, 143–44

Liverpool, Earl of, 44

Locke, John, 4, 12, 71, 109, 122, 143, 159, 171, 204; purpose of government, 193; doctrine of emergency powers, 209–10

Longinus, Dionysius: on the sublime, 90

Louis XIV, 79

Louis XVI, 211, 214

Love, Alfred, 206

Lovejoy, A. O.: on the hierarchy of being, 72

Lowell, John, 57

Luke, 22

Luther, Martin, 95–96, 169, 170

Lycurgus, 20, 125

Mably, Abbé de, 123, 126

Macaulay, Catherine, 16

McDonald, Forrest, 219

Machiavelli, Niccolò, 7, 117, 123, 125, 126, 211; primacy of foreign policy, 121–22

Mackintosh, Sir James, 43–44

Madison, James, 2, 39, 128, 180, 181, 209, 224; proposes to nominate JQA for a position on the Supreme Court, 40–41; on human nature and politics, 74; America as a workshop of liberty, 115, 266–68; republics and expansion, 116–17; indebtedness to Hume, 129; respectability of nations, 174; arguments as "Helvidius," 204

Magna Carta, 143, 149

Mahmud II, 135

Maintenon, Madame, 79

manifest destiny, 5

Manilius, 44

Marat, Jean Paul, 94, 107

Marshall, John, 58, 159

Martens, Georg von, 42–43, 229, 242–43, 244

Mary I, 170

Mary II, 150

Massillon, Jean Baptiste, 56

Metternich, Clemons von, 42

Mexican War, 197, 262–64

Middleton, Henry, 252, 253

Milton, John, 15, 100–101, 171, 172

Missouri Compromise, 59

Molière, Jean Baptiste Poquelin, 17

monarchy, 19, 21, 103–4, 105, 106, 124, 127, 177

Monroe, James, 46, 137, 240, 255, 259–60; appoints JQA secretary of state, 44; recognition of independence movements, 133, 135

Monroe Doctrine, 3, 5, 47, 117, 199–200, 250

Montesquieu, Baron de la Brede, 7, 117, 128, 162, 204; virtue and republics, 76, 123; equality, 76–77; revision of ancient and modern perspectives on foreign policy, 125–26; on modern commercial policy, 127

morality, 13, 53, 78, 108, 135, 216, 258

moral reasoning, 8, 226; and diplomacy, 270

Morgenthau, Hans J.: on JQA, 5; nature of statesmanship, 66–67

Morris, Gouverneur, 33, 220

Napoleon I, 28, 36, 40, 41, 136, 148, 237, 240

national interest, 2, 4, 26, 31, 50, 134, 226, 265, 271–72

nationalistic universalism, 29
natural law, 4–5, 60, 74, 98, 104, 111,
142–44, 146–47, 152, 153, 182, 247
natural rights, 179, 186, 214, 230
Nelson, Hugh, 259
Nero, 21
Nesselrode, Count, 240
neutrality, 27, 28, 37, 202, 207, 210,
212–13, 218, 254
new diplomacy, 202, 211
New England Confederation, 7
Newton, Sir Isaac, 12, 64
Nicias, 120–21
Niebuhr, Reinhold, 167–68; irony of
power in American history, 268
Nonimportation Act, 37
North, Lord, 17, 151
nullification, 153

Onís y Gonzales, Luis de, 46, 254, 257
original sin, 71–72
Otis, Harrison Gray, 57
Ovid: creation of the world, 88–89

Paine, Thomas, 7, 58, 107, 125, 271; and
Rights of Man, 26–27, 179–99 *passim*
Paley, William, *A View of the Evidences
of Christianity*, 92–93
Parsons, Theophilus, 24, 32
Paul, 84, 86, 107, 171
Pericles, 119, 121
Perkins, Thomas H., 57, 136
Perry, Ralph Barton, 77
Persius, 79
Peter the Great, 112
pharisaism, 22, 86
Pichegru, General Charles, 28
Pickering, Timothy, 33, 36–37, 39, 58, 221
Pinckney, Charles, 115–16
Pinckney, Henry, 60
Pinckney, Thomas, 28, 203
Pitcairn, Joseph, 205
Pitt, William, 17
Plato, 6, 56, 117, 167
Plumer, William, 155
Plutarch, 55, 80
political ethics, 1–2, 3, 5, 8, 23–24, 32,
37, 41, 49, 61–62, 73–74, 75, 139, 148,
162, 184–85, 207–8, 227, 231–32, 238,
268

Polk, James K., 63, 254, 263
Pope, Alexander, 18–19; immortal spirit
of man, 14; idea of duty, 68; Great
Chain of Being, 71; "Dying Christian to His Soul," 84–85; *Universal
Prayer*, 88
posterity, 162–63, 173
power, 100, 129, 139, 160, 166, 172, 206
Prescott, William, 57
Price, Richard, 182–83, 201–2
Protestant Reformation, 95–96, 169–70,
171
prudence, 95, 114, 141, 248, 253
public interest, 6, 7
public service, 25, 39, 44–45, 58, 144, 173
Pufendorf, Samuel, 22, 142
Puritans, 18, 153, 164–66, 170

Quincy, John, 9
Quintilian, 6, 24

Rabelais, Francois, 17
Randolph, John, 53, 136
realism, 2, 5, 67, 115, 125, 141, 203
reason, 64, 67, 70–71, 72, 81–82, 88,
110, 144, 153, 169, 185, 197, 235
reason of state, 116, 137–38, 211, 220–
21, 240–41
religion, 13, 14, 21, 67
representation, 195–96
republican government, 74, 116–17, 122,
126, 127, 130, 162, 176, 177, 181, 222,
232
republicanism, 29, 104, 114–15, 123
Rhea, John, 255
rhetoric, 38–39
right to petition, 78
Robertson, William, 16, 165–66
Robespierre, 220
Roland, Madame, 42
Rousseau, Jean Jacques, 17, 29, 123, 167;
critique of might makes right, 97–98;
on the social contract, 187; and right
to declare war, 198
Rumiantzov, Count, 40
Rush, Richard, 47, 251–52, 256, 263
Russell, Jonathan, 42

Sandoz, Ellis, 267–68
Santa Anna, Antonio López de,, 63

Sappho, 84
Schlesinger, Arthur, 238, 264
science, 5, 64, 67, 78
Selden, John, 152–53
self-love, 72, 74–75, 77, 87
Seneca, 80
Shakespeare, William, 15, 32, 55, 64, 68, 84, 98, 245
Shelley, Percy Bysshe, 249
Sheridan, Richard, 17
Sidney, Algernon, 7, 117, 126; *Discourses on Government*, 104–5; primacy of foreign policy, 124–25
slavery, 59, 61, 139, 263
Smith, Adam, 58–59; limits to free trade, 128
Smithson, James, 64, 65
Smollett, Tobias, 174
social contract, 7, 35–36, 99, 103, 133, 163, 164, 165–66, 186–87
Solomon, 79
Sorel, Albert, 220
sovereignty, 102, 103, 122, 151, 154–57, 159, 187, 218
Stamp Act, 10, 150, 153
statesmanship, 1, 5, 8, 31–32, 66–67, 73, 83, 111, 131, 153, 211, 227, 235–36, 239, 247
Steele, Sir Richard, 84
Stiles, Ezra, 234
Stoicism, 83–84, 90, 91
Strauss, Leo: primacy of internal policy in classical philosophy, 117–18
Swinburne, Algernon, 168

Tacitus, 163
Talleyrand, Charles Maurice de, 42, 240
Taylor, Zachary, 263
technology, 267
Themistocles, 119
theocentric humanism, 268
Thomson, James, 15
Thucydides, 7, 20–21, 117; *History of the Peloponnesian War*, 117–21
Tillotson, John, Archbishop of Canterbury, 56
Tolstoy, Leo, 39
Townshend, Charles, 150
tragedy, 66, 235, 274
Transcontinental Treaty, 46

Treaty of Westphalia, 226
Tuyll van Serooskerken, Baron de, 251, 260

union, 59, 132, 139, 144, 147–48, 261, 264

Vattel, Emmerich de, 22, 43, 204, 229, 242–44
Verac, Charles Olivier de Saint Georges, Marquis de, 11
Vergennes, Comte de, 211
Verres, 13
Virgil, 6; and example of Aeneas, 174–75
virtue, 2, 12, 13, 14–15, 18, 74, 76, 89, 95, 102, 111, 114, 123, 125, 128, 160–61, 167, 172, 176–77
Voltaire, Francois Marie Arouet de, 17

Waller, Edmund, 15
Walsh, Robert, 51, 136
war, 10, 11, 62, 118, 124, 150, 195, 204, 207, 209, 211–12, 246–47
War of 1812, 3
War of the First Coalition, 201
Warren, Joseph, 10
Wars of the Roses, 149
Washington, George, 5, 30, 37, 130, 174, 223, 233; Farewell Address of, 7, 114, 199, 204–5; and Proclamation of Neutrality, 218; on prospects of JQA, 239, 241
Watson, John F., 219
Watts, Isaac, 56; *The Improvement of the Human Mind*, 82–83
Webster, Daniel, 58; supports Greek independence, 135
Wickliffe, John, 169
Wieland, Christoph Martin, 30
William III, 150, 154
William of Normandy, 186
Wilson, Woodrow, 114
Winthrop, John, 77, 154; "Agrippa" and republican government, 127
Wirt, William, 136, 256
Wise, Henry, 60
Witherspoon, John, 75
workshop of liberty, 173, 266–68

Zouche, Richard, 222